You are the limiting factor:

That's good…

Find out why by reading and reflecting on the practical guidance provided in this book.

Success doesn't come to you, you go to it

First Published by
Outside The Box Learning Resources Limited
W6W Tougher's Business Park
Newhall, Naas, Co. Kildare
Ireland
www.otb.ie
Email: info@otb.ie

Classification(s): Business

Author: Blaise Brosnan (www.mriwex.ie)
Editor: Deirdre Eustace (seasoul@eircom.net)
Graphic Designer: Outsource Graphix (www.ogx.ie)

Printed & Bound in Ireland by: Johnswood Press Ltd.
4 Airton Business Pk, Airton Road, Tallaght, Dublin 24
Tel: 01 4522777 Fax: 01 4522818

First Published: April 2009

13-Digit ISBN: 978-1-906926-00-7

Management Resource Institute (Wexford)

Disclaimer Notice
This book offers personal development information and guidance only and is not intended as direct advice. The author and publisher have no control over the way that the reader uses the information contained within these pages – the reader has sole responsibility for the outcomes of any actions they take.

This book is a valuable guide; however it is recommended that the reader always employ qualified professional specialist advice. Remember, the way that the information contained in this book is applied is the responsibility of the reader.

To my wife, Delia
And my children, Caitriona and Padraig

The fact that **you** are the limiting factor in your personal life, your career and in your business is good. Why? Because the variable you have most control over is yourself. The person who has enough insight to admit to his/her limitations is the person who comes nearest to perfection.

This book focuses on **facilitating** and **challenging** you to achieve your optimum potential. By reading this book and reflecting on the concepts addressed herein, you can begin immediately to build your own capacity. With this enhanced capacity your personal life, your career and your business will improve, ensuring that you optimise your wealth.

Through the medium of this book. I will act as your mentor: someone from whom you can draw the wisdom and guidance necessary to facilitate you in achieving your optimum potential. My aim is to provide you with the knowledge and skills that will take you from where you are now to where you need to be. Great work is done by those who are not afraid to be great. You only live life once, but if you work it right, then once is enough. With this in mind I invite you to come on this life-changing trip and to reap the rewards.

> *"Ancora Imparo"- "I am always learning"*
> *Michelangelo*

CONTENTS

About the Author...iv
Preface...vi

SECTION ONE: You As A Person   1

Chapter 1   Putting the next stage of your Life Journey in context...................1
Chapter 2   Who are You and why is this Important? 6
Chapter 3   Compare yourself against Successful Management Profiles 48
Chapter 4   The Things that Keep You in a Rut 58
Chapter 5   What are the Secrets of Success?..61
Chapter 6   'No man is an Island' We all need Help - here's how to get it 66
Chapter 7   Survey Results – Messages for You 70
Chapter 8   Understanding why Businesses Fail 81
Chapter 9   Managing your Time to make the most of your Opportunities....90

SECTION TWO: Building Your Business Model   119

Chapter 10   Strategy: What is it about and what are its Implications for
             your Business...119
Chapter 11   Health Checking your Business 159

SECTION THREE: Understanding The Dynamics Of This Business
                        Model   189

Chapter 12   Flaunt your Propositions, don't hide them 190
Chapter 13   Being an Effective Salesperson 201
Chapter 14   The Art of Negotiation 227
Chapter 15   Pricing for Profit..235
Chapter 16   Building and Managing your Team 247
             Conclusions 258
Bibliography & Acknowledgements...260

About the Author

Blaise Brosnan is an independent management consultant, trainer and businessman. He possesses a unique blend of practical senior management experience gained over twenty three years in his role as Chief Executive of a number of large businesses. His successful completion of a portfolio of assignments in Ireland, the US and in Russia has gained him further national and international experience.

Born into a small rural retail business in Kerry, Ireland, Blaise gained hands-on experience of dealing with customers and with the other variables of business from a very young age. From there he worked in a range of summer jobs in the UK and the US to fund his college fees.

His first management opportunity arose at the age of twenty four when he was appointed CEO of a dynamic multi-purpose business. There he quickly learned to initially survive and then succeed in business and, as he learned by 'doing', his experience and success often arose through the school of 'hard knocks'. Blaise subsequently underpinned this practical business experience by successfully completing his post graduate studies at Trinity College, Dublin.

Fifteen years ago Blaise established his own Management Consultancy / Business Training enterprise known as the Management Resource Institute, Wexford (MRI). As Senior Strategy Specialist within the Management Resource Institute, Blaise facilitates business owners and their teams to stand back from the 'fuss' of their day to day activity and focus on how best to drive their businesses forward. This he achieves through a combination of direct consulting and focused training. At the time of writing, some two thousand-plus owner / managers have successfully participated in his Owner Management Development Programme **(OMDP).**

Blaise is also the founder director of International Dispute Resolution (Ireland) Ltd., which specialises in providing disputants with alternatives to the normal litigation routes in solving their commercial disputes.

Outside of his formal commercial positions, Blaise holds or has held a number of other influential roles. He is the former regional chairman of IMI (Wexford), founder of IDW, founder member of Enniscorthy Rotary Club and Board member of Wexford Festival Opera.

Blaise Brosnan B.Agr.Sc (Econ) M.Sc.Mgmt. M.Mgtl.

Sample Excerpts

Endorsements

Blaise works within a wide range of business areas: presenting at conferences, training managers, mediating commercial disputes and acting as business advisor. In all of these roles Blaise both challenges and guides his clients to increase their management capacity thus enabling them to optimise their desired output.

His vast practical business experiences equip him to reduce complex issues and models down to usable tools that you, the reader, can understand and use in ways that are relevant to you in your own forward journey.

By completing the exercises in this book and internalising their relevant messages you will convert this book into your own personal roadmap to guide you forward in your business.

Are you worth it?

Are you up for the challenge?

If so let's begin this exciting journey towards your business and personal enhancement.

Preface

This book is my response to the thousands of graduates of our **Owner Management Development Programme (OMDP)** who have asked me to present my unique practical guidance in written form.

The successful development of your career or business depends on your ability to manage.

Although you are the most important person in propelling your career / business forward, you are also the limiting factor. The reason I say that this is actually a good thing for you is because you have more control over improving your own capacity than you have over changing other variables which you may have little influence over.

We are all products of both our genetic map and our interpretation of our life experiences to date. The conversations taking place in our heads are influenced by both. These conversations often arise from criticisms of our past performances and circumstances; we fear standing out from the crowd, we want to be popular and ultimately, we fear failure. All of these limit our forward journey.

If you have a dream of becoming more successful in your career or business, this book is a must for you. It contains a unique opportunity for you to gain valuable practical exposure to a range of ideas, methods and techniques which will both challenge and guide you. By reading and internalising the issues addressed in this book, you will uncap your latent potential and substantially improve your competence for both self and business management. This enhanced capacity will better equip you to successfully tackle the opportunities and threats that may arise as you move your business forward. I am guided by the 'Trim-Tab' concept, where a relatively small absolute Trim-Tab (mini rudder) intervention has a major impact on the movement of the larger rudder which guides the ship in a pre-planned direction irrespective of the prevailing navigation variables.

By completing the various tasks and exercises, you will make this book your own personal roadmap to guide you along your chosen career or business path. It will serve to instruct, to inspire and to increase your knowledge of how to manage your career or business into the future. You will have a greater ability to release your brakes and instead of continuing to spin on the same spot you will be better able to drive your life, your career and your business forward.

As a result of your enhanced capacity, the quality of your input to your personal life, your career and your business will improve. Your output is a direct result of the quality of your input. Your improved output will ensure that you optimise your wealth. The market pays you based on your output, not your input. It doesn't care how busy you are. It just pays you for the output from that sweaty activity. From my experience there is very little relationship between sweat and business success. By internalising and adopting the key messages contained in this book, you will achieve a better output in a smarter way.

You can achieve whatever you want from your career or business provided you want it badly enough. Everything has a price. Are you prepared to pay the price? If you are, you can confidently change your dream into reality. You can achieve this simply through the quality of your input to your business and career. You are the most important input. If you can improve the quality of your own input, then your output will improve proportionally and this will be reflected through your enhanced value in the market.

Clarity of purpose is the first critical link in your future success chain. The challenges and guidance contained in this book will facilitate you in clarifying your purpose. You will then attract the resources and circumstances necessary to make it happen. This is accomplished via the law of attraction.

I have a very special understanding of the issues facing the owner /managers of businesses. At the time of writing, some two thousand plus owner / managers have successfully participated in our **Owner Management Development Programme (OMDP).** This programme focuses on challenging and guiding the participants to initially understand their own strengths and weaknesses, and then to develop their business capacity so that their vision for their business becomes a reality. This book is based on the range of experiences gained from working closely with and understanding, business people.

The focus of the book is on facilitating and challenging you to proceed to this enhanced output level. Through the medium of this book, I will act as your mentor: someone from whom you can draw the wisdom and guidance necessary to facilitate you in achieving your optimum potential. My aim is to equip you with the knowledge and skills to shift from your current position to where you and your business need to be. Incorporate these development steps into your life and you too can make those dreams of business success and wealth your very own reality.

You have to take RESPONSIBILITY for your future success. The word responsibility means the ABILITY to RESPOND; the opportunity or ability to act independently. Don't play a game of chance. Take your future success into your own hands. By implementing the guidance given to you in this book you will begin to manage yourself more professionally and to witness increased success both in your business and in your personal life.

The greatest pleasure in life is the act of giving; especially giving something that will really make a difference to the receiver. I have successfully come through the hard knocks of business life, from which I have learned very valuable practical lessons. It is my privilege to share these with you and to help you energise your dream. Please remember to recommend this book to your friends and colleagues and watch the positive changes both in their thinking and in their lives.

For those of you who already understand most of what this book teaches, perhaps the book may be useful for other members of your team. It may challenge and facilitate them in getting up to speed on a range of career and business issues so that they too can begin to optimise their individual and team contributions to your business.

Make this book your personal management manual which you should continuously dip into for inspiration and guidance. Keep this personal manual close to you. Let others get their own copy which they in turn can personalise by completing the exercises and challenges and reflecting on their responses.

Opening this book represents the first day of your new journey. We all know you can't change yesterday, but you can choose to make today a better day and tomorrow even better still.

Thank you for coming on this life changing trip with me - enjoy the results.

The journey starts with where you are now and finishes with the new you. This represents your journey to the next significant staging post of your commercial and personal life. When you successfully reach that point, a new cycle must be travelled and so forth.

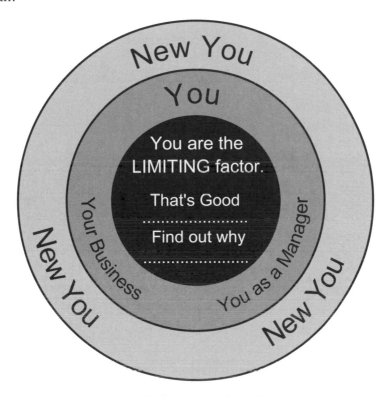

New You

The purpose of life is to live a life of purpose.

You are the **limiting** factor

You As A Person

Chapter 1

Putting the next stage of your Life Journey in context

This book is presented in three sections.

The opening section concentrates on you, both as a person and a manager. You are the most important person in your business but you are also its limiting factor. Whilst this may be difficult for you to either understand or agree with, it is nevertheless true. Having addressed this crucial issue, the second section looks in detail at building your business model from a strategic and a financial perspective. The third and final section focuses on the dynamics of your business model, exploring the operational guidelines required to make you a more effective and a more efficient manager.

Practical application

You all know what a shovel looks like, don't you? A shovel is of no use if you don't put it to work. It's not an ornament, it's a tool and it is only beneficial if you actually use it. Like the shovel, the 'tools' I am exposing you to in this book will be of no benefit to you if you don't put them to use for your own advantage.

Background
This book evolved from a successful Management Development Programme (MDP), which the Management Resource Institute (MRI) initially put together over twelve years ago and which has since been delivered to over two thousand businesses.

> I aim to challenge you to really look at yourself. If I can get you to think a bit differently about yourself and your business, you will act a bit differently. If you act a bit differently in your business on a consistent basis then you will achieve a different result. However, you can't have a different result in your business if you don't act and manage it differently, and you can't manage it differently if you don't start to think differently. You need to stand back a small bit from your business and look for a smarter and more effective way of working. That really is the basis of what this book is about.

The speed of change is limited by the speed of learning.

I don't want you to think of this as a textbook. You should view it as your personalised reference manual. Use the exercises to help you build your individual road map as you travel along your business/career route.

You should use your head at work and your heart at home.

Throughout this book, I will continue to challenge you through exercises and questions. My aim in so doing is to ensure that you internalise the issues in each section. Rather than listing pat answers, I want you to work out your own solutions. In this way you will learn a lot more. I will teach you how to fish so that you can feed yourself for life.

An ounce of commerce is worth a tonne of work.

What kind of a week have you had?

1. _____

2. _____

3. _____

I get varied responses when I ask business people this question, ranging from good, busy, terrible to relaxed and productive. How do these responses compare with your own?

How do you judge whether it was a successful week or not?

1._____

2. _____

You need to learn to differentiate between a victory and a defeat. If you set out to do something and you achieve it within your planned timeframe, then that is a success.

If you want to be more commercially successful, then you must understand and feel the difference between victories and defeats. You need to build a series of potential opportunities for victories into your commercial life. The achievement of these victories will become the building blocks for your future success. This book will facilitate you on that journey.

Your future focus must be on output, because this is what the market pays you for. The market doesn't care how busy you are, or whether you stay in bed all day. It just pays you based on your output. If you can achieve your planned output in a smarter way, then you are on the way to success.

• **Achieve your planned output in a smarter way.**

In most market niches, you tend to find that one third of the participants are very successful (A), one third are just about holding in there (B), and a third are on the way out (C).

Success

Which one of these mini niches do you currently occupy? Everything in life has a price. There is no reason why you can't be in that top (A) mini niche provided you are prepared to pay the price in a smart way. If you successfully implement even one of the strategies that I present to you in this book, then you will greatly enhance your possibilities.

• Are you prepared to pay the price?

Successful business people consistently look for a return on their investment (ROI). Your investment in this book is not its cover price. It is the time you will spend reading the book and reflecting on how best to implement the learning points addressed therein. You will achieve a good return on this investment when you start to think differently about your opportunities and threats. This in turn will challenge you to act differently, resulting in an enhanced output and better payment from the market.

Metaphorically, you are currently on one bank of a valley. As you read and reflect on the issues in this book, you will begin to clarify your vision for the future, which often tends to be located on the opposite bank across the valley. In order to reposition yourself you must manage your way across this valley in a smarter way. This valley is often labelled the 'Valley of Death' since so many dreams are 'drowned' on this difficult journey.

You are Here   **Your Future**

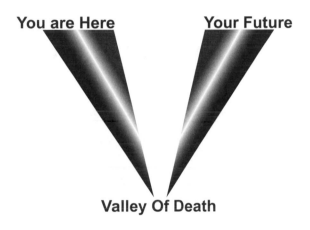

Valley Of Death

Using the exercises and challenges in this book, I will guide you in managing your way through this rather difficult valley of change.

I want you to feel uncomfortable about your current status. If you are not you will remain in your comfort zone. If you remain in this state then you are not going to exploit your potential and this will be reflected in your return from the market.

Chapter **2**

Who are You and why is this Important?

Initially, when we put the MDP together, this first personal development section was not included. As we worked with more businesses it soon became evident that you, the business owner/manager, are the critical ingredient in this potential success formula.

You are the most important person in your business. If you can't manage yourself and you do not have a clear understanding of what your role is, then you are not going to be very effective at managing anyway. As we in MRI began to understand this critical dynamic better we started to anchor the programme on the personal development section. That is why Section One of the book is focused on you. The focus is on what your strengths and weaknesses are, how you think, what your attitude is and many other personal characteristics. The future success of your business depends on your capacity and your increased awareness of how to enhance this capacity.

Having decided to read this book you may feel that the focus in the first section does not seem to address any specific business issues. However, the lessons addressed in the first few chapters are critical, as the focus is on you the person – the crux of the business.

'How would you eat an elephant?'

The answer is one bite at a time. It is the very same with the changes you need to make in your life. Take them on one by one and start to tackle them by 'nibbling at them in a forward direction'. It is the consistency of the forward direction which will ensure your progress.

'To plan for a year sow corn; to plan for a decade sow trees; to plan for a lifetime train and educate men.'

The company philosophy of MRI is built around this ancient quotation. The underlying principle of our approach is to teach you how to fish rather than give you a fish. This means facilitating the development of your own capacity so that you can progress to becoming who you want to be. If you become over-reliant on others to give you pat, instant answers, then you are risking your bright future. What if this source is cut off for any number of reasons?

I will challenge you to take more ownership and to uncover your own answers to particular issues. By so doing you are learning to enhance your fishing capacity and thus guaranteeing your own future growth. Development is a journey with many check-points and stops. You have to extract value from each of these interfaces.

Focus Area: Return on your Investment

As mentioned earlier, successful businesses are continuously focused on ROI. When asked what is the meaning of ROI the most common response from people is simply 'return on investment'. While this is correct, we need to deepen our understanding of the term.

If you want to compete with successful business people, you must imitate what they do in a way that is appropriate for your particular circumstances. What is the ROI of the activity you and your people are engaged in? This is how successful business people think. They do not approach business matters in an ad hoc fashion. They are aware that they are making an investment of their time and resources. So they consistently look at what return they are getting either in the short or long term. The more established and professional a business becomes, the more managers tend to look at the ROI over the longer rather than the shorter term.

When you first commence business and are struggling to survive, it is difficult to think in the longer term because of the day-to-day issues involved in becoming established. You can perform all the longer-term strategic planning tasks, but if you don't have the cash coming in today in order to survive, you might never reach that point further down the line. However, once you get over that initial phase you need to look at your business in a more strategic manner and understand where you are positioning it. For example where is your competitive advantage going to be established from?

Running a business is a balancing act between short-term success and longer term focus.

It is very easy to focus on the long term as a surreal place that we do not yet inhabit. However the reality is that we have to live and eat today in order to be there for the longer term.

Education in the broadest sense is critical for your business success. This book is not about education in the narrow sense of attending classes and sitting exams. It is about you acquiring knowledge, skills and tactics in relation to your business so that you can redefine the principles in your own mind and decide: *What is this going to do for me? Can I do something with this back home in my business tomorrow?* That is the acid test.

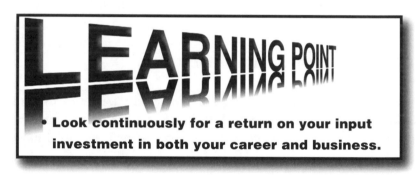

LEARNING POINT

• **Look continuously for a return on your input investment in both your career and business.**

As you work through this book you should challenge yourself:

Does this mean something to me? Can I do something with this? Can I re-juggle this to suit my business in some shape or form?

Even if you only take away and successfully implement two or three approaches from this book you will get a good ROI from your financial investment and your time spent reflecting and planning for your road across the 'Valley of Death'. Don't try and take away a hundred things from the book. Take away what is right for you and what will help you to make the necessary interventions to improve your capacity.

You must learn from the mistakes of others, since you cannot possibly live long enough to make them all yourself.

Give an example where you can apply this in your own life:

_____

_____

When we as consultants are invited to examine a business facing a financial crisis, within a short time period we can define the source of the problem. Clients often wonder how this is possible – 'How in the hell did you know that?'; 'Were you told?' My response is that no, we were not. The actual problems tend to be the same everywhere. Of course every company will have its own variations but there is a similarity and consistency regarding many of the mistakes which businesses tend to make.

There are about a dozen things that they all do wrong. As you go through this book, I will try and guide you around some of these obvious 'black holes'. With this guidance you should be able to manoeuvre your way around some, but there are also less obvious obstacles awaiting you. As you read on and reflect, I want you to look at your own profile and judge how you stand up in relation to these issues. We need to look at ourselves and compare how good we are in relation to whatever the 'better people' are doing. Is there a gap between what I am doing and what they are doing? How can I close that gap?

There is a management concept referred to as *'gap analysis'*. It is a concept which you can use to good effect in your own situation. You look at what somebody is doing well, look at how you compare and then define whether a gap exists between the two approaches. If the gap is on your side, then you have to decide how you can close it. This may be a simple concept but it can be difficult to apply and take corrective action.

Of course this approach is not specific to business situations but can be applied to any aspect of your life. We should always compare ourselves to the 'best in class' as this will drive us onwards and upwards.

'It's not what happens to you that matters, but how you react to it that counts.'

Do you agree or disagree with this statement?

Sometimes you will learn more by redefining the question in a way that is more relevant to your situation. For example you may agree to a point, but with a rider. For example, 'I agree but it depends on the severity of the issue'.

An instance might be a company which is faced with financial ruin. Sometimes it is more comfortable to blame others and bury your head. However I have never come across a situation where a company went bust overnight. The symptoms are generally there for a long time. Often we use the ostrich strategy of putting our heads in the sand. We don't really want to see the symptoms and so we avoid the issues. Often in our own business we approach difficult situations with rose tinted glasses and the symptoms aren't always glaringly obvious to us.

You need to be very careful with a business that you have created because you can get emotionally attached to it. Creating a business can be somewhat akin to having children. If you have children you will know what I am talking about. It is usually the neighbour's child down the road who is causing the problem. We find it difficult to be pragmatic and objective about our own children. Your approach to your own business can often be the same. Our emotional attachment can be both good and bad. It is bad if you can't see reality and the emerging facts. Sometimes we don't want to face the issues as facing issues often has painful implications, but that is the price we must pay.

LEARNING POINT
• Are you prepared to pay the price to address the issues facing your business today?

What are the five most critical issues facing you and your business at the moment?

1.

2.

3.

4.

5.

How long have you been avoiding addressing these issues?

What action plans are you now prepared to put in place to address these issues? Please include time frames.

Issue 1:_____

Issue 2:_____

Issue 3:_____

Issue 4:_____

Issue 5:_____

It is very unlikely that there is a business problem that doesn't have a solution. It is also unlikely that anyone reading this book will come up with a new problem that somebody hasn't previously faced. The only thing that is unique about your problem is you and your capability or lack of it.

An example is that of Intellectual Property (IP) rights. Having spent a number of years developing a product, many businesses face being exposed in the area of IP because they have not yet secured the rights to the product. While one might think of intellectual property as a black and white type of issue, there are still many legal angles which are anything but straightforward. A further issue is the high percentage of products that are protected by patent but which never make it successfully on the commercial market. It is quite frightening, taking into account the effort of the inventors and the investment of scarce resources in trying to protect that supposed potential asset.

Secondly, the value of intellectual property is only as good as your capability of defending it afterwards. What do you do if, for example, some Asian low cost operator robs your basic 'idea' and swamps the market with a 'me too' product? Sometimes they won't even go to the trouble of re-engineering it, they just copy it.

If you invent something which a big company becomes interested in, the big company has two choices. They can either re-engineer the product in such a way that you are left with a useless (supposedly protected) asset or, they can buy out your rights rather than risk legal action. Often the second option is the cheaper one for them and you get some tax efficient income, which appears relatively big to you but is incidental in the cost equation of the acquiring larger operator. They tend to be able to control the channel to the market and thus drive predictable volume into this business. If you can invent something that's attractive enough for some big operator to take on, this is the model you should consider. If you invent and you try to control the whole process you are unlikely to be commercially successful because they are two very different jobs.

Brand Recognition is another area to consider. Each brand is a statement. Cuisine de France is a good example of developing competitive advantage via market positioning and drive rather than just IP protection. When the IAWS bought it over they were able to pump the necessary resources into it and use it as their bridgehead to strategically build their food business. It is nearly always possible to build even a bad business if you have plenty of resources, but obviously it is easier to build a potentially attractive business.

All businesses need to have access to enough resources to enable them to live long enough to be successful. Many businesses fail at the initial phase because they don't have adequate resources, especially working capital. I am aware of businesses which went bankrupt before they ever reached the stage where they were in a position to write their first invoice. They focused on developing solutions which were going to revolutionise particular market niches but which burned off the investment capital faster than their planned output. In other words they failed to convert their 'fantastic ideas' into tangible outputs which could provide an income stream within the timeframe that their investment capital took to burn.

LEARNING POINT

- **Your business must live long enough to allow it to be successful.**

When I was starting out as a green graduate, one of the best pieces of business advice I was given was: *'Manage the business variables you have control over or can influence and don't get too concerned over those you have no control over'*.

As manager of your business you have to take responsibility. There are lots of variables out there you have no control over. However, irrespective of the way those variables come at people, some handle them better than others. For example, if the European Central Bank raises interest rates by another quarter percent there is nothing any of us can actually do about that – it is an uncontrollable issue. However every business person will adopt a different strategy to that common issue. While they have no control over the actual quarter percent, they have some control over how they manage the working capital of their own businesses. They can adopt different management tactics to nullify some of the ill effects of the interest rate rise.

We actually have more control over many of the variables than we give ourselves credit for. *As a professional manager start taking responsibility.* There are people who make a career of just surviving on somebody else's payroll, but (un)fortunately when you are on your own payroll you don't have this option. The market is a ruthless paymaster. It pays you based on output, not on promises of what you are going to do. It is clinical!

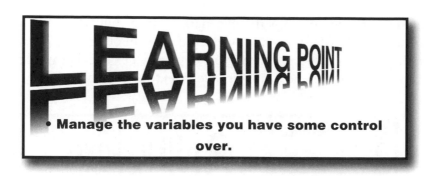

• **Manage the variables you have some control over.**

You must understand that you are the **driver.** You need to plan but you must also implement.

Focus Area: Attitude

How would you read this phrase?

Opportunityisnowhere

Opportunity is now here? Opportunity is nowhere? It depends on how you are looking at it. Is that glass half full or half empty?

If you weren't an optimist you would probably be working for somebody else. That doesn't mean you don't have bad days and you don't hit rough patches. The feeling of isolation is one of the biggest problems business people must contend with. Some of the most lonesome business people I know are actually physically located in enterprise centres but they are still very much islands. It's not the physical isolation; it's more a mental isolation. I recommend getting involved in appropriate networking activities. When you worked in the corporate world you were probably part of 'cells', where there was (in theory at least) a range of supports.

The opportunity of a lifetime must be taken during the lifetime of the opportunity.

Can you think back over your own life and identify opportunities you didn't take within the lifetime of that opportunity?

Opportunities are very transparent when we look backwards but they are very hazy looking forwards. There are opportunities around us all the time. There are as many opportunities today as there were last week or over the last twelve months. You should never be too fussed about the opportunities you have lost. Your opportunities are now and in the future. I think the biggest problem with people who run small businesses is that they try and grab too many opportunities simultaneously.

Picture the following scenario. If you went out at night into a field hunting rabbits how would you bag the largest number possible? Snare them? Lamp them? Shoot them? It is important to remember that you only have one lamp, a field full of rabbits and you want to come home with the greatest number of them.

The correct answer is to hunt just one at a time. This will give the most beneficial results. If you go out with your lamp shining all over the place trying to catch them all, the rabbits will scatter and you won't catch any. However, if you go out and focus in on one, kill it, focus in, kill, focus in, kill, you will come back with a bag full. Act like a sniper!

One of the biggest mistakes we find with small businesses is that they try and snare too many rabbits at the one time and finish up not getting any. You just don't have enough resources in a small business for too many fights at the one time. Invariably, the reason they finish up with nothing is indecisiveness - people can't decide which of the options available is best. So, rather than making the decision to run with two or three, they do a bit of this and a bit of that and a bit of something else and finish up doing nothing right.

In business you often have scarce resources and if you spread your resources too thinly you are not going to optimise your bottom line. You are not giving yourself any chance to really exploit the identified opportunity. The resources I am talking about here include time, money, technology, facilities and reputation. They are the resources that you as managers have and you must manage these resources on a daily basis. There is no business (big or small) that has enough resources to do everything it would like to do.

There is a strategic option known as **"the funnel or the tunnel option"**. The funnel option is to take the broader view and the tunnel option is to take the narrower one. In business you must adopt both options at different times so that you can successfully optimise your targeted opportunity within the timeframe of that opportunity.

If you take the funnel attitude which is to start out wide with the intentions of refining it down, will this work for your business? It can, but if you spread yourself too wide and don't focus in a short period of time your resources will get wasted very quickly.

Can you think of situations in your own business where you had two or three fires going on at the one time and you failed to put them all out? I think if you are honest it has happened. Big companies do it as well, but big companies get away with it because they have enough resources to bury their failures and nobody will ever know about them. If one or two projects go wrong together your relatively scarce resources get burned off and your business is left with 'insufficient blood' flowing through it. The next logical step in the absence of a blood transfusion is death!

To achieve you must first win the battle in your own mind. You have to talk your way into the discipline of the change. You won't always get there but if you think and talk that way, you are far more likely to achieve what you set out to do. There are many opportunities out there but you have to focus in on 'killing' one at a time.

Why did you choose the business / career you are currently in?

_____

_____

_____

Knowing what you now know, would you make the same choice again?

'It's never too late to become what you wanted to become.'

It is important to have an interest in the type of business you are in. If what you are doing doesn't turn you on in some way you will have a serious problem in making a success of it. It's hard to make a success of something you are not pumped up about in some shape or form. Would you admit it, even to yourself, if you are not really switched on to whatever your business career is?

If you let nature take its own course and if you are not very disciplined, the parts of your business that you don't like will not get done. We all have parts of our business that we don't like doing. You might not like doing the books, someone else might not like doing some other aspect, but if you are not very careful those areas that you don't like doing (which are often the most important areas of your business) will tend to get put aside.

'If you do what you have always done, you will have what you have always had.'

What message does this give you in relation to your business?

_____

_____

_____

Many people wish for a better return from their business. They talk about wanting a better return from their business but are not prepared to change their inputs. Whatever outcome you have from your business is a direct result of the quality of your inputs. You are by far the most important one of those inputs. If you want a better return from your business, you must to do something about it. *Wishing it to happen won't make it happen.*

The quality of your inputs on one side directly relate to the quality of the outputs on the other:

Let's say that you are making a net profit of 10% at the moment but your business is capable of delivering a 13% net profit. You have to do something about the quality of your inputs. You can talk forever about getting 13% but it won't happen on its own. You have to make a change at the inputs levels. You have to manage the situation more effectively; you have to buy in better, manufacture more efficiently and do something different in order to have a different output.

There are two ways of doing this. One is to do more of the same but to do it faster. This is one strategy – the hard way. The other strategy is to stand back, take stock and realise that there is a better way of doing this – the smart way.

One is sweat, the other is the *smart* way of doing it. Probably in excess of 70% of the businesses which are not going well would suggest the solution is to work harder.

LEARNING POINT

- **There is little correlation between sweat and business success.**

The successful people that we see out there are not sweating; they are working their heads. They are looking for a smarter way of achieving. We are all creatures of habit, just like the cows coming into the milking parlour one at a time in the same rotation. Today was Thursday, how much different was today than last Thursday for you? How much different will tomorrow be from today in the way that you go about your business? Or are you looking at your inputs here and saying, hold on a minute there must be a better way of doing this. This book is about *trying to challenge you to stand back a small bit from your business and look for a smarter and more effective way of working.*

You have put that investment into your future by buying this book and internalising the issues it has raised so far. That's about being smart.

I want to tell you about John, who had a very mundane kind of business which was going nowhere. He was just about making a living and was at the point where he was under intense financial pressure, but pride was stopping him from really letting it go. Participation in the programme challenged him to look at his business from a different angle. He came up with a different business model in relation to the management of that business. That was four years ago. That business today is super-successful: same guy, same product but a different way of doing it.

John didn't get into this change mode in a voluntary way; he did it out of complete necessity to survive. He would now say that if he had been smart enough he would have challenged himself many years earlier and would be a millionaire today. The model he came up with is interesting. I will profile it for you later.

You might say okay that's fine, but it's not typical - it's more of a once in a lifetime thing. I don't agree. What's more, you know people similar to John in your own locality; they are in your own circle. I challenge you now to write down the name of somebody who you consider is a good business person. (I don't want you to write your own name down!)

My identified person is:

_____

Why did you choose that person?

_____

_____

Why do you believe he/she is a good business person?

_____

_____

_____

_____

Is it:

- Complete passion about what they do?
- Constantly re-inventing themselves by generating good ideas?
- A very good manager and good with people?
- Natural ability?
- Somebody you would aspire to be like?
- Someone who is very open to change or can adapt to different types of markets and can see opportunities?

The following is a listing of the parameters identified by one of our **Owner Management Development Programme** groups who were asked to identify a business person they admired.

	Your Total Score		
	1	5	10
Self Belief			
Understand the issues very quickly			
Passion			
Focused			
Capable of re-inventing their business			
Communication ability			
Ideas Person			
Able to close sales			
Professional in the way they do things			
Consistent			
Good at delegating			
Your total score			

I want you to score yourself against each of those criteria on a score of one to ten - one being very poor and ten being excellent. There is a total possible score of 110. I want you to score yourself against that profile. Be honest in your scoring. As it says in the Bible, '*to thine own self be true*'. Honesty should have been included in this list. Honesty to oneself is one of the ingredients for success in business.

Add up your own scores and see where you are in relation to that profile. Not all the ingredients of success are on that profile but there are some very fundamental ones there. You should add your own identified ones to the blank spaces in the list and let it become very personal for you.

What does that exercise tell you?

_____

_____

_____

It is a gap analysis. It is a gap between where others are and where you perceive yourself to be at the moment. You should re-score yourself at intervals into the future. Your change of score under the various traits will indicate your upward movement. Reading and digesting the lessons from this book will enhance this journey for you. If you scored yourself particularly low under any of the above traits there is a message there for you. You need to work on those areas of your development in order to better equip yourself to manage your business and career.

All these ingredients/traits impact on the quality of your input into your business. You are the most important person in your business. You might say that's obvious if you are only a one person operation, but I would still say it even if you had a hundred people working for you.

You are the most important person in your business but you are also the limiting factor.

Your business is actually as good as you are. No better, no worse. That is a sobering thought for all of us but I believe it to be a good thing. It is easier to do something about ourselves than it is to do something about other issues. So when I say that you are both the most important but also the limiting factor, I believe that this is actually a positive and not a negative statement.

I aim to challenge you to really look at yourself. If I can get you to think a bit differently about yourself and your business, you will act a bit differently. If you act a bit differently in your business on a consistent basis you will achieve a different result. However, you can't have a different result in your business if you don't act and manage it differently, and you can't manage it differently if you don't start to think differently. That really is the basis of what this book is about.

I am referring quite a lot to the concept of 'change'. However, consistency is also an important concept. If you are flexible enough about making the initial change you then need to **anchor** it in order for it to take affect. If, after making that change you haven't the necessary discipline to stick with it until it becomes a new habit, you will naturally drift back to your original ways with no positive result for you or your business. It will have been a waste of your scarce resources.

Change is difficult because what you are doing is breaking habits. You have to be very conscious of trying to keep at it until it becomes a new habit. We must consciously repeat a new change at least twenty one times before it anchors itself as a new habit. A habit is something that we repeat unconsciously.

Any of you that have tried to give up smoking will realise that it is not easy. Neither is it easy for you to change the way you are currently operating your business. Your daily sequence involves a lot of repetition and unconscious movement in your activities which have become part of your subconscious; you are engulfed in your comfort zone. Although the comfort zone may not be that 'comfortable', it is more comfortable than changing - and that's the problem. If you don't change and if you don't anchor that change, then you will be back again to where you started.

There is no business that cannot be improved and as managers you must keep challenging yourselves to optimise your commercial results. One of the traits identified above was consistency. This is critical if you are to achieve sustained improvement.

Elastic band

When you stretch an elastic band it changes shape somewhat, doesn't it? Now if you leave the pressure go again what happens? It goes back to where it came from. A change in your business and change in your life is similar. Many people are good at the initial burst, but if you are not consistent and don't anchor the better business tactics, then it goes back to more or less the original shape. You will not improve if you feel that you are okay. My aim is to challenge you to look at where you currently are in relation to your business cycle and to decide how far you want to drive it on. You need to define where the gap is between where you are at this moment and where you want to be. For many of you the changes will only be small but for some of you larger changes may be necessary. A combination of small changes, in an organised way, can have quite an impact on your business.

Your brain

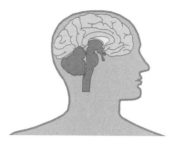

The brain is divided into a left side and a right side. The right is the creative side and the left is the more logical side. Each of us uses a degree of both the logical and creative sides of our brain in our daily lives.

When you were at school you will have come across the concept of the normal distribution curve, or the bell shaped curve at it is better known. Essentially, this means that two thirds of the population fall within one standard deviation from the mean. In the brain example, it says that two thirds of us have a reasonable balance between right and left brain. At both extremes you have a smaller proportion of the population who tend to be either very left brained or very right brained. Very left brained people tend to be very black and white in their thinking and very structured in their approach to activities. Generally people with this left profile tend to be attracted towards precision type work such as accounting or engineering. For example, somebody who designs bridges has to define and measure all the stresses, loading etc. to exact detail or otherwise the bridge will fall. This type of work requires them to be more left brained. On the opposite side there are people who require innovative and creative traits. In theory it would be very unusual for a left brained person to come up with a new creation for a vivid garden layout because they see the world from a slightly different viewpoint. Obviously the more right brained an individual is the more likely they are to be 'big picture' people in their approach to an activity and they are generally less focused on the organisational and operational end of things. They tend to see the creative end results and aren't as focused on the smaller details.

I believe that it is very important to stress that difference is a good thing – it would be a very dull world if we all had the same focus.

Considering the above, which do you think is the best type of brain profile for business?

Right _____   Left _____

Outline the reason for your answer below.

_____

_____

_____

_____

Ideally a mixed combination works best, with the traits of both brain profiles complimenting one another. However, this is one of the real weaknesses in smaller businesses. As there is less opportunity of balancing your brain profile due to lack of numbers within your business, you have to put a bigger effort into doing the things you are not naturally good at. If you are right brained the last thing you want to look at is your balance sheet and the detailed messages leaping off the page. In such a situation you will obviously have to be a lot more disciplined in making sure that this side of your business is well managed. Bigger companies put project teams together who bring a good cross-section of all of these kinds of characteristics to achieve a balanced approach. In businesses where it is possible to have a team with a combination of brain types working together the end results are usually better.

When starting a business it is important not to focus too heavily on the left hand side approach where 2+2 always equals 4. There needs to be room for innovation and creativity.

Phases of Business Cycle

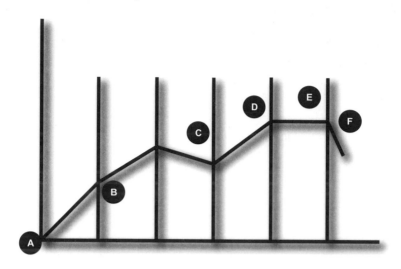

Time

Every business starts out at point (**A**). Someone has an idea and gets it up and running. To achieve this you must have a reasonable innovative vision. When the business gets to a certain mass (**B**) you need somebody to actually start managing it more professionally. Innovative people are great at starting businesses but they are not naturally good at the day to day management issues. Once an idea moves into production they tend to lose interest and move on to the next project that interests them. Innovative people are fantastic provided there is a team behind them to pick up the project and run with it, thus allowing the innovative one to get the next good idea off the ground.

If you keep jumping ahead without killing off whatever you are doing then what **output** will you have to deliver to the market? Remember, the market pays you for delivering **needed output**, not promises.

You require a different style of management for each of the time phases of your business cycle. Your natural style will be suitable for some of the business cycle phases, but not all.
Which phase does your style of management suit best?

Personnel Profile Exercise

		Circle Appropriate Figures				
	The more accurate the description fits the higher the score					
1	I am a very confident person					
2	I like problems and see them as challenges to be overcome					
3	I am an enthusiastic and optimistic person					
4	I take action rather than delay a decision					
5	I get things done					
6	I have untapped potential					
7	I make thing happen rather than just let things happen					
8	I have a good impression of myself					
9	My upbringing and life to date does not limit me					
10	I get a great 'buzz' from my work					
11	I always strive to do the best I possibly can					
12	I know exactly what I want from life and work					
13	I am highly motivated					
14	I know who I am, where I am going and what my values are					
15	Write just five lines describing what your business/career will look like three years from now:					

Instructions:

This is just a short profiling exercise for you to complete. It will help you to get to know yourself better. The first statement is: 'I am a very confident person'. If you think you are a very confident person score yourself 5. If you think you are the opposite score yourself 1. Otherwise choose whatever number in between that you feel best describes your level of confidence.

Complete the exercise up to Question 14 and just leave Question 15 for the moment.

We are applying this section to your work life so please answer the questions with work in mind.

People display different characteristics, depending on whether they are at work or outside. A client of ours who owns a very successful commercial business presents these contrasting characteristics in a very stark way. Sociably he is very good company but when you meet him in the morning in a work environment he is focused and pragmatic. His interest is solely on the business issue at hand. He is extremely intense when he is working but outside of work he is actually a lamb. From a personal perspective he would see himself as a tough guy - very focused. In his mind if he has struck a deal, whether the deal has been written down or not, that is it. However an important learning point for you to note is that in his situation it would always be written down. His business was the first business that I encountered which saw the value of good documentation and filing. If you had a meeting with him, there was always a note put in the file. It is a lot more common today for contact notes to be filed, aided by electronic communication facilities etc. I have seen those files make or save a lot of money for his business because his company had a far better record than a lot of people they were having disputes with later on.

Question 15:
I want you to think about Question 15 above and write just five lines describing what your business/career will look like three years from now. I want you to really think about this. It is a very important question. Now consider, was it by design or by accident that I left this limited space for your answer? Was I trying to spare paper or was there some other reason?

_____

_____

_____

_____

Consider the following story: There was a young Irish man many years ago who was spending his first Christmas away from home. His only means of communication with his mother at home was by letter. He wrote a twenty four page letter describing how he was doing, what he was at and giving an overview of the countryside. At the end he added a P.S. Can you guess what was in the P.S.?

 • That he was missing home?
 • Asking for money?

In fact it was none of these. His P.S. simply stated:
'Mum I'm sorry for writing such a long letter, I hadn't time to write a short one.'

There is a real message in this story. If I had left a whole page for you to complete the answer to Question 15 you would all ramble in order to fill the page. It is human nature to do so. It's far more difficult to get your thoughts down in a focussed and very short format. It takes a lot of discipline to do so.

Many of you may be finding it difficult to answer Question 15. Don't worry about it. I would expect that at this stage, but it is actually the critical question that you need to answer. I would suggest that one of the greatest motivators in business life is **clarity of purpose.** If you know what you want out of your business there is a much greater chance that you will achieve it. I believe that vagueness about what you really want out of your business is the biggest de motivator.

Establishing this type of clarity is quite difficult for many people. I probably have never yet seen a successful business where the owner or the driver of the business was vague about what he or she wanted. I strongly believe that a vague idea of where you want to go and a successful enterprise cannot actually go together (if they do it tends to be by pure accident).

Question 15 is a challenge to you in relation to the shape of your business. Put the book down now and reflect and debate with yourself and trusted others on what your answer to Question 15 should be. Capture the output of your reflection in the space left for you next to Question 15.

Some people are afraid to be clear in case a better version will come around the corner. However they need to think about the fact that it may or may not come and even if it did come, would they recognise it? It is always easier to get a good idea up and running rather than a bad idea, but there are many good ideas that are unfortunately in the wrong heads. It all really comes back to the person. There are plenty of good ideas and opportunities but there is a shortage of implementation. Ideas need somebody to grab them and make them happen.

Take a look at the picture.
What do you see? Why have I included it?
There is one finger pointing out, while three are pointing back at you. What is the message for you in this symbol?

LEARNING POINT

• I am responsible for what's going on, the buck stops with me.

You can't point a finger at somebody without having three pointing back at yourself.

We in MRI are often invited by financial institutions to go into some of their troubled business clients and see what the real financial disease is. Like in the medical world, the disease is generally well anchored by the time we get there and often the only medicine is the knife. In business language this involves putting the business into receivership in order to protect the finances of the secured creditors, which are generally the banks.

I have often sat with the owners or directors of such businesses and you can imagine that in these difficult situations everybody is very emotional. I have never yet heard a director of a company saying *'I was responsible for this mess; I managed this bloody company badly'*. However, what you will hear is: "*... the banks screwed us, the government ...they are terrible! Staff - you couldn't get them to work for you ... nobody would pay you...*" - a long list of excuses with everybody pointing a finger at somebody else in relation to their impending demise. These people never think about the three fingers pointing back at themselves. They are the owners and managers of the business but they don't take responsibility for the evolving business funeral. They just keep blaming 'others'; pointing the finger. In business you are responsible. If you break down the word responsibility it means having the ability to respond to your emerging opportunities and threats. Do you use you ability to respond (your responsibility) adequately for both your own career and your business? Yes_____   No_____

List some examples below.

_____

_____

_____

If you want to be more successful in your business you have to understand that nobody has a better vested interest in its success than you do. To achieve success on a consistent basis you have to make the necessary investment of your time, thoughts and other necessary resources. It's your gig; you can't depend on other people to do it for you. Nobody will come and knock at your door and say, 'Can I help you?' Life is not like that. Strangely enough (and particularly for smaller businesses), there is more outside help available today than ever before but you have to set yourself up to avail of it. Programmes like the Management Development Programme (MDP) wouldn't have happened fifteen years ago because there were no County Enterprise Boards. There was no specific business training for people like you. To start your own business at that time wasn't a 'cool' thing to do.

Today there is a lot more support for smaller businesses through local agencies such as the County Enterprise Boards (CEB) than there is for medium size businesses (excepting those positioned in the high export growth category). Several years ago the support agencies decided that they would concentrate their scarce resources on identified high growth export type businesses and let everybody else sink or swim. I think there is a message for you in that strategy. You too have scarce resources so you have to be careful that you don't spread those resources too thinly on the ground. You should concentrate them on the good sections/elements of your business. What are the good sections/elements of the market for your business to go after? Where should you be putting your scarce resources so that you can get the 'biggest bang for your buck'

_____

_____

_____

Focus

It is very tempting to try to be all things to all people, but you can't be. Nobody can be, particularly a small, start up business. That is why you must be selective. Of course it is always easier to say I am going to do this than to say I am not going to do that. In fact saying no is actually a more difficult decision to make for lots of people. What often happens is something between those two extremes. The indecision arises and results in you doing a bit of everything and spreading your scarce resources so thinly on the ground that you get little response and no competitive advantage.

The person you identified earlier as being a good business person, one of his/her characteristics I suggest is that this person wasn't all things to all people. They tried to specialise in something. They may have tried a few things before they hit on the right one, but once they hit on it they focused in and tried to do it better. Am I correct?

Yes_____   No_____

> *'If you think you can or you think you can't, you're right.'*   Henry Ford

Responsibility

I believe that we all have to go through a learning process. A lot of the mistakes we make tend to be repeated mistakes. It's not smart to continue to make the same mistakes all the time but unfortunately, it happens quite a lot.

'If you are going to make a mistake, at least let it be a new mistake'

This is a very strong statement and one worth remembering.

Within a large organisation the system controls us to a large extent. There is a flow and a momentum there. When you are running your own business you don't necessarily have these controlling systems, therefore you must consciously manage yourself in a disciplined fashion and learn from these mistakes while trying not to repeat them. You have to be far more self disciplined now than when you were working within a large organisation. You have to hold your shape. You don't now have the same support mechanisms around you. (It's a lonesome journey, isn't it? Yes_____ No_____.) It is easy to be down on yourself and that's why I think that anything that encourages you on or gives you 'a leg up' is so important. After all you are the critical person in your business.

'If at first you do succeed, try something harder'

There is a message here for you. You owe it to yourself to say: 'Is there more in me?' If you decide you are fine where you are, without reaching your potential, then that's okay, but many of you are at the stage where there is at least one or two good kicks left. Perhaps sometimes your ambition or your vision is not big enough. I believe you have to think big and plan in blocks towards your future. It is important to have some reasonable clarity about your long term journey or long term vision. That journey is made up of a sequence of steps. You need to be very specific about the steps you want to take. Your answer to Question 15 is basically your best guess (at this stage) in relation to your end point three years down the road. This is a reasonable timeframe to be aiming towards. Now you have some documented view about where you want to be in three years time. That's good. There are lots of steps along that journey that you have to plan for. You need to have a written Action Plan, signalling certain staging posts along the way so that you can reach your planned output within the agreed timeframe. That's really what your business plan is about. It's about first crystallising your thoughts and then putting down on paper the various staging posts you need to be at in predetermined timeframes so that you can achieve your end goal. Circumstances may change as you travel this journey but it's better to have the map than to be without it.

Success Metrics

Some people make things happen; some people watch while others make things happen and some wonder what happened.

Which of these three characters do you think you are?

_____

Realistically, there is an element of these three characters in all of us. When you are running your own business with the market as your pay master, you need to have a strong streak of that first character, because if you don't make things happen, who will?

Eating the Elephant

Using this **Issue Template** will facilitate to consistently take this journey in a forward stepping manner.

Issue Template

1.   **Identify an issue.**

2.   **List three reasons why you haven't addressed this issue before now:**
   A.
   B.
   C.

3.   **Set objective(s) re this issue.**

4.   **Flesh out an agreed Action Plan to address this issue.**

5.   **Agree how you are going to monitor progress.**

I recommend that you use this template to facilitate you in tackling the issues in your career or business. I want to ask you now to identify just one issue and write it down under the first heading. It should be something that you know you need to deal with but haven't done so for whatever reason. Next I want you to list three reasons why you haven't successfully dealt with this issue before now. Then I want you to set some objective for tackling the issue at hand. This could be a time or money objective. Now flesh out your action plan which is the means by which you intend achieving this objective. Finally, to know whether you have achieved your objective or not, write down how you intend to monitor it.

WORK SPACE.

For example: Let's take a typical business issue such as your debtor accounts which are gone out of order. One of the reasons for this is because you have ignored doing the snag list. This allows your debtors to have a useful excuse for not paying you. It's another example of the working of the cause and effect principle. The effect here is that your debtors are gone out of control. One of the causes is your inability to 'kill' off the job. The objective here could be that you are going to do the snag list by Friday and collect the money by Tuesday.

Next I want you to flesh out your action plan. In other words, how are you going to achieve the objectives you have documented above?

Finally, how will you know whether you have achieved it or not? How you are going to monitor the situation?

When you have successfully completed or 'killed off' the identified issue, then use a copy of the above template to work your way in a stepped manner through another issue and so on. I want you to get into the habit of doing this exercise. If you set out to do this and you have a measurement to show you achieved it, that's a victory. It's very important for you to have victories, because victories help you to build confidence in yourself. You need a series of them and you need bigger ones as you go on.

Good organisation skills are critical

I am advising that you should open a file and name it the **Issue File.** Have one divide only in the file. Put all the issue templates you are working on at the front of the file and the issues which you have 'killed' at the back of the file. As you read and digest the challenges in this book, you will identify a number of issues you need to address. Fill out an Issue Template for each and insert them in the Issue File as suggested above. This will get you into the habit of addressing issues in an organised way. What is behind the divide is killed off and completed. What is in front of the divide is work in progress (WIP). Make sure it is work in progress within the timeframe that you had set for it. It can be work in progress if you have done nothing with it, but that's not really what I am talking about. If you give yourself three weeks to do something, you should be moving that sheet to the back of the file after three weeks. This is where the monitoring step comes in. If you do this on a stepped basis you will surprise yourself at the progress you will make in relation to killing off issues.

You might be thinking of issues as negative things that need to be addressed but this is only one side of the equation. Issues can also be opportunities that you haven't yet addressed. For example, there could be a customer out there that you need to chase and this would be a positive issue.

Of course you don't *have* to do any of the exercises but I would suggest strongly that you complete these exercises and reflect on the learning points from them. If you get into this way of thinking you will be a better manager.

Planning

Did you have a good week?

How you respond to this question indicates what **measurement type formula** you have in your head. This is a critical issue because these mental formulae regulate your follow-on actions and thus your **tangible** outputs. The market in turn pays you based on these tangible outputs.

I am trying to get you to think about success or what a good week is. A good week is one where you have successfully completed whatever you set out to do. If you have achieved your goal then that's a good week. A bad week is a week where you don't really set out to achieve any specific goal but instead have a very vague idea of what you want to do. That by definition has to be a bad week because you are not too sure; there is no measurement in there, no focus and you are just putting in time. A bad week is also one where you just didn't achieve what you set out to do, you just flunked it. You should be very annoyed with yourself if you commit yourself to doing something specific for a particular week and then you don't genuinely go after it. Of course circumstances can always arise and get in the way but for the most part you must try to control these to the best of your ability and ensure that you achieve what you set out to do.

I believe that the language you use is a reflection of the way you think. If you talk in very general or global terms like 'I was *busy*', it is generally a reflection of the way you think. If that is the way you think then it is probably the way you act as well. So, as a discipline for yourself, be a bit more precise in the language you use in relation to your business. This will undoubtedly have a direct impact on your follow-on business actions. What do you set out to do? It's not to be busy; it's to achieve some specific objective. You should judge yourself then based on its success or failure. That is why I am asking you how your week was.

So did you have a good week?

_____

_____

_____

Benchmarking

Those of you coming from the corporate world will be familiar with other forms of benchmarking - from an efficiency and an effectiveness perspective. Many larger businesses take this process very seriously and allocate huge resources to optimise their value from the process. Large companies use consultants to audit an industry type. Everyone who wishes to participate has to pay. The consultants constantly gather all this information and put it together in a statistical format and then pass those performance figures back to the participating companies. In turn each of these companies can compare themselves and their performance against the average for their industry. The consultants present the figures into, for example, the lowest third, middle third and top third, so that when the participating businesses get those composite figures back they can compare themselves against whichever performance section they are in.

Smaller businesses cannot afford this strategy but the concept is still very important to them. I suspect that most of you are at best comparing yourself with yourself. You are comparing this year's performance against last year's or this month's against last month's. If you continue only to compare yourself with yourself you really don't know whether you are doing well or not. Last month's performance wasn't very good anyway, so if you are up five or ten percent this month, so what?

What we suggest is that you should try and identify a like-minded business, similar to your own but one which is far enough away that you will never be in competition with them. You should then set up a relationship with them over a period of time and start to share information and work it from there. Compare their performance against your performance under a number of relevant headings. I am including two examples below to show you just how well this can work.

Case 1

There's a furniture designer I know whose name is John. John thought this concept was worthwhile. He looked around and one of the first decisions he made was that there was nobody in the twenty six counties far enough away from him because of the nature of what he was doing. He identified a guy in Northern Ireland named William. They met a few times over a six month period but it didn't really work for them. The reason it didn't work was that although William thought the concept was good he was by nature a very closed person. It was against his nature to be too open in relation to figures and drawings and the relationship just didn't work. However John decided that it was still worthwhile and he went looking around and came across, through research, a company in the US that were into a similar type of design as his. They made contact, spoke on the phone a few times and exchanged brochures. Eventually they decided it would be worthwhile meeting up. So John flew to the US and spent three or four days. They started to build a relationship and they now go across the water both ways every year. It has been fantastic for both companies in relation to design ideas and many other aspects of their respective businesses. If John was speaking directly with you he would say that it was one of the best things he ever did. They have a very open relationship and share everything. While their cost structures would be different in both countries, sharing other aspects of their business has been great. They brain-storm each other in a very open relationship and it worked very well for them.

Case 2

There is an auctioneering firm I know in the Midlands who thought this concept was worthwhile and they looked around and eventually identified two auctioneering companies a long way from them that they thought might have potential. The first company they approached weren't interested but the second one thought there might be something in it, and over a period of time the principals came together, had a drink and some initial chats. They have taken the relationship to a very sophisticated level over the years. They now meet formally four times a year and not alone do the principals meet but the heads of various departments meet their counterparts also. They alternate visits to each other's offices and have a complete open book strategy between them. It has been fantastic learning experience for them. When one firm compared their performance with the others they found some of the things they thought they were good at, the others were even better. That kind of comparison has been fantastic for both firms in relation to genuinely identifying performance deficits and opportunity potential. Another message here is: No one has a monopoly on good ideas.

Gap Analysis

In management language, the above process is known as **gap analysis.** As mentioned previously, it is the concept of defining the gap between your performance and somebody else's performance. If you have been running at a certain level of efficiency in your business and you think you are doing all right but then suddenly realise that somebody else in roughly the same business type is far better than you, you are left with two choices. You can either ignore it, or you can try and close the gap.

In order for this benchmarking management tool to work, the companies must be distant enough so as not to be in direct competition. For some, the next parish might be far enough away, for others the next county, but others may have to go abroad.

I know a girl called Mary who participated in this Management Development Programme (MDP) a couple of years ago. She had a very good laundry business but thought this benchmarking management tool was worthwhile. She identified another operation down in Cork and approached them, explained what the concept was and asked would they be interested. They were never going to be in competition. After some consideration they decided they were interested and the courtship process began. They now have a completely open book exchange of information and ideas. It has gone fantastically well in the last five or six years. Again Mary found that areas she thought her business was excellent at, the others were even better and vice versa.

If you continue to compare yourself solely with yourself you are not going to create the tension that is required to beat the resistance to change and to kick yourself out of your comfort zone.

I will give you one last example of a manufacturing company (A), that has benefited from this concept, although through a different methodology. They don't benchmark like the above examples, but they were still exposed to the advantage of benchmarking through their access to our consulting services.

We at MRI had another client (Company B), operating in the same type of business as Company A, but they were not in direct competition. Company A had been earning a 5% net profit for the previous three years and felt they were doing okay. We knew from our other client that this 5% margin was in fact very poor. Company B was consistently earning a net profit margin of 15%. For two years we had a real battle with Joey, the commercial director of Company A, to try and convince him that this 5% margin was a lousy performance. We heard all the usual nonsense about the market and competition etc. We kept trying to convince him that 'others' were making net margins of 15%+, but Joey didn't believe that this was real. We had many arguments over it. Joey had to win the battle in his own head first. Eventually, he got so tired of us he said, '…okay, we'll have a go and see what happens, but you will be responsible if it doesn't work out'. We agreed to increase the target for the first year from 5% to 7.5%. Not alone did they come up to the 7.5%, they actually reached 8%. That was about six years ago, and they have never been below 13% since.

Like many of us, Joey resisted change when it was being imposed on him. He had been a commercial director for ten years and felt that he was delivering a good performance at 5%. When I came in from the outside and told him it was a poor performance, it was natural for him to defend what he had been doing. His expressed concern was that they would lose business if they worked at a larger margin.

As you will see in later chapters, there are many variables in the composition of this Net Margin figure. Many of these variables can be managed better, not just in Company A, but in most businesses. Joey was defensive and not really open to suggestion. I am fully convinced that if we hadn't had access to Company B's financial accounts which showed that this 15% was possible, Company A would not have experienced this improvement. It's another example of gap analysis. Company A is very successful today.

The defining of the gap and its eventual acceptance by Joey is a most important learning point. If we are really down and someone puts a challenge in front of us, there is something in our psyche that drives us on to have a go at it against the odds. When you know that there is a negative gap between your business performance and the better operations, you have to first win the debate in your own head so that you can put in place an action plan to close this defined gap. The problem is you don't know what those gaps are because you currently don't have access to that kind of information.

I appreciate that we in MRI are in a privileged position in that we have access to a lot of information from a wide range of businesses. Your accountant or auditor should have some similar information but most of them won't volunteer it unless you challenge them. You can also access the lodged accounts of companies similar to yourself via the Companies Registration Office (CRO), which allows you to compare your performance under various headings. The only problem with the accounts filed is they are bulk figures; you don't get the breakdown so you have to do a fair bit of manoeuvring and analysis to get at the real guts of it.

Banks also perform some of this analysis from a lending perspective. While you cannot get the information directly from them, they may be able to assist you generally through what they have learned in their dealings with companies similar to your own. The banks have a range of businesses profiled under a number of key performance indicators (KPI). Access to these would give you useful benchmark figures to compare your own performance against. Your accountant should also be able to source these types of benchmark figures for you.

However, a better way is to adopt the benchmarking process I am suggesting above. If you can build a relationship with a non-competitive yet similar type business, you will not just get figures, you will get access to their brains as well. Different people have different views on things. If the relationship is honest and open - which it has to be, otherwise it won't work - it's a really worthwhile and rewarding process.

I came across another case where two large companies amalgamated to form a very large corporation. The purchasing department of one of the companies had built up a reputation over the previous twenty years as the best purchasers in the country, and it was accepted within the industry that the guy heading up this department was the best purchaser in the country. Nobody questioned it, it was just accepted that they were the best. It was very interesting when the two purchasing departments were put together and started to compare like with like. They found that the other organisation was actually buying better than the company that was supposed to be the expert in the field, and often buying from the same sources.

Could the same be happening to your business?

Yes_____ No_____

Explain._____

_____

_____

_____

What is the message for you in the above example? One company had built up a reputation; everybody assumed they were the real professional buyers in the country. The company themselves thought it, everybody thought it! The suppliers played into that ego and kept pumping them about how tough they were while at the same time they were giving better deals elsewhere. This company wouldn't improve because they felt sure everybody else was benchmarking themselves off them.

If you are comparing yourself solely with yourself, at best you will only have incremental changes. If you compare yourself with the best in class and there is a gap between both, there is something in that gap that will make you go after it.

I wouldn't expect anybody to identify a partner immediately and build an instant relationship. Those shotgun marriages don't work. You have to go through the courtship period to make it work. However, I would be very disappointed for some of you if you don't energise this excellent idea. You will all intend to do it but the reality is that probably only about 20% of you will actually do it. For some it will be easier because you don't have to go that far, for others you will probably have to travel a long distance because of the type of business you are in.

'*If it's to be ... it's up to me.*'

If you keep doing what you have always done, you will get more of what you have always got. If you are happy with your current performance, keep with it. If not then change your attitude, the way you operate or your strategy. I don't think any of you would have purchased this book if you were totally happy with your current performance. There is no point in reading and digesting its concepts if you don't actually do something about it. It's an input/output model. If you want a different output from your business, then you have to change the quality of your input, and always remember, you are the main input.

Success / Risk Taking
I will give you an example of what is possible.

I was at a black tie ball recently for a company who were celebrating their twenty first anniversary. The four guys that own the company were working with another company many years before and were looking for a bit of the action, but the owner told them to forget it so they decided to go it alone. They had no capital but set themselves up with very little. When I got to know them first around that period, they were working out of the back of one car. They now have 350 employees and a turnover close to €50m, making a net profit of 12%. Four ordinary guys - nothing at all extraordinary about them - but they just had the 'get up and make a go of it' mentality. They had a vision about what they wanted to do. It was great to see how proud their parents were of their achievement. One of their mothers was telling me stories of praying and offering up rosaries and masses because the four lads had left safe jobs to start out on this dream. They had young families with nothing (basically), and at times she felt sure they were going to starve. However they had a determination to succeed and they proved it can be done. I can imagine the praying my own mother did for me during the 'hairy times' on my own commercial journey.

There was a girl at the same function who started off fifteen years ago as a one person sole trader. She is still a sole operator today, but that is what she wanted to do. She runs a very small and efficient business and for her that represents success.

My point here is that success is different for all of us. It is doing what you want to do and doing it well. The girl in the above example did what she wanted to do. She does it well and has a very a good small business, but at the pace and the level that she wants and to her that's success. For the other four lads it's different.

For each of you reading this book success is what you define it to be, not how I define it for you. But don't think too small. Stretch the elastic band some bit at least. Go for it. Whatever that bit is, it can be done. The lads in my story were four ordinary lads. I am emphasising the concept of ordinary here. They did nothing new. All they did was set up a similar type business but just did it a bit better. So you don't always have to hang around waiting for the 'big idea' to get going. Just do whatever it is you are going to do but do it a little bit better than Joe Soap down the road and you will be successful.

I think it's fantastic to see people like those I've described above, having a go and making a success of it. They had a few crazy times in those twenty one years. Everybody looking from outside would say, 'Wow, they were unbelievably successful' which they were, but there was lots of hardships in that business as well. They have over three hundred and fifty employees now and managing that is not easy. I was just doing the figures the other day and it is costing them €38,000 to open their business door every day. That's a lot of money to think about every morning when you turn the key, isn't it? There was a time they hadn't thirty eight cents. I think it's great to hear and see these successes. You don't have to be a genius to be successful in business. Ordinary people can be very successful too.

Commitment

'It's doing what you said you were going to do, long after the mood you said it in has left you.'

Can you empathise with that? That is why I am trying to get you into the discipline of doing some of these exercises. Essentially, you will learn from the messages jumping out of the page at you. You need to develop the discipline of actually finishing off what you are taking on. You need to commit yourself to doing it and killing it off. If you can get into the discipline of actually finishing off things, killing off things, then you will increase your capacity. The four lads profiled above had commitment to their mission.

For some people, the only thing that gives them a buzz is starting off something new. After starting it the buzz wears away and there is nobody there to pick up the slack. In bigger companies that's fine - you have the support mechanisms around you to do that. Unfortunately in small companies you have to do many things that you don't naturally like doing and which you are probably ill equipped to do. You have to wear several hats at the one time. In your situation you may have to be the production person, the marketing person, the cash flow management person, the PR person and many other roles. You might have to wear up to fifteen different hats all in the one day. You need to grow your business beyond that point so that you can afford to have the support staff around you that will take on those tasks. For most of you commitment is: 'I'll do what it takes until ...' and that is usually until something less painful appears. I'm bored, nobody will see me skiving off, I'm my own boss now. The only one that sees you skiving off is the market.

- Remember- The market pays you for output not input.

Killing Things

Bacon and eggs

Can you see the link between the bacon and egg and the concept of commitment?

The pig is more committed, since he must die to give the bacon. The hen is just naturally dropping the egg and moving on to new pastures.

You can't have a rasher without having a dead pig. The pig is committed, but the hen is only just doing what she normally does. In business you need to be far more like the pig than the hen.

There are many barriers facing you in your business. The question is, are you committed enough to break through those barriers and still be resilient enough to drive your business on? You need to be resilient to get your business up and running. The opportunity is out there but it has to be availed of; it has to be worked and worked consistently.

I challenge you to get into the habit of doing things and 'killing off' things. How committed are you to driving your business on?

_____

_____

_____

Where is the evidence? _____

_____

_____

_____

Luck is defined as *'Opportunity meeting Preparation'*.

Do you believe in luck?

Yes_____ No_____

Arnold Palmer once said '… the harder I try, the luckier I get'. Even with the lotto, you can't win if you don't buy a ticket. It's a game of chance.

The same rule applies to business. You have to make things happen. You have to decide what you want done and you have to pursue it. When the economy is buoyant, the circumstances and environment you are working within are attractive. It's easier to get things done in a rising tide situation. However, there will be people out there who will make more money and more wealth in a falling market than in a rising market.

There are always opportunities. I'm sure you've heard people bemoan the fact that they weren't around five years ago or in a position to do so and so ten years ago or suchlike. I believe that is utter rubbish. There are as many opportunities in front of you today as there were five years ago. Opportunities look far more transparent when you look back than when you look forward. In fifty years time our children will have as many opportunities in front of them. There are opportunities in front of us all the time but sometimes we don't see them.

Chapter **3**

Compare Yourself against Successful Management Profiles

In this chapter I would like you to look at yourself against the following successful management profile.

1. Mentally Tough

Management is a tough game. If you are to score yourself on a scale of one to ten on mental toughness, what would your score be? To get a business up and running successfully is a tough game.

2. Self-confident

If you want to be a successful manager you have to be self-confident but not falsely confident. You have to be genuinely self-confident and that is achieved through a series of victories; setting out to achieve something and accomplishing it. That is a victory and you need to build up those victories because they are the path to true self-confidence.

3. Assertive

There are three modes of behaviour you can adopt. You can be weak, assertive or aggressive. There is no room in business for being weak. If you are perceived as being weak you will be used as a doormat and people will wipe their feet on you. Neither is there room for aggression. There are two types of aggression. One is emotional aggression and the other is contrived aggression. Emotionally aggressive people make poor negotiators because they get very emotionally intense and lose their shape very quickly. If you are negotiating with this type of person it is easy to hit their 'weak underbelly' (provided you can handle their outburst). Contrived aggression mode is different. In this scenario the person is using aggression as a tactic to 'soften you up'. They are fully in command. As a negotiator you need to recognise the difference and respond accordingly. Assertive people are very strong people. While they may be mild people, they know and you know just how far they are prepared to move. They make excellent business people. Which is your natural mode?_____

4. Ability to Sell
Everyone in business has to be a salesperson. Some of you might say I'm a production or a logistics person, but that is not the end of the story. While you may not consider yourself a natural salesperson, that doesn't mean that you are not a potentially good salesperson. Everybody in business has to sell to someone. You are selling yourself every day in some shape or form, and it's just a cop out to say 'I'm no good at that'. When you are on your own pay roll you don't have the choice to opt out of these things. You have to organise yourself to become an effective salesperson.

5. Good Negotiator
The art of negotiation is addressed in a later chapter. When we talk about negotiation, we tend to think of just the big negotiations we are faced with every so often, but in reality you are negotiating every day. This morning you negotiated with yourself whether to get up or stay under the sheets. Purchasing is a formal type of negotiation which you need to be very good at and when you are selling, you are negotiating as well. When you delegate and allocate jobs you are negotiating with somebody to take these tasks away from you. If you are recruiting somebody you are negotiating the purchase of that person's time and experience. You are constantly negotiating and you need to be good at it. There are tactics that one can adopt in order to become a better negotiator. We will discuss these later in the book.

6. Setting Priorities and Sticking with Them
This is where consistency comes in. If you don't have your own priorities then everybody else's will come in on top of you. If you don't have a shape to your day you will be at everyone else's mercy. They are only interested in their own agenda. If you don't have an agenda of your own you will be thrown all over the place. If you are being thrown all over the place you won't be very successful.

7. Doing the Right Things Better than Anyone Else
Just go back to the four lads we spoke about earlier. They didn't do anything extraordinary. They just took the same type of business that they were working in and did it slightly better. Now their former employer is not in business any more. A hundred percent of nothing is nothing. He would have been better to cut them in

on part of the action. They would have been just good, average employees. They wouldn't have done for him what they have done for themselves, naturally enough. So we all have more talent than we give ourselves credit for. If you had met those four lads twenty one years ago and asked them if they had any notion of going into business on their own they would have responded in the negative. Realistically they just wanted a good week's wages. **It's not what happens to you that is important, it's how you react to it.**

If you were faced with the same scenario as the four lads, how would you have reacted?

_____

_____

TASK

I want you now to score yourself against the seven criteria we have just discussed. Mark yourself 1 if you consider that you are weak under any of the parameters. Mark yourself 10 if you consider that you are very strong under any of these. Mark yourself between these two extremes as you judge yourself under each of these parameters. There is a total possible score of 70.

	Task	Your Score
		1 5 10
1	**Mentally Tough**	
2	**Self-confident**	
3	**Assertive**	
4	**Ability to Sell**	
5	**Good Negotiator**	
6	**Setting priorities and sticking with them**	
7	**Doing the right things better than anyone else**	
	My total score	

What are the messages for you here?

_____

_____

_____

Do this exercise again in six months time and see how you score yourself. Look at it as a gap analysis between your current position and your position six months hence. Of course it's very subjective, but it's a judgment call about you.

If you go back to the Henry Ford quotation, '*If you think you can, or you think you can't, you're right*'. If somebody else scored you they might score you differently, but that's not the issue.

Management Definition

Results are the key to good management and results are based on output. As a manager you must set the objectives and then develop the appropriate strategy to achieve them. That's a long-winded way of saying that the job of the manager is *to decide what you want to do, cause it to happen and measure what has happened.*

I recently had the opportunity of delivering the more advanced Business Development Programme (BDP) to a group of business people who had previously completed the MDP. It was interesting to see their development from the time they had been on the MDP some years previously. The one common thread that came through was that most of them had moved from being good operators to becoming better managers. They were modelling their management style on the definition above.

Over the next couple of years start to manage your business, as distinct from doing it. Of course I appreciate that this is easier said than done. You have to take your own particular circumstances into the situation, but that is the direction in which you should be going, and at a pace that you can handle. You need to work for your business rather than in your business. Your business must be a means to an end rather than an end in itself. It is your chosen vehicle through which you can grow your wealth. What you choose to do with that wealth is a different issue.

Man cannot discover new oceans until he has the courage to lose sight of the shore.

You are at the shore at the moment in relation to your business/career. Do you have the courage and ambition to look at the shore from afar? You will have different ambitions to others but I think you should stretch that rubber band a small bit. You have far more capacity than you give yourself credit for.

The speed of change is limited to the speed of learning.

At the start of the book I mentioned that I don't want you to think of this book as a text book but rather as your personalised reference manual. You are an adult and are responsible for your thinking, your follow-on actions and net results. Nobody knows it all. You must also learn from the mistakes of others since you cannot live long enough to make them all yourself. There is a lot of latent talent and information around you. You must be proactive in assimilating this and re-digesting it in a format that suits your circumstances. You should then use it as a better input to your decision-making which will ultimately lead to a better output for both you and your business.

There are many cross pollination possibilities within the small business world. This sharing of information and experiences will ultimately improve your self confidence. You don't have to be a genius to be successful. Very ordinary people can be and already are, quite successful. I want you to name three people you personally know who you consider to be successful.

1._____

2._____

3._____

Do you think that you are as well equipped to be successful as these three people?

Yes_____ No_____

What are the messages for you relating to the success of these people?

_____

_____

_____

Defining Success

Success is different for everyone. You should have a picture of what success is for you. There needs to be a gap between that picture and where you are currently at. The tension of that gap should drive you on to realise your potential. The following profiling exercise will help you to better understand your decision-making style.

Instructions:

The exercise consists of twenty sets of contra statements. You should read both contra statements and decide which statement is most reflective of you. Take a look at the first set of contra statements:

1. Often make decisions before gathering available facts.

2. Always meticulous in gathering available facts before deciding.

If statement 1 is most like you, then mark yourself 1 or 2. If statement 2 is most like you, then mark yourself 9 or 10. If you decide your natural work style is between these two extremes, mark yourself between 3 and 7 accordingly. Continue down through the other nineteen pairs of contra statements. The emerging profile will indicate how decisive a decision maker you are.

Decision Analyser

Name:_____   Date:_____

	1 2 3 4 5 6 7 8 9 10	
1. Do you often make decisions before gathering available facts?		Are you always meticulous in gathering available facts?
2. Are you almost always right in the decisions made?		Do you often decide and then have to alter decisions?
3. Are you highly objective in decision making?		Do you often let personal feelings influence decisions?
4. Do you often fail to follow up on decisions?		Are you excellent at following up decisions made?
5. Are you an impulsive decision maker?		Are you a highly cautious decision maker?
6. Do you have highly crystallised goals against which to make decisions?		Are your goals vague and have little effect on the decisions?
7. Do you often make decisions without considering all the implications?		Are you aware of the far reaching implications of the decisions?
8. Do you practically never look back once a decision is made?		Are you often worried about decisions made and mull over them?
9. Do you seek help in making difficult decisions?		Do you prefer to make difficult decisions alone & live with the consequences?
10. Do you rather make a decision now rather than later?		Do you postpone decisions that should be made?
11. Do you know yourself, where you are going and what your values are?		Are your self-structures poorly defined?
12. Do you have a high degree of common sense/judgement?		Is your judgement often theoretical and impracticable?
13. Do you have courage to make decisions no matter how unpopular?		Are your decisions often influenced by what others will think?
14. Do you often make decisions, subordinates should make?		Do you delegate all decisions that should be made by subordinates?
15. Do you make decisions fast and stick with them?		Are you highly deliberate and systematic in decision making?
16. Do you often decide before all the alternatives are developed?		Do you formulate many alternatives before deciding?
17. Are you too easy on people where decisions are concerned?		Can you make tough decisions involving people?
18. Do you pay little attention to the importance of timing in decision making?		Are you highly sensitive to the importance of timing in decision making?
19. Do you have a vast reservoir of experience for use in decision making?		Do you have a limited reservoir of experience for use in decision making?
20. Do you have a broad general education for use in decision making?		Do you have a limited general education on which to draw for decisions?

The rational fall back for you if you don't want to make a decision is to say to yourself, 'I haven't enough facts yet. I am not ready to make that decision'. But this is really just a cop out. If you don't want to face something you will never be ready, but you won't admit this or be honest enough with yourself to say 'I flunked it'. Instead you will make the excuse that you haven't enough facts or the timing isn't right or whatever. But you have to be able to make those hard calls in business and you have to make them on time.

In general, I believe that men are poorer decision-makers than women because they rely more on facts than on intuition. Although there are always exceptions to the norm, women are generally far more intuitive than men – and intuition is a highly beneficial tool in so many areas of business (such as negotiation and conducting interviews to name but two).

Your intuitive feeling is right most of the time. You should trust it more often. It is the combination of all your experiences to date which comes into play when you are faced with an issue. I would always advise people in business to listen to their gut. If you are faced with a set of circumstances and your gut is saying the opposite to the data you have analysed , the data would want to be very convincing before I would go against my gut feeling or intuition.

In business you have to be wise enough to actually play whatever game you are faced with in order to win. If you are a bit more aware of the games played against you, you can be more proactive in adopting the appropriate contra game.

For things to change, you have to change.

For things to happen, you have to make them happen.

If not you, who?
If not now, when?

This is a very powerful challenge.

_____

_____

Responsibility

In reality you have to make these things happen. Nobody else will do it for you. Who else has a vested interest in improving your situation other than yourself? It is your responsibility. I came across the above quotation years ago. It was in Russian and I had someone translate it for me. It's the most powerful challenge I have experienced. Forget the words, but reflect on the message jumping out at you. There is a real challenge there, and if you are any good at all you must react to it.

How is this challenge hitting you?

_____

_____

_____

_____

Are you embarrassed re your inaction in the past? Yes_____ No_____

Is it painful? Yes_____ No____

Change

I believe that you have to win the debate in your own head before you consent to making a change, otherwise you will drift back to your norm when the pressure of the challenge has passed. Remember the elastic band I addressed earlier? When you take away the pressure it goes back to its original shape. If you can actually change the way that you view situations and win that debate in your own head, then you are more likely to anchor the change. Change is a process, not an event. It takes time to anchor the change by building it as a new habit.

If you really reflect on the issues in this book they will initiate change in you. You may not be conscious of the sequence of these changes, but the people around you will. You will be that little bit more assertive, that little bit more definite in your decision-making; you will see the bigger picture and have the confidence to go that bit further. Others won't take you for granted as much either. You will now be better prepared.

The Secret is Knowing What you Want

When you know what you want you can prepare for it and by the laws of averages you have a better chance of getting it. That's a victory. A problem is nothing more than an opportunity disguised in working clothes. Some of us don't like the pain of change, but I am not for sweat, nor for working harder; I am for using your head. That's why over a period of time you will have moved on quite a bit in different ways - more than you will actually realise. When you do these things on an incremental basis, they actually build to quite big steps when put together. Stretch yourself a bit beyond your comfort zone.

Risk-taking

If you have no fear in yourself or in your business you are actually doing nothing new. You are not stretching yourself. Every time you do something new there is naturally an element of fear. The only way of conquering that fear is to get out there and do it. Recognise that each accomplishment is a victory and this will provide you with the motivation to take an even bigger bite the next time.

Chapter **4**

The Things that Keep You in a Rut

If you are not changing, you are in a rut. The following are some of the things that keep you in a rut.

1. Blame
We are very good at blaming other people. Remember the three fingers earlier in Chapter 2?

2. Anxiety
People get stressed because they get caught in a position and are afraid to move. There is a strong correlation between indecision and stress.

3. Indecision
Indecision leads to stress. The most stressful time in your life is always the period before you make a decision, particularly a big decision. We have all been faced with big decisions in our lives. Think and write down an actual decision making time in your life.

_____

_____

_____

I bet the most stressful time for you was the pre-decision time. After making the decision your stress levels reduced. You then had to focus on trying to implement the decision. If this hypothesis is correct, why do you prolong this indecision time period and continue to suffer stress for longer periods than is necessary?

4. Making Judgements

You do have to make judgment calls in your business. Men in particular have to be careful in this area because we are generally not good at making those calls. This is because we naturally tend to be very factual in the way we make our judgement calls. Other dimensions in relation to this are addressed in Chapter 7.

5. Perfection

There is no such thing as perfection. People can have elements of perfection in certain aspects of their lives. You are blessed if you are not a perfectionist in certain aspects of your life. Perfectionists can tend to be a disaster in other areas because all the focus is on their Achilles heel. You have to perform the full circle of activities in business and not just focus in on a particular aspect or aspects.

6. Feeling Sorry for Yourself

There is very little sympathy in business. Business is a factual game. You should use your head at work and your heart at home, not the other way around. I believe that if you do that you won't go too far wrong either in your business or your personal life.

In business the beans are counted based on facts. There isn't too much room for heart at work. People who are quite emotional or soft tend to be abused a lot in business. You will never be successful commercially if you allow yourself to be a doormat. You are like a mirror. The law of reflection indicates that people reflect back to you how you reflect out to them. How do you reflect out to your business world?

_____

_____

_____

_____

What is your game plan to change this?

_____

_____

_____

Chapter **5**

What are the Secrets of Success?

The secrets of success are not secrets at all. There are a number of pillars you need to be guided by if you desire more success in the future. You should judge yourself against each of these parameters. Identify the areas you need to focus in on, and with a game plan in mind improve your score. Know what you want to achieve and start with this end in mind.

These pillars are:

1. Set Objectives or Goals
I will guide you on how to set SMART objectives in a later chapter.

2. Excellence
Excellence is a descriptive word, but it is all in the eye of the beholder. One set of customers might see your package as excellent and another might see it as poor. In business I think you have to position yourself slightly ahead of your competitors but not too far ahead. You might find this strange advice. If you are too far ahead, it is going to cost you too much to be that far ahead. You must be perceived by the customer either to be ahead, or to be 'different' - but not too different because if you are too different you are seen to be offering a different product or to be in a different niche in the market altogether. The message is to be meaningfully different as your targeted customer perceives. The term Michael Porter gives this concept is 'Differentiation'.

So the essence of business is to look at who your customer is and what perception of you do they want. What are their needs? You have to respond to that profile and not to what you would like to respond to. That is why there are so many solutions formulated and worked on for nonexistent issues. This happens quite a lot in the software business - massive solutions for nonexistent problems.

I recently came across an IT person who struggled to describe his business proposition in simple terms. His long winded response was far too technical. If you are coming from a very technical background and you have put a lot of effort into building a solution of some sort, you naturally want the whole world to know the details. However, your potential customer doesn't really give two hoots. They only want to know whether it will solve their immediate pain/problem or not. Your technical ego has to take second place when you face the market. You have to be a solution provider, full stop. I know it's very difficult for technical people who have spent half their lives developing something not to shout about it. But is this what you customer really wants? To the customer, the technology is only a means to an end and not an end in itself.

It is so important to stress that you have to reflect your targeted customers needs and wants. One of the things that we in MRI do when looking at selling and the essence of selling is to use the 'law of reflection'. You need to reflect back to your client what they really want. So, if you are dealing with a factual person or somebody from a technical background, you present your proposition from their angle. The next potential customer that you present to might just want a unit that looks good. If you get into technical jargon with this type of customer you will drive them mad. So you have to act differently at every stage of the selling cycle. **While you may not be a natural salesperson, you can be an effective sales person if you understand what your client wants.** Use your intuition to pick up those vibes. There are ways of equipping yourself to become better at operating this vital link of your business chain. Just be careful that some of these supposed potential customers are neither tyre kickers nor brain thieves.

3. Concentration of Resources
One of the biggest problems for business is that you all have scarce resources, be they brain power, capacity, machinery, technology, time or money. They are all the resources that you have to play around with and no company has enough resources to do everything they would like to do. If you don't have the resources to do everything you would like to do then you have to make decisions. This is where being decisive comes in. What often happens to people is that instead of deciding 'I won't do so and so', they say, 'I will do a bit of this or that and a bit of the other thing'. That's actually indecision. What you are doing is you are spreading the very scarce resources you have over too many areas with the result that you are not doing any of them right. You have succumbed to indecision, not being capable of making the decision yes or no.

One of the worst things you can do is try to be all things to all people. You can't do it. You don't have the resources to do it. There are always more opportunities out there for you than you can ever handle. So you have to be clear in your decision making about where you are going to concentrate your relative resources.

I remember facilitating a business workshop out in the Kursk region of Russia, prior to the Berlin Wall coming down. Towards the end of the conference I conducted an open forum which provided the participants with the opportunity to question me about life and business in the West, particularly in Ireland. The Kursk region has a fantastic depth of excellent black soil which is ideal for grain growing. The participants were asking me about grain yields since their yield of wheat at that stage was about 30% of the yield in Ireland. During the discussion we tried to tease out the reasons for this difference. While they had potentially excellent black soil, they had no herbicides or fungicides. The quality of their seed was very poor and they had limited availability of fertiliser.

The management issue for you from this scenario is: If you had just one tonne of fertiliser would you try and spread it over the whole farm, or would you spread it over part of the farm at the recommended rate? If you spread your limited fertiliser over the whole farm you will spread it so thinly that you will not get a growth response from your crop of wheat.

It's the same with your business. You also have a limited amount of resources (or fertilizer) in your business. You have two choices: you can spread your limited resources over lots of supposed opportunities or you can concentrate them on one or a few opportunities and enhance your chances of getting your planned yield. Your strategy has to be to concentrate your resources, to allocate them to do whatever you decide to do, and by definition you are also saying what you are not going to do. Be decisive.

So many people are not decisive about what they are doing. Indecision and inability to say **no** is the root cause of a lot of problems in business. Saying no in a positive way is about being assertive about where you decide to concentrate your resources. If you don't give enough fertilizer to your crop/business, it just won't grow; it will half grow and be useless. You will have another useless crop in the next field and the field after that. You will finish up with a number of useless starving projects rather than a well nourished good one that will eventually come good for you.

It is happening every day in business, believe me. I am sure it's happening in your business too - a bit of this or that and not being sure about where you want to focus in order to afford that part of the business the opportunity to grow.

When people start off in business they do a bit of everything, but that's the market research part of their business cycle. There is generally no serious business until two to four years in. When you start off a business all you are really doing is testing the market. That phase is a pre-trading phase in one sense. Now it can last different time periods for different business types. No matter what market research you do you never really know until you come to the market and you ask somebody to write a cheque. That's the acid test. If you look at businesses six or seven years down the road, many are doing something that is quite different to what they started out at. Their original theoretical market research probably indicated that they should focus in a particular niche. When the business got out into the market they found different opportunities and threats, resulting in their decision to focus on angles different to their first idea. This is healthy since nothing is forever. If I was speaking to you in five years time I would say you will be doing something reasonably different to what you are doing today. You probably will be in the same industry type, but positioned at a different angle.

4. Review your Progress
Monitoring is very important. **What gets measured tends to get done.** If something is not worth measuring in your business you should seriously consider whether it's worth while doing or not.

5. Energy
There is no scarcity of energy out there, too much of it maybe. In my view there is little correlation between sweat and business success. The successful people are smart, not sweaty.

6. Time
You need to put a timeframe in place in order to achieve your objectives. Deadlines are great. I will address this issue in greater detail later in the book.

Review of your Secrets of Success

	Your Score								
	1 2 3 4 5 6 7 8 9 10								
Set your Objectives									
Excellence									
Concentration of Resources									
Review your Progress									
Energy									
Time									

Score yourself from 1 to 10 for each of these six parameters, to give you a total personal score out of an optimum score of 60.

- How good are you at setting goals?
- How good are you at generating output in relation to your competitors?
- How good are you at being decisive in relation to concentrating your resources?
- How good are you at measurement?
- What is your energy level?
- How good are you at managing yourself and your business within the planned timeframe?

Your current score is your benchmark score. It would be useful for you to complete this exercise some six months down the road when you have completed reading this book, digesting its contents and changing the quality of your inputs to your career or business. Observing the movement in your scores under the six headings will indicate how far your have travelled. Again this is your personal challenge.

Chapter **6**

" No Man is an Island"
We all need Help - here's how to get it

We all need help. In business you need help. You cannot do it all on your own. You have suppliers on one side and customers on the other; you have staff and many other variables to manage so that you can achieve both your business and your career objectives. One of the important skills you need to develop is to learn how to get help. I want to give you a few guidelines to improve your chances of getting the necessary help.

1. What do you really need?
Clarity of purpose about what you want is critical. I can't help somebody if I don't know what they want. So if I am dealing with you and you are not sure what you want, I have no hope of helping you, have I? Help me to help you. It's the same if you are going down to the bank or to a supplier and you are hazy about what you want: they can't help you. So decide what it is that you really need.

_____

_____

_____

_____

If you are clear about what you want you are halfway towards solving your issues.

2. Who can help you?

There is no point in looking for help from somebody that hasn't got the capacity to help you. Of course those who have the capacity may or may not help you, but at least they have the capability.

3. How can you make your pitch?

You may have already put together a business plan for your business or a C.V. for your career. That is one form of putting your case forward. You only get one chance to make a first impression, so understand its importance. The qualities of proposals made to banks are often very poor. They don't reflect the real strength or potential of the business. You also find the opposite, where somebody is very good at presenting their proposition, but has very little real capacity to deliver their promise. Often it is a lack of preparation that causes you to make a poor first impression.

I recently spent time with a board of directors who were about to go into very serious negotiation over the following three months. We spent half the day preparing for that negotiation. They knew the game themselves, but they had to be prepared for all eventualities. Remember that there is a fair chance that the people on the other side of the table are preparing as well. They may never have to use a lot of the negotiating tactics that I was exposing them to, but then again they just might. It is like preparing for an exam. Do you just prepare for three or four questions and hope they will come up or do you have a broader preparation done in order to shorten the odds in your favour?

Seeking assistance from somebody is essentially just another form of negotiation. You need to be prepared for it. Your capacity to negotiate is critical. You may only think of negotiation in terms of the big negotiations but you are in fact negotiating many times every day. You negotiate with yourself about various activities and situations during the day. You have to negotiate with yourself whether to continue reading this book and whether you will make any meaningful changes as a result of your exposure to it. These are all mini negotiations and you need to equip yourself better in this area.

4. What are the give and take possibilities?

Again this is very important. In any negotiation situation there is always give and take. You need to work this out for yourself beforehand. Once again you must start with the end in mind.

5. How can you overcome being shy?

There is no point in being shy in business. If you want something, go and get it regardless. When I sit down with clients and they are talking about what they are going to do with their business and wondering what strategy or tactics they should use, the basic question I keep asking them is: **How badly do you want it?** A lot of people talk about wanting something but do they want it badly enough?

What do you really want?

_____

_____

_____

_____

Are you prepared to pay the price? Yes_____ No_____

Where is the evidence?

_____

_____

_____

There is always a way of achieving what you want provided you want it badly enough and you are prepared to pay the price. You need to be a lot more like the pig than the hen. Try visualising what you want and then put in place an action plan to make it happen. Use the Issue Template as your crutch during this journey of change.

6. How can you ask in a professional manner?

In different ways people reflect back to us how they see us. You are a reflection of the other people you interact with. If you are dealing with the public service or bureaucracy of some sort, you need to be very careful because they have what we call "positional power". If you ruffle their feathers too much they may be less than helpful so you need to be mindful of that.

7. How can you avoid creeping on your knees or begging?

Never beg. Even if you are hungry, don't beg. If you show weakness there are lots of people who will trample on you and go for the kill. You need to present yourself professionally even if you are on your last legs. People sometimes use begging as a game or tactic in order to get sympathy. In such situations, you need to understand that you are using this purely as a tactic and that it is only genuine from your teeth out.

8. How can you show respect?

It is important to show respect. If you are dealing with an equal on the other side of the table and they have the power to say **yes** or **no** to you, you need to show them respect for that. There is a difference between respect and being weak.

9. How can you maintain resilience?

Again resilience is a critical trait you need to have. You have previously heard the saying *'the drip on the rock wears the rock'*. If you want it badly enough you will have to be very resilient. Is that a problem for you?

10. How can you go beyond 'me' to 'we'?

You will have won the argument and the support if you can get to the point where you are both striving for a workable solution; for example, *how are **we** going to solve this problem? What are we going to do about this?* You have won at that stage. Just observe good salespeople operating and how they get to the point of 'what are we going to do about this?'. When you hear that language they are very near the end game. Some people try to get from the 'me' to the 'we' too quickly. You have to build trust in order to get to that point. If you have specked out the proposition with your customer and explained the relevant details, you must 'test the waters' by using such sales closing tactics as: "What colour will I put you down for?" You have to assume that the deal is done and you are empowering them to choose the colour. It's a bit cheeky, but it works. And what works wins.

To succeed in business you have to be very careful that you are not isolated. You need support and you have to be able to obtain that support in an artful way. The squeaky wheel gets the grease and the crying child the attention. You need to be resilient if you want something, but artful in your approach.

Chapter **7**

Survey Results - Messages for You

I now want to show you the results of some survey work that we completed a few years ago. The purpose of the survey was to draw out learning points from the successes and failures of existing business managers so that you can benefit from their experiences.

As mentioned previously, *you can learn from the mistakes of others*. During this survey, we interviewed and worked closely with forty Irish businesses who were engaged in a range of commercial activities both in manufacturing and the services. More than half of them were very successful companies and the balance were just hanging in there. The following is a flavour of the critical traits which surfaced during the interview process.

1. Courage and Vision

The companies that were successful not only had great courage but they also had a clear vision of where they were going. The companies that weren't successful were afraid to take the next step.

If we go back to these specific businesses which we interviewed for this survey, some of them were planning very definite big steps ahead (quite risky sometimes if they didn't work out) but they were determined to go through with them. To me that is courage. Everybody has failures. If you are not prepared to accept some failures you will never move forward. Some of the weaker companies were actually afraid to make a decision in case they would fail, which indicated their indecision style. It was one of the determining factors between the successful businesses and those that were struggling.

Your vision must be reflected in your business plan. However good a business plan is, it is only a written reflection of what is in your mind. You all have a business plan by the way. For a lot of you it is just in your head while others will have it committed to paper. Every business needs three types of people within its team. You need a visionary type person, a business person and a 'son of a you-know-what'. Now can you put names to these three characters within your business?

	Person in your organisation
Visionary person	
Business person	
Son of a you-know-what	

Unfortunately in a small business, you probably won't have enough numbers to wear these three hats, so you probably have to wear them all yourself at different times of the day. That is the main reason why it is so much more difficult to manage a small business as opposed to a larger one. Some people are quite naturally visionary, but they can be hopeless in relation to being a son of a you-know-what or a business person. You might have somebody else happy to be a son of a you-know-what but he or she might have no vision whatsoever and might not necessarily be good commercially either. None of us have those three characteristics naturally because they are poles apart.

While it would be very unusual to have these three traits in the one person, as MD of your own small business you need to have them. Some of them won't be natural to you but you need them when you are making the hard calls in relation to credit control, staffing and other issues. I would suspect that a lot of the outstanding issues in your business relate to people in some shape or form. This would indicate that you are not as hard-nosed as maybe you should be.

I came across a company recently whose major customer is exploiting them to the hilt. In reality they are making no money from their business. In fact I would say they are subsidising this customer in some ways. They need to make a hard call on this situation and they have known this for a number of years. Some of the smaller customers are subsidising the major customer. What is happening is that the hard calls are not being made and the business continues to live with those kinds of weak situations until a crisis hits. Then it's panic stations. You all have a variation of that in your own business. Have you got the courage to make those calls?

In smaller businesses people tend to be very good at the operational side of the business but weak at the commercial side. The reason for this is that most people who start their own business come into it because they are good at aspects of the operational links of the business chain. To succeed in a small business you need the courage and vision to be good in all areas.

2. Ability to see ahead

This trait was very striking in the better companies amongst those surveyed. I came away from interviewing these better businesses with a sense that they had real clarity about where they were going. I was speaking to the Chairman of a PLC in the UK today who I had done business with last year, I was trying to encourage him to come back on board again and I said, 'Sure you have done this in the past.' He said 'I have made lots of mistakes.' In business, as in life, anyone that has done anything worthwhile has made lots of mistakes. If you have stretched that rubber band out at all you are somewhat into foreign territory. You will make mistakes, but if you make more good decisions than bad, you are still winning. The reason some businesses don't really go anywhere is because they are afraid to stretch that rubber band out. Within our sample of forty there were a few businesses that were quite successful in a particular timeframe but then lost their nerve to go any further. They put their hands around whatever they had accumulated and missed the opportunity to drive forward. Economists call this concept *Opportunity Cost*. The opportunity cost of not driving forward these businesses was the value of their missed opportunities.

It takes courage to change and drive on. For those of you reading this book who came out of the PAYE system and established your own business, you had to have courage and win the *opportunity cost* debate in your own head. That was a good move and a courageous one. You came out from under the umbrella into the rain or sunshine, depending on your commercial success to date. That's courageous, but would any of you go back?

I would suggest that eighty percent of the people that came out would not go back even though this life is far more challenging than where they came from. But it also has pluses that the past career didn't have. You will never create wealth for yourself while working for somebody else (the system just won't allow you), but you have some chance if you set up your own enterprise. You really need to get your head around wealth as distinct from income. They are two quite separate issues.

3. Being confident, realistic and willing to learn from all experiences

The people from the successful businesses in our survey were very confident people but they were also realistic. The one thing that I was really surprised about was their desire to learn more. The more successful the businesses were the hungrier they were for information. They would squeeze me for any bits of information/advice that may be of relevance to them. This was in very stark contrast with our observations on the less successful businesses, where we were never challenged with that type of questioning.

While I was surprised at the time, perhaps I shouldn't have been. Maybe this was one of the very reasons why they were more successful. They had a real hunger for new and better ways of running their business and were using any opportunity they could grab to enhance their capability.

I would profile a strong entrepreneur as someone who is willing to have a go, willing to go broke and will do whatever is necessary to achieve their objectives. They are willing to pay the price.

4. Need to be multi-skilled and knowledgeable

Our survey also showed that the smaller the company the more multi-skilled the people in it needed to be because they couldn't afford to surround themselves with a management team populated with the necessary range of specialists.

5. Building up networks

Another thing the more successful companies put great emphasis on was relevant networking. It was part of their strategy in order to build their business. They were quite clinical in their approach to networking. A number of them told me that they were happy to involve themselves in various non-work organisations, provided they could see a return from their investment of time and effort (ROI). This focus on the ROI (while chilling) was informative. One of the interviewees explained it as follows: *"If I am involved in an organisation I am more likely to give it more valuable input if, in return, I can see some value coming to me or my business."* At the end of the day business is done between people from one company interacting with people in another company. For them this was networking as part of a positive strategy to build their business.

Networking takes time and it is an investment. While it may not take a lot of money it is your time which represents your major investment. Your networking needs to be relevant networking. You can attend functions and shows, but when you attend do you try and get a pre-determined return on our investment?

Derry who was one of our OMDP participants shared with us the following gem:

"Someone advised me to do the following every day: Hand out four business cards, send out four letters or quotes, make four phone calls and make four follow up calls. If you do that, you will have made contact with over three thousand people in a year."

I believe that structured networking is really worthwhile. I'm not here to sell it; I am giving it out as a tool. But remember my comment about the shovel: it's not an ornament. You have to use it in order to achieve your planned output.

We were doing some consulting with a national retail organisation some two years ago. The participants were the top operators in the country and they tend to win most of the prizes. While facilitating a brainstorming session with the top ten operators, I asked the number one person to share one nugget of wisdom with his colleagues. His advice was to come outside the counter and look in. 'You will get a completely different view of your business, the view your customer sees. If you are inside the counter looking out you have one view; if you are outside and looking in you have a different view.'

I thought that was insightful and excellent advice. I recommend that you too come outside your counter equivalent and get the same view of you business as your customers have.

In a way, you are coming outside your business by reading and participating in the exercises and challenges in this book. You are mentally coming outside your business and being exposed to some different ideas and reflecting these back into your business from outside in, rather than inside out. You vision can be clouded by your own environment. You are tied up in the day to day activity of your business, often putting out recurring fires which can get very dull and which can be very isolating, even more so mentally than physically. When you have to make those hard calls and decisions, who do you talk to? Again, this is where the support from your networking relationships can be very useful.

6. Keeping up with technology

Very few of the MDs in our sample of forty were actually into technology themselves. Evidence of that was how many of them had those post-it stickers stuck on the monitors of the desk PCs. But what they had was an appreciation of what technology could do for their business. They were really hot on that, even though most of them were not technological gurus themselves. There were a few engineers in the sample of forty so naturally they were into technology. The others were more business people rather than technological specialists.

7. Ability to manage and delegate

Management involves leveraging yourself though other people. Effective delegation facilitates you to gain the necessary multiplier impact.

8. Prestige

The more successful entrepreneurs surveyed had a lower need for prestige or approval, which was interesting. The less successful managers were more concerned about prestige. How would you judge yourself in relation to this observation?

The more successful managers within the sample read people very well. This is important because what is a motivator for one may not be a motivator for another. Different things turn different people on. The better managers often used prestige as part of their tactics, to motivate individuals and certain teams. These managers were very single minded about the success of their business and they used whatever appropriate tactics were needed with different people in order to achieve their planned business objectives. This often just involved giving someone a fancy title which they craved.

A good sports coach would do the same. In any good football team the manager will understand the individuals within the team. While they are getting the team to perform, the team is made up of individuals and it's the synergy and balance within the team that is important. They might be abusive to one player, coax another and use different tactics at different stages in order to achieve what they want. They are single-purposed about results. Clarity about what they want is the linchpin.

9. Achievement

The more successful managers surveyed had a high desire for achievement and a pride in killing off a job. They were very focused on measured planned output. That's really what I'm trying to get you to do if you want to get real value out of your relationship with this book. You need to start to think in terms of **measured planned output** as distinct from just being busy. You need to focus on important versus urgent jobs. I'll pick that up when we are looking at time management in a later chapter.

10. Good Judgement

What is good judgment? It is bringing together all the intuition, experience and database information you have to guide you in better decision making. You will never have enough information if you are indecisive. You have to make the best judgment call based on what information you have at that particular time. Timing of decisions is often more important than getting it a hundred percent right. If you are waiting to be a hundred percent right all the time you will never succeed because you will just procrastinate. If you are prone to procrastination at all you will use the fact that you are not a hundred percent certain as an excuse for indecision.

Message from another Survey

The major banks had enterprise units, whose terms of reference were to try and encourage small businesses to get up and going. In order to facilitate this mission, the criteria they were to use for such focused lending was less demanding than the pure commercial alternative. Naturally, as it was more attractive funding they were bombarded with applications, far in excess of their budget capability. The result of this was that only about twenty percent of the applicants were funded. We in MRI worked closely with one of these banks to review their lending criteria in order to ascertain the reasons why some applicants were successful while others faced the waste paper bin.

Why some applicants didn't get the 'nod' from the bank:

1. Portrayed an attitude that they had a 'right' to succeed

You might think that's a funny one to come up with. Such bankers are in a strong position. Imagine their scenario: they have a pot of money but only have the capacity to give the nod to twenty percent of the applicants. They have no problem in spending their budget but they are also bureaucrats. The applicants were approaching the situation with very high expectations, in the sense that there was this block of money and some of them felt they had a right to get it, irrespective of their position. In reality, if you go into a large organisation with an attitude that you have a right to get something, you'll soon find out that this tactic doesn't work. The bank people said to me that if somebody came in and banged the table demanding something, they certainly didn't approve of such an approach. I questioned them on how they handled such situations? Their typical response was: *"We kill them with a smile. We just smile at them and delay. We have all the time in the world. If we delay an application long enough they will probably be dead before the decision is made."* That is the reality of how some bureaucrats handle awkward people.

2. Vision

Some of the applicants had very little immediate vision or if they had it was very vague. Some of them had great vision for ten years down the road but they had no idea what was in the forecast for the next twelve months. A lot of the business plans or applications were very poor and this made it easy enough for the banks to screen them out and justify not supporting them.

3. Ability of the promoters

The banks really focused in on this. Their view was: it's not the Business Plan that's the most important, but who is going to drive it. As an example, they showed me the business plan for one of the projects they had supported. It was a business plan for a very young business which had just barely started and was a one person operation. The individual had a good business idea and presented the idea very well. The critical point from the bank's point of view was the guy himself. The banks enterprise manager opened this page of the business plan specifically and invited me to take a look. It was the organisation chart for the business. Remember this was a one person operation at this stage. He had presented a full organisation chart for the business for the following five years. While he had no names for any of these boxes, he was indicating what the future structure of the organisation was going to be. He had titles and specs for every one of these jobs. Now that's a guy that was looking ahead! The potential was oozing out at that early stage. That guy just had something different. He was thinking ahead, not in a vague way but in a very specific way. 'I'm not there yet, but this is how I am going to do it' was his mission. He didn't try and fool anyone that he had all of this here and now, he was quite open about it but it was very impressive. It was one of the best presentations of a case I have ever seen, so simple yet so effective. Indeed the proof of the pudding is the massive success of that company some ten years later. You all know that company today for all the right commercial reasons. That's where it started. I think there is a real lesson there for you. You do need help from many sources but you also have to put your own case forward in a strong and effective manner.

4. Lacking drive and motivation

The banks rejected applicants that they felt just didn't have the innate drive that was required to successfully turn their idea into a hard commercial reality.

5. Lacking know how

Many of the rejected applicants really didn't know what they were about, or where they wanted to go.

6. Failure to work in a smart fashion

Many of the rejected applicants didn't have a successful track record. The bank people would say to me, *"If somebody hasn't a successful track record how are they going to be different now? Where is the evidence that they are going to be successful in the future when they haven't anything to show in the past?"* Inevitably your past record is important, irrespective of what you say, because leopards don't tend to change their spots too easily. If you have a poor enough track record and you are projecting to do X, Y and Z, you have to have some evidence and some credibility about how you are going to do it differently than you did in the past. The point the bank people were making was: *"It's the promoter behind the paper who is the most important element."* They were making a judgment call on the person as distinct from the project. They were backing people as distinct from projects. They backed the guy I was talking about above. He was a jockey. It was a good call on their part, but it was a very obvious call to make; he could be successful in any number of areas.

Operational to Management – Is there a correct sequence in the shift?

Circumstances will usually dictate the sequence and for smaller businesses, the normal route to management is via the operational route. But they are two different jobs, requiring two different mindsets. When you move from operations to management you must reinvent yourself mentally. This bank applicant guy I profiled above is a useful case history. While he was very strategic as he has proven since, he was doing the operational things which needed to be done at that early stage, since it was a one person operation then. He was also smart enough to understand that he needed to get funding into the organisation very quickly so that he could start to build his shadow team behind him and release his capacity to address the larger strategic issues. After that initial injection of funding he went the venture capital route in a stepped way. This required delivery against pre-planned measurable targets, so as to continue to encourage venture capitalists to keep putting up more funds for less and less equity. He moved very quickly from wearing all the hats into trying to have those hats worn by other people. The pace of that cycle will be different for different people.

Many people are more comfortable starting in the operational side before delegating the tasks out to others. It can be hard to delegate a job you don't understand. You are not too sure of the parameters of that job. People are a bit more comfortable about delegating something they understand. Also, when you are in a more powerful position and you know the job, it prevents someone bluffing you.

What about financing this delegation? It costs to do it and it costs not to do it. What is the answer?

The bank applicant guy I just spoke about had a fully integrated plan. Running parallel with his HR plan was his plan to manage the other variables and then it was all pulled together into his financial projections. While it's easy enough to put figures on paper, the banks were looking for the assumptions behind those projections - *were they credible and where was the evidence to back them up*. It is that credibility which they are concerned about. They are so used to seeing slapped up figures with no meaning that they can be quite suspicious about figures that are produced for them. They are no fools either. One thing that banks have is a lot of information. The banks have what they call the 'Big Red Book' which contains profiles of most business types. They continually build these profiles from the information in their databases. When you submit an application to the bank, their first task is to compare your proposition against their relevant profile under a number of critical parameters. If your proposition is off beam versus the norm, you need to know that and the reasons for same. For example if you are projecting a gross profit of ten percent above the norm, you have to show how you are going to manage the relevant variables better than the others. Is this credible? Where is the evidence that you can do it?

Banks look for the four C's:

Character
Capacity
Creditworthiness
Collateral

1. Character
That's the jockey thing I was talking about. They do make a judgment call in relation to you. How good a business jockey are you?

2. Capacity
What is the capacity of your business? How robust is your business model? Whatever proposition you have, how does it compare with whatever benchmark figures they have?

3. Creditworthiness
This is self explanatory.

4. Collateral
Banks love security. Believe it or not they are not in the risk business. They have a very simple formula. They buy money from either depositors or in the money market, they take as big a margin on it as they can and then they proceed to lend it to you. No matter how big a margin they charge you, if they don't get the principal back it is still no good to them. So their first issue always is can we get this money back? If we can get it back then how big a margin can we get out of it when we are getting it back? They are no different to any business. They are in the business of buying money, lending it and taking a margin.

In terms of the assets in your balance sheet, they will look at your assumptions underpinning the figures and what your depreciating policy is. The book value is likely over time to be lower than the market value. This is why banks may force you to get your assets re-valued professionally. This will give them a more realistic picture of your true financial position at that moment. They will then have more transparency relating to the value of your fixed assets for their security purposes. They will have a panel of professional valuers that you will have to use and pay.

Have you by any chance signed a personal guarantee on behalf of your business or anybody else? Most people think that they are signing a personal guarantee against a specific loan because that's the way it is sold, but in reality you are signing a personal guarantee against any loan that might be outstanding for that business or person. When the said loan is paid off, insist that you receive back your original guarantee or get a dated letter from the bank, confirming that it is cancelled. Be assertive in this area and be very careful.

Chapter **8**

Understanding Why Businesses Fail

Businesses fail for a number of reasons. While each failure will have its own particular reasons, there are a number of generic reasons which seem to be present in most business failures.

1. Late payments
This occurs where your customers decide when they will pay you rather than you insisting on collecting your money within the agreed timeframe.

2. Directors lacking crucial business skills
Do you have the critical skills required in order to make your business successful? Do you understand your business?

3. Poor management information system
This is very prevalent in small and medium sized businesses. Their management information systems (MIS) are often meagre, inaccurate and out of date. Many have a poor understanding of how to interpret the information in a meaningful way in order to make more informed decisions. Managing businesses blindly is prevalent.

4. Too much debt

5. Under-capitalised
What I am referring to here is a situation where the initial investment and the reserves that have built up in the company are not strong enough to support the business, particularly a fast growing business. The faster you grow your business (unless you are in a cash business) the more finance you need. This is where a lot of companies get caught. Again I will go through that in a lot more detail when we look at finances in later chapters.

6. Inadequate business strategy

Generally there is not enough focus on the strategic positioning and direction of businesses. Lack of clarity regarding what your business is about, what market you are after, what package you are planning to bring to this market niche and how you plan to build your competitive advantage are all critical strategic decisions. What we in MRI often find disturbing in businesses is that they are not clear as to what they are about. They are doing a bit of this, that and the other with a total lack of clarity as to what they are really about.

7. Poor cost controls

Our experience would indicate that cost controls tend to be better managed than the revenue controls in smaller business. A lot of businesses make a fair effort to control the obvious costs but there are a lot of hidden costs that seem to pass them. Much of the waste in your business tends to be invisible. If you are in a business where you are selling labour, the hours that are not charged, the extra hours spent on projects etc. all cost money but tend not to be measured via proper timesheet procedures. Over-stocking, poor warehousing, damaged stock and poor procedures and documentation are all other forms of invisible costs.

I know of a business that took in a general manager two years ago. While there he cost the company over one million euro. In order to get rid of him the company had to pay him a large severance package, even though his management performance was dreadful. The reason it cost the company so much was because he had far better records about the disputed issues than they had.

8. Excessive domination by a single executive

If you are a very domineering person in your business, it can be fantastic for the business at a particular stage of your business cycle but it can be a disaster later on. Different management styles are required at the various stages of your business cycle.

Is your approach appropriate for the current / future stage of your particular business cycle?

_____

The stronger your character, the more critical your answer to this question is going to be.

9. Price cutting

This is one of the major weaknesses in smaller businesses. Many of them don't realise the impact that discounting has on their bottom line. This concept is fleshed out in detail in Chapter 15.

10. Poor marketing and selling

If I went out and did a survey of a hundred companies, in excess of eighty percent would tell me that one of their major weaknesses is marketing and selling. I don't believe that's correct. I think you are probably a better marketer and seller than you give yourself credit for. The reason you think you are poor is because you are comparing yourself with the wrong benchmark. You are not doing the same as the big boys. You have to be careful not to fall into the trap of saying to yourself: "I can't be good because I am not doing it like them." That's not correct. What is right for one is not right for another. Your business is unique and the way you promote and market yourself could, and probably should be, quiet different from your neighbour. It's not a situation where one stroke is suitable for everyone. I will develop this argument later in the book.

11. Diversification away from core business

Be careful about getting involved in opportunities that are strategically very far away from your core business. I am not saying that it won't work for you but it's a higher risk, as every business has its own peculiarities. The fundamentals are the same in every business but you have a steep learning curve to travel when you invest in a non-core business proposition. As already stated, every business has its own peculiarities, which is the reason why it is so difficult to amalgamate two businesses and squeeze out the theoretical synergy that was supposed to be there. These mergers often tend to be a disaster because the acquiring company try and impose their own culture and controls on the acquired business, which often results in stifling it. If you look at a lot of amalgamations nowadays the smart acquirers are leaving the purchased businesses to be run and managed as they previously were, but with obvious help in sourcing and marketing coming from the corporate headquarters. This is a far better formula than imposing a solution. Principle Number Seven in Tom Peters' '*In Search of Excellence*' states: 'Stick to the knitting.'

12. Non-sensitive to the changing business environment
It is very important for you to look at your business strategically in relation to relevant changing trends. Do you pick them up and interpret them quickly enough?

_____

Where is the evidence? _____

_____

13. Choosing a business that's not profitable
There are certain businesses that are just bad businesses to be in. Other businesses are by nature quite profitable and even if you run them badly, you will probably still do okay. You need to examine whether the business you are in is a profitable business. The worst type of business to be in is a business that's too easy to get into. If it's easy for you then it's likely to be easy for every Joe Soap. The more cowboys that come into your patch the quicker the exiting margins will be eroded. Here the entry barriers are low and the exit barriers are high. The best type of business to be in is the business type which is difficult to get into. In management jargon, we say that this business type has a **high entry barrier** and a **lower exit barrier.**

The professions, such as solicitors, pharmacists and accountants strive to control the numbers of new entrants. They all have high artificial entry barriers. They use the state exams points system as an artificial entry barrier. Traditionally there were a limited number of places for pharmacy students every year in Ireland. By controlling numbers you control margins. Some of these barriers now are being challenged and eroded due to more and more anti-competition laws coming from the EU. The professions are very strong and they are fighting a real battle in all manner of ways to try and keep these artificial barriers in place and thus maintain the status quo.

14. Who is your customer?
You need to identify your customer category; otherwise you will waste your scarce resources by adopting the scatter gun tactic. There is often a mismatching between your customers needs/wants and your product offering which makes successful selling impossible.

15. Knowing your competitors
Do you know who your competitor is? I often go into companies and ask who their competitor is. Sometimes they don't know or they might be able to give me a

couple of names. Then I'd ask what are their strengths and weakness vis-à-vis their business. This question gets a varied response. There is often a real lack of knowledge about your competitors. Could you do a detailed analysis about the strengths and weaknesses of your competitors?

Who is your competitor?

_____

_____

_____

_____

What are their strengths and their weaknesses?

_____

_____

_____

_____

Every one of your competitors has a 'soft underbelly'. Have you identified it?

_____

_____

_____

_____

Having identified it, what is your action plan to exploit it?

_____

_____

_____

Businesses often have a very narrow definition of who their competitors are. They think that it is somebody in the same business as themselves but this is not necessarily the case. Your competitor could be any business fighting for the same income stream that you are fighting for. I remember we were doing work for a national sporting organisation some years ago. When I asked the local managers who their competitor was their response was the similar type facility down the road. This was an incorrect analysis. Other events which were fighting for the same purse like the local hotel, sports centres, concerts, foreign holidays etc. were all competitors. Sometimes you have too narrow a view about who your competitor is.

Based on this hypothesis, who now is your competitor?

_____

_____

_____

How are you going to gain a competitive advantage over them?

_____

_____

_____

Coca Cola recently revealed who their main competitor was. I challenge you to guess what it is.

The answer is milk. Interesting, isn't it? Everybody would assume that it would be one of the other fizzy drinks.

16. Being all things to all people

From our experience I would say that one of the major weaknesses in smaller businesses is that they are not certain where their competitive advantage lies. Because of this they adopt a 'being all things to all people' type tactic. This is a very poor strategy.

17. Over-dependence on a single customer

Under normal circumstances this is dangerous but there can be circumstances where it may be a strength. If you can latch on to a strategic partner who is growing strongly and build a mutual interdependence, then you reduce this supposed risk. The important question is who owns the basket you are putting your eggs into.

18. Over trading

Over trading means selling too much and not being able to finance the credit transaction cycle. It is responsible for killing in excess of half the businesses that go bust.

19. Poor delegation

This issue is addressed in detail in Chapter 7.

20. Putting up with a poor team

It's critical not to go ahead with this albatross around your business neck. It begins with putting up with your own poor performance and expands outwards from there. In smaller businesses there tends to be a reluctance to face personal issues.

How would you score yourself (between 1 and 10) in this area? _____

Over reliance on anything is dangerous for both you and your business. Good employees know their worth and they have that priced. If they are good for you, they are probably good for somebody else as well. The same applies to good customers. If your competitors are any good they should be targeting your good customers, but equally you should be targeting theirs.

21. Managing your banking relationships

Banks are a supplier of capital to you and you should treat them just as a supplier of capital, no more or no less than any other supplier of inputs to your business. You should build a professional working relationship with your bank manager so that they know they are dealing with a professional person rather than just a number on a computer screen. As I indicated earlier, business is never done between two businesses; it is done between people in one business interacting with people in the other business.

22. No surprises

Banks don't like surprises, good or bad. Keep them informed as relevant issues evolve. This will help build confidence which you will need when a quick decision is required.

Banks are always aware and watching. Have you ever noticed that when you borrow more you seem to get on better with them? They are managing their risk and the real trick is to get in very deep.

I know a farmer who borrowed one hundred percent of the cost of a large additional farm he purchased in the late1980s. Agriculture went through a very bad time and the bottom fell out of the value of agricultural land. This guy had plenty of neck and he was suave, but he had no money. He was able to talk his way into influencing a liberal bank manager to give him the money to purchase an expensive farm. He never made any payment on it. The bank did all the usual things to put pressure on him, with no positive response. Eventually he was called into a crisis meeting in the bank. When he went in the local manager looked very frightened. His bosses were also there. Paddy went in, sat down, turned to the bank manager and said: 'Are you worried about my account?' The bank manager of course was worried because his job was on the line. Paddy went over and shook the manager's hand. 'There's no point in two of us worrying' he said, and he walked out. That's a true story. The banks tried to sell the farm but he organised a boycott and they failed to sell it. Eventually there was a non demanding repayment schedule agreed. Paddy was in so deep they couldn't do anything about it. Plus there was the added problem of the bank's lack of security. Banks are far smarter about security today.

23. Quality of loan applications

Many loan applications show obvious weaknesses. They don't address issues which concern the lender such as lack of research, inexperienced management, under-capitalisation and repayment capacity. Banks always look at the potential repayment capacity of the business. Their first priority is to get the money back; their second priority is to get the money back with the optimum margin and their third priority is they don't want any problems associated with the loan. I think you should accept that they are mercenary in their business dealings and you should be just as professional. There is little room for sentiment in these transactions.

As part of your business plan you should build in buffers regarding the assumptions underlining your projections. Nothing ever turns out quite as predicted. The planned buffers will insulate you over those bumpy patches. From a banking perspective, if your business owns its fixed assets it is perceived to be safer than if it is just a trading business operating out of leased premises. In the latter situation, banks will focus in more on personal guarantees.

In your loan application you should be specific about the amount and purpose of the loan; the security, the repayment source and schedule and the details of the project and equity contribution. Banks are always looking at your proposed equity contribution. In other words, what exposure are you going to carry? Banks don't want to carry one hundred percent of the exposure. They want to know what element of the risk you are taking in the event of the proposition not working out commercially.

Now, let's briefly recap what I have outlined so far:

1. Successful people tend to have a common profile as detailed in our survey results.
2. You should judge yourself against this profile type. Naturally, there will always be a gap between where you are at under the various parameters, and where they are at. Your objective is to build your capacity and close off these gaps.
3. Banks are purely a supplier of capital and you should treat them accordingly. You need them, so manage the relationship rather than fight them. If you are not getting on well with a bank manager because of some personality issues, leave. A bad bank manager can destroy you and a good one can make you. One of the biggest property development companies in the country owes their existence today to the initial £2,000 business loan they received from their local bank some twenty years ago. The bank manager bet on them as potentially good jockeys, even though they had no horse to ride at the time. If they were faced with the wrong bank manager at that time the story would certainly be different.

I know of a current case where a client company are proposing to invest eight million euro in the next phase of their business. They have banked with their existing bank for ten years. The bank just won't support the project. They are using all the business excuses in the world for not supporting the project but the real reason is that the local bank manager and the business owner just don't hit it off and consequently, he won't support the proposition up through the credit department of the bank. If the company didn't have an alternative option this local banker could potentially destroy them. Fortunately for them they do have another option and are proceeding with their attractive investment.

Chapter 9

Managing your Time to Make the Most of your Opportunities

I want you to complete this analysis for yesterday or your last work day. Break that working day into the allotted time slots and next to each slot record what you were actually doing. You might have blocks of time that you were doing the same thing. If so, you can block a number of timeframes under the same activity heading. Your memory should be able to go back that far. If not you have another developing problem, which the medical people have a name for, but which I cannot remember!

Time	Activity
7-7.30	Sleeping / dreaming –visualising my future!
7.30-8.00	
8.30-9.00	
9-9.30	
9.30-10.00	
10-10.30	
10.3-11.00	
11-11.30	

It is imperative that you keep referring back to this analysis because I will be challenging you to look at how you are managing yourself within the timeframes available. If you are honest most of you are actually quite poor at it. You can't organise other people until you are organised yourself. If you find that you are badly organised and you don't have a structure to your own day or don't have priorities, then how can you expect that you will be able to organise others? If you don't have your own agenda then everybody else's agenda takes priority. Others will try and get you to do what they want you to do. If that is typical of your situation then you are unlikely to be very successful in business.

Time is a scarce but equal resource

The only thing that we all have an equal amount of in life is time.
We are different in every other way: we have a different genetic make up, different personalities, different brain power, different everything. The only aspect of our lives that we are equal in is time. We all have the same twenty four hours, so if somebody says to you that they don't have time to do something that is an incorrect statement. They have the same twenty four hours as everybody else but the difference lies in the way that they manage themselves.

Time is a scarce but equal resource and it is also perishable. If you look at your analysis of your last working day, the time that you wasted that day is gone. There is nothing you can do about it. You can't put time in a freezer and use it tomorrow. It's gone. Any time you have wasted today, any time that was unproductive from your point of view, is now gone. That's a sobering thought. It's a bit like an unsold hotel bedroom at ten o'clock at night. It's a perishable product. If it is not sold that night, that particular space cannot be resold the following night. If you had the nerve to wait to book a hotel room until nine or ten at night you will get it for at least half the normal rate. If you look at it from a hotel's point of view, the cost of the room is there anyway; probably the cost of cleaning it is there regardless, since they will have block contracted for the room cleaning. If the room can be sold, even at fifty percent of the pricelist rate, it will still be making a contribution to the overheads.

You might believe that it is great to have flexibility in your day. However, it generally doesn't lead to optimising your productivity. You have to acquire the discipline of putting some structure into your working lives, otherwise you can easily come to the end of the day, week or month with very little achieved. Now that doesn't mean you weren't busy. There are lots of busy people out there but doing what? If you look at your analysis sheet above, you were probably quite busy on the day you analysed. But the question you really have to ask yourself is: *what was the outcome of the day?* What was your outcome of the last week or the last month? You need to start to think of yourselves in relation to output.

The market doesn't pay you for activity; it pays you for planned output. If you are on someone else's payroll you probably don't have to develop any of these diciplines. The survival strategy you have probably perfected over the years is that you can appear busy and stay out of trouble. You are paid for membership of your organisation, that is, you are paid to turn up in the morning. This type of strategy and attitude will not satisfy those of you who have the marketplace as your paymaster. The marketplace is a hard but fair master. It pays you for output, not for talking about what you are going to do.

It's cutting edge and it's great
Everything you have to do requires time. The better you manage it the more success you will have. If you strip out from an eight hour day the really productive work, what percentage of your day was productive? _____%.

I want you to look at your analysis sheet above and work out the percentage of the day that you would consider was actually productive. I want you to see how near it is to the norm. Just work out whatever number of hours you've worked and express the productive hours (the real worthwhile hours) as a percentage of the worked hours. What percentage of that day was productive for you? _____%

Does this figure shock you?

Do you know that out of a standard eight hour day the average productive hours worked by the average person is three?

What about travel time?
As you start to become a bit more conscious of the value of your time as a resource you will find that you will be more inclined to organise yourself to travel in non-productive time. This is the time you can't be in front of a customer or doing something worthwhile. You will start to travel early in the morning or late in the evening. If you start travelling long distances in the middle of the day, you just don't get in front of enough customers.

In MRI we have a different approach to this concept of time. In our view it's not about time management, it's about the self management of the time you have available. You might say there is only a subtle difference but I think it's quite an important one. When I asked you to analyse your day, I did it to challenge you to break your day into slots. That's more like a time management approach, but that's not the way I want you to do it.

I will be suggesting that you adopt the concept of self management. I want you to understand and appreciate the importance of your output and start measuring yourselves in relation to your planned output. That's far more important than managing the slots of time. A slightly different focus but I think a critical difference.

You manage your job within the timeframe that you have planned. Do not let it manage you. If you don't manage yourself, if you are not far more au fait with the importance of time and your focus on planned output, then you are allowing everybody else to manage you.

Being busy doing something that's unproductive is a very bad use of your time; it's the worst use of your time. You would be better to be idle than to be busy doing the wrong thing like servicing a bad customer. You should cut out bad customers. Your bad customers shout loudest, they shout most often and they probably don't pay you anyway at the end of the day. If you are honest with yourself being busy servicing these is a real waste of your valuable time.

You have many more examples of being busy in wasteful activities within your business/career at present. Can you identify them here?

_____

_____

_____

There is a certain satisfaction in being busy but I believe that it takes nerve to be idle. I think you should have the nerve to be idle and decide to use the freed up time to tackle more important issues in a more planned and professional manner. When you are at work you should act professionally.

Your motto should be: ***When out of work relax. When at work use your head, when at home use your heart, not the other way round.***

For those of you working very close to where you are living, whether in the same yard or same house, you have to have more self discipline. If the demarcation line between your living and working spaces is only an imaginary line, then you need to be more disciplined than if you were going into a structured work situation. Does this lack of defined spaces bother you?

Some people just can't handle it. They need some bit of a crutch to facilitate a structuring of their working day. The following are examples of 'crutches' adopted by people I know who work from home.

Mary was an artist/designer who worked with a number of the big agencies in London and Dublin. She married a guy down the country and the commuting wasn't viable. She built a proper studio as part of their new home. She found it very difficult to adjust from the corporate world to having the self discipline to go into her studio and produce. There were too many 'other' things to do. She found that her creativity and design quality was deteriorating. I remember talking to her at one stage and she was seriously considering going back to commuting, just to get the creative juices going again. Their new house was about three hundred yards back from the road with a lovely sweeping driveway. She decided that when ready for work she would walk out the front door, down to the road gate and back and into the studio. At lunchtime and in the evening she would walk out of the studio, down to the road gate and back into her house via the front door. She was now closing the door of her business in the evening and going home or opening the door in the business in the morning. Psychologically she found that crutch helped her a lot.

A further example:

I know a professional who lives over his practice. He walks out the front door every morning, goes down to the shop to buy the paper, walks back and into his practice. He repeats this route the opposite way in the evening. Even though there is an internal stairs he is now disciplined enough never to use it.

Self discipline on a consistent basis is very important. You have to establish the guidelines otherwise you will have other people's agendas imposing on you. When you are at work be professional. When you are out of work, stay out of it.

There is a direct relationship between how you feel and perform and the amount of control you have. In other words, if you feel out of control and you are fighting fires all the time, that's a stressful situation. You will continue to fight fires if you don't stop and quench the root causes of some of those fires. We are all victims of it at certain times but if you are a victim on a continuous basis you will just burn out. You do need to put some effort into restructuring your operation.

Do you remember Jack Charlton when he was manager of the Irish team?
It was a great era for Ireland. He was a very simple man in lots of ways but a very determined man. He had two very simple coaching themes. Can you remember them?

Keep them under pressure was the first one. He also kept preaching: keep your shape. If you have a team under pressure they tend to lose their shape. Everybody panics and start bunching and running around like headless chickens. I am saying the same to you. You need to have some shape to your day, week and month. If you don't then you are no better than the players that are panicking around many play pitches every day. Nobody is able to keep their shape a hundred percent of the time; I am not suggesting that for one minute. However, if you can keep your shape for ten percent more of the time than you currently do, it will be very beneficial both to you and your business.

That won't happen of its own accord. You have to make it happen. I am not giving you any solutions yet. What I am currently trying to do is to get you to think about how badly you actually manage that very scarce resource known as time. If you don't feel bad enough about your current performance you are not going to change. I will give you two very simple tools towards the end of this chapter which will help you to develop both the discipline and the technique to start to self-manage this valuable, perishable time resource. These techniques are very simple but very effective. I use them all the time, as do most of our past programme participants. Neither they nor I could manage without them, they are that important. If you consistently use them they will work for you the same as they work for lots of others. If you don't follow and use these two techniques, then it's a missed opportunity for you, like the unproductive part of your day.

Managing your time puts you in control. It gives you inner peace and well being and achieves a winning attitude. Not managing it can be a source of stress and anxiety. Are your feeling stressed?

Do you find yourself out of control in relation to people imposing on your time and your agenda?

Panic manifests itself in all sorts of ways. It can manifest itself health-wise if you are under stress. It certainly manifests itself in poor economic performance.

I recently came across a business owner who is very stressed. There is about a seventy percent chance that his business will go bust if he can't find a solution in a very short period of time. He had been working twenty hours a day for the last twelve months. He never stopped even once to put some bit of shape on either himself or the business. He has guys working for him and they are doing very little. He is so busy himself trying to create cash flow that he cannot manage them or the business. The whole situation is crisis upon crisis upon crisis. They have orders in the books for the next nine months, can you believe that? And that business is going down the tubes.

This guy is a bit of a genius in many ways but he is not an effective manager. His marriage is in trouble and banks have refused to honour any more cheques. When they return the first cheque marked 'Refer to Drawer', the business won't be around long after that.

This business is viable if you could get enough time to actually manage it out of its crisis. Between work in progress (WIP), debtors and stock, there is enough working capital to rescue the company. It's just all in the wrong place at the wrong time. But this guy and everyone around him are so stressed out that they are making a successful solution impossible. What he is trying to do is to run faster with the same formula that hasn't worked in the past.

The key is to put structure into the way that you are managing yourself in the first instance, and then your business. Managing yourself within the timeframe available is a problem for you because you have a choice. If you are working for a large organisation they will have procedures and regulations in order to keep their people in some kind of shape and control. They have certain deadlines in relation to meetings and reports and certain targets have to be met. So what they are doing is trying to impose a structure on a whole mass of people in order to keep the whole business model moving forward in a particular direction. That's what bureaucracy is about. However that can also get to the point where it becomes unproductive.

When you come out from that type of environment into doing something for yourself, you don't have a boss. A lot of people say to me that the reason they started their own business was that they wanted to be their own boss. Being your own boss is great in theory but it carries all the liabilities with it as well. If you are not able to make that transition and start to manage yourself, there is no great joy in being your own boss. If you can make that transition and put some discipline and structure on what you are doing, then it's great. Being your own boss gives you different choices but life can be tough if you can't consistently manage those choices.

Time is a perishable resource. It is consumed as you use it. Many people fight time and lose it. If you fight something in a panic situation, with the same formula, you will end up like the stressed business owner I just mentioned. He is fighting with the same formula that didn't work in the past but he is still trying to use it, only more quickly. If you are in a hole and want to get out of it there is no point in digging any faster. What you need to do is build a stepladder of some sort in order to climb out instead of going deeper. My client is not unique by any means. I am sure you have been there at different stages of your life, doing something wrong. But doing it faster is still wrong - twice as wrong.

What if you can recognise that, but cannot formulate a plan of action to get you out of it?
If you can identify and define the real problem/issue there is always a solution. While you may not know the answer there and then, there is a better solution out there and you must go after it. Did you ever hear your grandmother saying *'when the student is ready, the teacher appears'?* The same logic applies here. The issue must be painful enough in your own mind that you are prepared to pay the price to have it fixed. This payment involves the pain you need to go through in order to make the necessary change. Identifying and defining the real issue is the first and probably the most important step in the rescue journey. You have to get to the real root cause of the issue and not be tempted to come up with a solution that only addresses a symptom of the issue. If you do that you are trying to quench the flames without attending to the cause of the fire. All you are doing is heaping more expense onto a burning fire.

Many of the things you see wrong in your business are merely symptoms of more deeply rooted issues. For instance, if a financial person went into the business referred to above, they would see a cash flow problem. Now there are two choices: You can put more cash into the business and keep it going (which often happens), or you can look at it another way and say okay, there is a cash problem here but what is the root cause of that cash problem? When you go back and de-layer it, you will find that it's poor management basically: jobs not finished, repeat jobs, money not collected; too much stock built up, too much work in progress, snagging not completed and so there are plenty of excuses for customers not to pay him. The cash flow problem is just the external symptom of the real issue which is poor management.

Let's use a leaking bucket as another example. If you do nothing about the leak the bucket will go dry. But you can keep the bucket full of water in two ways. How would you do it? Would you plug the hole or keep filling the bucket up?

Many of the quick solutions are the equivalent to continually filling up the leaking bucket rather than plugging the hole. Looking for the hole can take time and some level of expertise, which tends to be more difficult than just refilling it with water. Sometimes the worst thing you can have available to your business is a ready supply of funds because it is so tempting to throw more money at a problem without addressing the real issue. It takes discipline to address the real problem. It takes discipline to address the real underlining issues.

Now that you have your own business you have two buckets, the business bucket and your own. You should pay yourself first and well in your business. Keep your personal bucket topped up. The reason I give you that advice is that it forces you to actually manage your business more professionally. If you start to pay yourself first then you have to manage the commerce of your business because your creditors will force you to do it. If you are not well structured and managed and you decide to pay yourself last, there is a real chance there will be very little left for you. This is another invisible way of subsidising your business. If, in the early days of the business, the cash flow doesn't allow for this, I suggest that you still write the cheques but don't either date or cash them until a healthier cash flow stage of the business is established. You are setting up a paper trail to show that the company is liable to you for this debt and thus its trading account is more genuine and transparent.

Recently I looked at a set of accounts of a company who were proud of their performance. I don't think they should have been. The profits were shown before drawings. While they were showing a bit of the profit, it was false profit because they hadn't taken drawings. Had they paid themselves they would have shown a loss. In a way they were fooling themselves. By not paying themselves they are actually subsidising their poor management performance. Now they have sources of income from elsewhere, but that's beside the point. We were looking at the specific business they own. There was a bit of ego there - aren't we great, look how well we have done! The reality is they haven't done well at all.

I don't have any problem with a company showing a loss in the earlier years if it has planned to show a loss for a particular purpose.

Exercise
I want you to work out what value you are to your business on a per hour basis. I am not asking you to put down what you are paying yourself out of the business on a per hour basis, I am asking you what value you are to the business on a per hour basis. What is it? -€_____

You are not allowed to either value or pay yourself less than the minimum wage. If you don't put a monetary value on something you won't value it. If you think small, you will act small. It has to be realistic as well. There is no point in setting a figure that you haven't a hope in hell of achieving as that would be de-motivating. So whatever figure you have, I would say stick with it because it will facilitate you to do what I want you to do.

Look at the door from where you are currently sitting. Let's assume there was a window open which was blowing air through the corridor, creating a vacuum and sucking air from the room you are sitting in. If there was a €50 note on the ground and you saw it being sucked out under that door, what would you do?

I assume you would go after it. The hourly value you wrote above represents some multiple of this €50 note. How many €50 note equivalents were sucked out under your business door today? Every block of unproductive time you have is the equivalent of whatever value you put on your time. I would expect you to fight if there was a €50 note being sucked out under your door because you have some value on a €50 note. You have no problem wasting the equivalent in time because you don't see it like that. The reason you don't see it like that is that you don't have a monetary value in your head in relation to time. The higher the value figure you have written above the better. That figure should become a turning point for you in the way you decide to use your time.

If you could internalise that value figure and challenge yourself - when you find yourself drifting or disorganised   how much has it cost you during this unproductive period? I think that will sharpen you a small bit. The message I want you to take away from doing this exercise is that you have a value. I would suggest that you stick that figure up on your office wall where it's going to be within your eye line, so you can see it several times a day. I am loath to tell you to put it on the dashboard of you car in case it is a distraction. Perhaps you could put it on the bathroom mirror where you will see it first thing every morning.

Other ways of looking at this are:

1. If you had to recruit someone to replace yourself, what would that person(s) cost you?
2. What could you command if you offered yourself to the jobs market?

Economists have a nice term for this; they call it the **opportunity cost** of you staying in your business. The opportunity cost of you being in your business is the money you are foregoing by not being in employment. The gap between both represents the degree that you are subsidising your business by not paying yourself enough. There can be other things in that equation of course. You might like what you are doing; you might like being your own boss and it's hard to put a monetary value on that.

You should think of your business **as a means to an end, not an end in itself**. If you agree with that, then your business should be a vehicle for you to create wealth as distinct from income. They are two quite separate issues. There are different strategies which you can adopt in order to manage your business and create that wealth for yourself.

We in MRI meet a lot of people who have been in business for over twenty years. They generally would have worked very hard all their lives and would have very little financial reward for their efforts. They have sweated a lot over those years and still have very little to show for their effort. Compare these with other people who have worked their businesses a bit smarter to create a nice bit of wealth for themselves. When you compare and contrast the two, what are the messages?

_____

_____

_____

_____

They have all gone through the pain but some have a completely different output than the others.

A guy who comes to my mind is a man named James who is fifty eight years of age. He has worked like a slave for the past twenty five years. He has about thirty guys working for him and he hasn't a wrap. He doesn't even own the house he is living in, which is very sad after giving that much employment for so many years. I remember him saying to me one day, 'I have helped to make millionaires out of a few people along the way.' And it's true.

He was soft and was trampled on by various people through the years. He was abused in lots of ways. He is in a tough enough businessman but he was so busy trying to keep going and doing the right thing commercially that he forgot about himself. Now I know that had that guy been exposed to the concepts in this book ten years ago he would be a millionaire today, no problem. And that's the sad thing about it. A lot of business people have the wrong focus and that is part of what I am trying to get across to you in this book.

You shouldn't be in your business just for a wage. If you wanted that you should probably be working for somebody else. You should be trying to create something for yourself. If you focus in and understand the dynamics involved in managing your own business, you have a good chance of working it out for yourself. You are where you are based on the quality of your previous business decisions. You have some choice about the future. Remember that the word SUCCESS has the letter U in it. **'If it's to be, it's up to me.'**

Complete the following profiling exercise. It will challenge you to have a 'felt need' to focus in on your use / abuse of this very valuable time resource.

Profiling of your Time Management

1.   How far ahead do you plan?

2.   What parts of your life are most important to you?

3.   What could you do, starting today, to enhance your enjoyment in each of these areas?

4.   In what areas of your life do you need to practice more self discipline to assure a better future?

5.   Taking the short view, into what time periods do you divide your day?

6.   What are the most important activities that you engage in each day?

7.   What activities do you engage in that contribute little or nothing to your goals? What should you learn to say 'No' to?

8.   What do you do that does not pay your desired hourly rate? What should you start delegating or out-sourcing?

9.   How would you spend your time if you learned that you had only six months to live?

10.   If everyone was watching you and using you as a role-model for excellent time management, what would you do differently?

Take a few minutes to do this exercise. Let's look at the first question: How far ahead do you plan? In other words: **What kind of time perspective do you have?**

As an employer, you need both a long and a short term perspective in relation to your business. Business owners assume that employees have the same perspective of time as themselves. However the majority of people working for a wage don't actually think beyond Friday. Give employees instructions for the next four or five weeks and it is generally beyond their comprehension. They may appear to agree with your viewpoint, but most employees don't have the discipline to think it through. You as a manager must break that four or five weeks into what is to be done today and tomorrow. That is as far as most employees can actually handle and therefore the timeframe they work most effectively in. You may think I am being unkind to employees, but I have seen the evidence of this every other day in client companies. They have a different mind set, which is why they are working for you rather than winning the contracts themselves.

Time horizons depend very much on your standpoint. To realise the value of a year ask a student who failed a grade. To realise the value of a month ask a mother who gave birth to a premature child. To realise the value of a week, ask the editor of a weekly newspaper who has deadlines. To realise the value of one minute ask a person who has just missed a train. To realise the value of one second ask a person who avoided an accident. To realise the value of a microsecond ask a person who won a silver medal in the Olympics.

You are managing your own personal life and your commercial life. Your commercial life may or may not be a fully-fledged business. Even if you are working for an employer, you must still manage the commercial aspects of your life.

What is the timeframe in your head? Do you think in terms of an hour, a day, a week, a month, a year, or five year stretches?

What monetary value do you place on this timeframe?

What is the hourly rate that justifies your participation and input?

It is crucial that this value is embedded in your conscious mind at all times. It is the 'tool' which will keep you focused. It will give you the necessary benchmark to judge your activity and determine if you are getting your desired return.

You have to be successful in the next six months in order to be there to achieve your long-term vision. It is easy to talk about that vision, but you have to live and manage in the shorter term.

The long term is made up of a sequence of shorter terms. It is these shorter terms that you have to have in your head, and you have to know your value figure on them. You have to keep challenging yourself to see if the output of your activity, within your mental timeframe, is earning your stated hourly value. If not, then you have a decision to make. I am focusing here on your ability to ask yourself these questions and facilitating the building of your capacity to address them.

What kind of company would it be if everyone managed their time like you? In other words what kind of a role model are you for the people around you? Are you a good role model or a bad one? If you are disorganised and stressed the people working for you will be just as bad. You must lead from the front and lead by example. It is your business and it is your prerogative. If you are disorganised the people you interact with have a license to be disorganised as well and the whole thing becomes chaotic. If you are disciplined and have more structure the people around you will fall into line. A good example of this is how the supermarkets dictate to their suppliers when, where and how they are to deliver their stock to the warehouses. Suppliers then have two choices, either discipline themselves to be able to operate at the dictated standard or opt out. Similarly, part of your time is imposed on by other people. As I've mentioned previously, if you don't have your own agenda then others will impose their agenda on you. The extent of their imposition depends on how weak and disorganised you are.

Some people feel that they are contributing just because they are putting in long hours. Their internal rational is: '*I work fourteen hours a day therefore I must be great.*' They could be a pure disaster for those fourteen hours. The critical question is not the length of time *but was the planned output achieved or not?* It is so critical for you to have the appropriate measurement type in your head. Remember, 'what gets measured tends to get done'. Your mental measurement focus has to be on a planned output and not on activity or length of time at the office. I stated earlier that there is very little correlation between sweat and business success. You must give yourself space in order to plan to work smarter.

If you had the misfortune of being given just six months to live, how would you change your life? None of us know for certain if we'll be around in six months time. We all have some friends or people close to us who have been through that situation. How did it change their lives?

People often say they would go on a world cruise or do something similarly out of the ordinary, but all the evidence is actually to the contrary. People faced with this dilemma actually don't do those 'wild' things at all. What they do is they put their house in order. They face whatever decisions need to be made and make fabulous use of that time. But none of us knows if we even have six months to live. Why aren't you putting your house in order? What are you waiting for? Do you have to have an imposed external crisis to start to concentrate your mind on putting your house in order? This is where self discipline comes in. Everyone has unfinished business. If you weren't able to work in your business tomorrow morning would your business survive? Is your business your pension? If it is then you need to manage it well so that it will provide adequately for you down the road. You have an obligation to become more professional.

Relaxation is a good use of your time, provided you have earned it. I am all for people taking holidays. I am all for people shutting the door on their business, because I think if you can do that and not feel guilty about it, you will be more professional at managing your business and your personal life. Sometimes I hear owner/managers nearly apologising for going on holidays. I think that's dreadful. You do yourself no favours in business by being available all the time. If you are too readily available you won't be valued by your customers. They will eventually just take you for granted.

Success becomes barren if you lose your ability to enjoy life. You will actually enjoy your free time and enjoy the fruits of your labours far better if you have managed your affairs well and got a good output for your input. *I achieved what I set out to achieve and I feel great about it'*, that is a victory and I say relax and enjoy it!

Your ability to say **'No'** is critical to how you manage yourself within the time frames available to you. You are going to be faced tomorrow with a number of situations which won't pay you the value that you have already written down above. What are you going to do? If the task does not contribute a higher value usage of your time, then you have to either say 'No' or re-engineer it in some way. As time goes on, you have to challenge yourself: 'Do I have to do this?'; "Does it need to be done at all?'; 'Is this the second or third effort at doing the same job?' It's only by implementing this self challenging strategy that you will consistently recharge your improved change process.

Recent research indicates that we handle the same piece of paper at least six times. This is quite frightening when you think about it. The post comes in; somebody looks at the post, opens it, it's thrown there, you pick it up. How many more times do you pick it up before you kill it?

If you start a job and half finish it, then you have to go back and re-start again next time. How many times do you start the same job? Now you can be very busy, but what is the productivity of that business? You are going to have to start challenging yourself a small bit. If you find that you are doing an activity that a € 10 per hour person could do, that is wasteful. How does this € 10 compare with your hourly written value above? This gap should shock you into focusing yourself on prioritising and reorganising your activities. You might be getting some innate pleasure from being busy, but that's not what you should be about. If you want to be more successful, you must consistently start to play to your strengths not to your weaknesses.

When you reviewed your activities in the profiling exercise above, how many of these activities were capable of paying you your stated value? Do some of these activities really need to be done at all? There are lots of things that you are doing that don't need to be done or could be done in a better way. If you take the time out to come up with a better way of completing an activity which is performed daily in your business, you will get a return of at least forty to one from that investment of your time over a twelve month timeframe. That's a fairly startling figure. The cheapest thing you will ever buy for your office is a good filing system. There is an old saying, *"a cluttered desk reflects a cluttered mind"*. I believe this to be true; I see it in businesses we go into all the time. Clutter doesn't mix with efficiency. You also have the other extreme where someone is so perfect with organisation that they forget to do the business! There is a happy medium somewhere and that is probably not where you are at right now. How much time do you spend looking for files, tools and other things? What is the opportunity cost of this inefficiency?

I remember being in a tyre depot on a wet Saturday evening some months ago. I was getting a new set of tyres fitted to my car. The other two bays were also occupied. There was a commercial vehicle in the far bay. The guy working on the commercial vehicle started shouting, 'where is the lump hammer?' I just stood back and observed the evolving scenario. Five employees and two customers spent twenty minutes looking for this lump hammer before they found it under a coat near their feet. I assume these guys were costing about € 15 per hour, so you had five people at € 15 per hour for twenty minutes, which is equivalent to a hundred minutes or € 25 in lost time. I don't know what the price of a lump hammer is, but it's certainly less than the cost of the time that was wasted looking for it, particularly if this was happening regularly.

How many times in the week does the equivalent happen to you due to disorganisation and what is the opportunity cost to you? Write down your best estimate here, so that it will start to bother you. €_____

Your hourly rate = €_____

I would expect that you will jerk the next time you find yourself drifting because of the actual hourly value figure you recorded above and which is now constantly in your head. That is actually what it is costing you to be disorganised. I want that figure to bother you and bother you badly because if it doesn't you are not going to improve.

I want you to examine the time management profiling exercise you completed earlier, then to look at the following options and decide where you spend your time. Are you driven by the panic fires rather than by the important tasks in your business? As previously indicated, if you are not clear about your own priorities and have your own agenda to energise same, then you will be the victim of the agendas of others. What percentage of your time do you spend under the two headings below?

Your Name	Panic/ quenching fires	Important issues

It really is a sign of professionalism if you decide that you are spending a higher proportion of your time on important rather than on urgent issues. How much of your time do you spend drifting into doing things which are either panic fires or are not important? This is a place you will drift to if you are not focused. It is a nice comfortable place to relax, but it's a disaster. You should relax outside your business. If you have achieved what you planned to achieve I would say go and relax and do it formally, don't steal it.

Your Name	% of your time spent on issues which are neither important nor very urgent

Are you a victim of having to react to something which is now urgent, but is not that important? The deadline has mysteriously appeared. Are you proactive or reactive? It could be something that you have to get out today but you knew that three weeks ago and you weren't disciplined enough to have it killed off then. So it has to be done today, probably at the expense of doing something that's far more important to your business.

One of the things which should annoy the people involved is the panic in trying to hit contract tender deadlines. Tenders have to be in by certain times, which often tend to be twelve noon on a Friday. I have frequently seen people going around like headless chickens at eleven o'clock trying to cobble together this tender. I think that's dreadful, it's suicidal in a business. If the business cannot get it right at this stage the whole thing is a washout. In most of those situations the companies would have had at least a month's lead-in and no matter what else happens in the business that day, that tender has to be in by twelve o'clock (and often at the expense of maybe getting it couriered to wherever it had to go). There is a lack of discipline, a lack of structure, disorganisation and potential for disaster. The real cost here is not the extra courier cost, but getting the specifications and pricing wrong due to the panic.

It's not because there was no time to do it. That's really what I'm talking about. If you want your business to be productive, you have to start putting some self-imposed discipline, deadlines and structures into what you are doing. Otherwise you are playing to everybody else's tune. The following advice, given by Justice Charles Russell to his son in the 1890's when he qualified as a solicitor, indicates the importance of having a structured approach.

'Dear son,

I have been thinking over some rules which I think you should follow:

1. *Begin each day with a memo of what is to be done, in order of priority.*
2. *Do one thing only at a time.*
3. *Take good notes at all meetings for corroboration in any future difficulty.*
4. *Arrange your case in the order of time.*
5. *There is no need to say you don't know to a client, but go and seek it from those who know.*
6. *Role model yourself as a tradesman who prides himself on his work.*
7. *Never fail in an engagement made and observe rigid punctuality.*

The challenge I am throwing out to you is to improve how you manage yourself within the available timeframes by ten percent. I am not asking you to turn yourself inside out, but that ten percent is critical. If you could bed down that ten percent and then take another bite, you would amaze yourself about how structured you could become. You will get quite annoyed with yourself after a while in relation to the time you waste. Wastage can come in many guises. For instance if you are doing something such as writing a report or a letter and somebody interrupts or the phone rings, by the time you get back to the task there could be two hours gone. You should aim to kill the task first before you go on to something else.

I'm a great believer in killing things. Of course I appreciate that you won't be able to kill everything but you can kill a lot more than you currently do. I have a thing about handling paper only once if at all possible, but it took a lot of self discipline to create this desirable habit. If you don't get annoyed about wastage of time and if you don't put your stated hourly value on it, you probably won't improve. Putting your stated hourly value on the time wasted should concentrate your mind. You have to create an artificial boss for yourself in order to keep you focused. Keep your stated value up in front of you so that it's annoying will do the trick.

What about the phone? Should you not answer it?
The answer really depends on how much time you spend on the phone yapping. I feel that the 80 / 20 rule applies here. This means that you get 80% of the business done in 20% of the time you are on the phone. Much of the 80% of your phone time is wasted. What is the value of this wasted time to you?

A survey was conducted a few years ago in a county who were participating in their first All Ireland Final for a number of years. They were trying to estimate the total amount of business time that was spent discussing the match in the two week pre and post match period. The figures were staggering, especially when an average valuation was put on the time. The conclusion was that the county couldn't afford to be in an All-Ireland again. Obviously this wouldn't stop them if their team was good enough to contest another All Ireland in the future!

Focus on reducing time wastage on your phones for the next twenty one days until you establish a better phone habit. There are a lot of time wasters out there, many of whom are lonesome people. Now it's great if you are on a premium line and you are getting paid while you are coaching or mentoring, but that's probably not your game. One of the reasons they have lots of time is because they are on somebody else's payroll. If you keep your value figure in front of you, you will get smarter on that phone and won't allow them to impose on you. You can be very professional and say, 'there is another call coming, sorry', or 'I'm going to a meeting' etc. You have to take the initiative and take charge, otherwise they are in charge. I see it every other day in businesses. The internet is another potential time waster. It just absorbs time, plus there are associated health and safety risks also.

You need to be quite assertive in relation to how you manage your time in your business. There is very little room in business for people who are either aggressive or weak. Assertive people can be mild mannered, but they know and you know how far they will move. If you are not assertive then other people's agendas will control your time. Say **'no'** to any demands that take you away from your most important tasks. The basis of being assertive is being clear about what you want. This clarity of direction is the real anchor upon which your business will be successful. If you can establish more clarity of purpose for yourself, you will have received a good return from your time investment in this book.

Many business people are prone to completing tasks themselves rather than delegating because they feel they will complete it quicker themselves. Of course you may be quicker but if you continue to do those things yourself, you become the limiting factor in your business. The question you must keep asking is: 'Is this activity worth my hourly value number?' Does it need to be done, or can you delegate it? Are you good at delegation? Most employers are not, but they don't realise it. I had a typical example of this recently with a client company.

These clients are an internationally traded business. They have successfully come through stage one of their business cycle but they are struggling at stage two. They are not struggling because of the market but because of the MD's management capability. He knows the theory of exactly what should be done but is finding it very difficult to let go. He has hired all the right people, but he is still doing all the things that he was supposed to off-load to these people himself. Having made the investment in his shadow team he is not now getting the return. The shadow team members are not sure what their jobs are, because he's not sure what he expects of them. He has never sat down and drawn up targets in relation to those people. He was always away travelling and when I queried this he admitted that it was easier to be away than to face up to his responsibilities. He said that deep down he knew he was running away from his responsibilities. He thinks he has delegated but he hasn't. He has abdicated. If these people are any good he will lose them. If they are of no use they will stay. People that are useless are like wet leaves, they stick around.

If I could give you a motto for the next twenty one days it would be:

'Do the most important things first, do things one at a time and be decisive.'

Failing to plan is planning to fail

It is not necessary to plan your life too tightly but you must put some shape on it. If you plan too tightly that stifles initiative as well. Don't make excuses, make plans.

Remember: ready, aim, fire rather than ready, fire, aim as often happens.

The 4D Strategy

The following stepped recommendation is very important. It is known as the 4D Strategy. I want you to analyse yourself against these four recommendations:

D ---- Do it
D ---- Delay it to a specific time
D ---- Delegate it
D ---- Dump it

Most houses have an attic. Attics tend to be filled with items we can't decide what to do with. The extent of our indecision is reflected in the stockpiles in our attic. The only two times an attic is ever cleaned out is: (1) when you have a house fire or, (2) when you are moving house. Now I think there is an attic or the equivalent of an attic in all your businesses.

Delegation

If you find you are spending a huge amount of your time doing something that is not worth that hourly value figure, then that has to be delegated. There are three golden rules to be followed if you want to be better at delegation.

1. Define the job and its expected output clearly

This was the problem of the person in the previous case study. He hadn't worked out the real parameters of the jobs for his shadow team. Look at the difference in the following case study.

A well managed business I know have a very clear strategy in this area. They never tell somebody how to do his / her job. What they do is sit down with the employee and agree the measurable outputs for this job. I remember having a discussion with the MD a number of times about why they approached it like this. He said that if you agree the measurable output of the job with somebody, then they know and you know what the actual performance is. The reason they don't tell people how to do the job is because they expect the person, when challenged, to come up with a smarter way of doing the job. The background assumption is that the person is equipped to do the job in the first place. The other thing he told me was, that at their weekly performance meetings the employee comes and reports on his/ her measurable outputs, rather than management presenting performance results to the meeting. This forces the employee to monitor his own performance and report on it.

If you set targets with somebody it is far more effective if they monitor themselves so that they are then coming to you reporting on the defined gap. They are not coming in waiting to see what the gap is. As managers you have no problem in giving responsibility but you can sometimes be very slow in giving the appropriate authority to go with it. You will never be effective at delegation if you are not prepared to give responsibility, authority and resources to the person to get on with the job. If you don't do that you are not giving them the full set of tools required to do the job.

2. Observe from a greater distance
As they get a bit safer and more comfortable with the job, give them more space.

3. Resist upwards delegation
This is where somebody comes to you and says, 'how do we do that?' and you show them and then they come to you again tomorrow with the same question. You have to stop at that stage. If you have to continually show them how to do the job then why bother having them on the payroll? You have to set the standards in your business. A standard ceases to be a standard the day you cease to insist on it. If you don't become the guardian of that standard in your business then you are not doing your job.

My advice to you is to have as few rules and regulations as possible in your business, both for yourself and for the people under you. But the few that you do have you must insist on one hundred percent. The best companies that I see are the ones that have very few rules but the rules that they have are sacrosanct. There are no excuses and everybody knows that.

You have peak energy times in your day when you are at your best. For some it's the morning for others it's the evenings. What is your peak energy time?

You should tackle the most important tasks in your business during your high energy periods. Try and delegate or outsource as much as possible. Tasks like book-keeping for example, should be possible to outsource. It is like something that is home baked; it doesn't necessarily have to be in your home that it is baked. There is a fabricating company I know who insist on fabricating every component part themselves. They don't have to do that, but they like to say that they manufacture everything themselves. Now, while that can be very laudable it is not very economical in their circumstance. Commerce must win at the end of the day.

Managing is not about hanging on to what you should be delegating and by default, giving away what you should be focusing on. If you hold on to things you should be delegating your brain power is not available to focus on the things you should be focusing on.

Time Wasters
If somebody comes into your office and they are wasting your time, stand up. Don't invite them to sit down. You have to start managing your time. Be professional about it, be quite nice about it but start managing your time. The amount of time

that is wasted in allowing other people to manage your time should not be underestimated. The amount of time that you can be in touch with your customers in any one day or week, be it face to face or on the phone, is actually quite short and you have to optimise that time. The following is a list of other time wasters.

1. Travelling
One of the things that I myself do is to try to travel as much as possible in non-customer time. If you travel at twelve o'clock in the day you are wasting valuable customer time. You must keep challenging your time allocation to such activities as travelling against your hourly rate written on your wall.

2. Unproductive meetings
If you have come from the corporate world I would suspect you spend a lot of time at meetings about meetings. There is probably also too much irrelevant reading of paper work. Try and cut to the chase. Browsing the net can be another form of time wasting and should be controlled.

3. Doing the same job twice

4. Servicing bad customers
My definition of a bad customer is somebody who shouts loudest, shouts most often and doesn't pay you. You probably give them far too much time. You need to cut off twenty percent of your customers. Nobody wants them, so why should you?

5. Socialising
I am referring to business networking. You should be conscious of what you want to achieve from it.

6. Disorganisation
Finish those important tasks and deliver your promise. Don't over-promise because it will come back to haunt you.

Now I want to show you two 'tools' that I think will pull together everything I have spoken about here.

Do you use a 'To Do' list?

How could you make it work better for you?

Here is a very straightforward way of managing your 'To Do' list. Get a one page per day diary and, for each working day rule off a left column about one inch wide as shown in the diagram below.

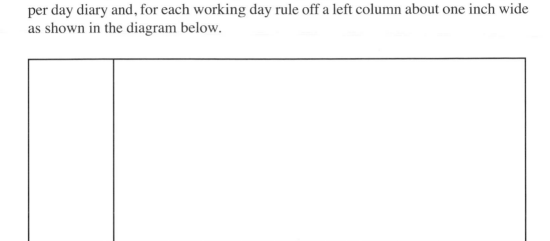

You then use that column as your 'To Do' column and use the rest of the page for your general diary purposes. At the day's end go through the 'To Do' list and cross off whatever is done. From the remaining list identify the two or three most important issues and designate them as **'A'** issues. Meeting customers, who may only be available at certain times, should be **'A'** issues. Designate the rest as **'B'** issues. You must now apply the **4D** formula to this list.

From your list decide which issues you are going to **DO** tomorrow, which ones you are going to **DELAY** to specific dates; which issues you are going to **DELEGATE** and which ones you are going to **DUMP.**

Decide which issues you can delegate and forward a note in your diary to remind you when the person you are delegating to is to report back to you. Transfer to tomorrow's diary page the **'A'** issues you plan to address tomorrow. If it's not appropriate to address some of these **'A'** issues tomorrow, don't put them into tomorrow's list, instead forward them to the delayed date you decide and forget about them. They will be there when you come to that date. Do the same with the 'B' list of issues. If you decide to DUMP some issues do so now. Today's list is now fully managed with nothing left outstanding. All the issues are either DONE, DUMPED, DELEGATED to somebody or DIARISED forward to the appropriate dates.

Your 'To Do' list gets finished today. You need to do this task during the last five minutes of your working day. The reason for this is twofold. Firstly, it is a way of signing off the day - particularly if you work from home. Secondly, you are challenging your sub-conscious mind to work on this list during the night, so when you go into work tomorrow you already have twelve hours of subconscious brain power put into addressing these issues.

Irrespective of anything else, you must do the most important 'A' listed items; those few critical things that will probably only take up twenty percent of your time but will give you eighty percent of your return. You have the rest of the day to work the 'B' issues. As the day progresses, other issues will be added to the list. You must manage this list during your last five minutes of work each day in the future.

If you find that you are diarying forward the same issues from one day to another it means that you are not making decisions. If this evening you diary something forward to tomorrow and then find that tomorrow evening you are diarying the same thing forward again, that is failure. You are not actually tackling issues. You are abdicating your responsibilities. But if you do it the way I am suggesting then you won't have a problem; this method works one hundred percent.

The diary is the equivalent of having a boss; it puts organisation and structure into your working day. But don't make the mistake of having two diaries. Have no diary rather than two diaries. Don't have an electronic diary and a hardback one, because you will have some things in one diary and some in the other and this can lead to serious omissions and mistakes. I have tried all of the electronic methods and I still find that I come back to the hardback diary. The physical act of sitting down for five minutes and just crossing off something or delegating something is far more penetrating that just deleting something on the computer.

You can use the system as described or adapt your own variation of it. Whatever system you decide on will be of no use unless you apply it consistently. The principle I am trying to get across is that of deciding this evening what is important tomorrow. If you are not dealing with the important things then you are not managing your business. I know people who have been using this method for the last ten or fifteen years and they are just as dependent on it as I am. Use this system for a month so that you build the habit. Make up your own mind at the end of the month. It is only after doing something twenty times or more that you will be able to see its benefit. It is important that you build and entrench good habits. You may have too many things in your head but if something is in your diary you don't have to worry about forgetting it because it will be there in front of you.

There is one further 'tool' that I want to describe. I want to suggest that twice a day, at random, you challenge yourself. This doesn't sound like much as a statement, but it is one of the most effective ways of focusing your business. Twice a day, say to yourself: *What is the most valuable use of my time right now?* Then look at what you are actually doing at that time. If you find that you are doing something which is not capable of justifying your hourly value figure, it forces you back on track. I suggest that you put this challenge on your screen saver or a notice facing your desk. This 'in your face' challenge will make you think and refocus on the important rather than the less important issues.

If you use both of the above tools consistently you will see the results. You will start to work the 80/20 rule by default. The net result is that you will be more productive. If you are more productive, your business is going to be more productive. One of the biggest angles is that when you are signing off for the day, you have tomorrow and part of the days ahead already pre-planned.

Are you now wondering what should really drive your business on a day to day basis? We have talked about various tools and how to apply them, but what should really drive your business? Clients are the main thing that should drive your business and that is where you should be focused. Support services must be managed, but revenue comes from your clients. You have to manage that client relationship well. Sometimes clients manage you instead of you managing clients. It is really the 80/20 rule again. If you don't make an issue of finishing a job or you don't finish a job yourself, that gives a licence to everybody around you not to be too bothered either. That is where the issue of deadlines comes in and the management of those deadlines. A lot of your deadlines are imposed on you externally. These 'tools' will help you to put deadlines on yourself. They help concentrate the mind on the important things, whilst also giving you the flexibility to do other things. I do not believe in having every section of your day planned. I don't believe that works in most cases. It is different if you are running a production line. If you are on the move a lot, then my suggested 'tools' will be of great benefit to you, **provided you use them consistently.**

You are the **limiting** factor

Building Your Business Model

Chapter 10

STRATEGY:
What Is It About And What Are Its Implications For Your Business

I want to reflect for a moment on just how difficult it is to run a small business. In the course of any one day you need to be an administrator, operations manager, motivator, planner, trainer, problem solver, physiologist and a guardian of your bottom line among other things. You have a lot of hats to wear. You have natural strengths for some of these tasks but you also have natural weaknesses in other areas.

Unfortunately, when you are operating a small business all of those bases have to be covered so you have to pressurise and discipline yourself to do a lot of things that you are not naturally good at doing. This is where the diary system described in Chapter 9 and all the other tools discussed earlier can help. They will give you a structure and a plan so you don't just focus in on the things that you like doing.

Understanding is only step one of your necessary change process. You have to follow this with an appropriate action plan and manoeuvre its successful implementation.

If you let nature take its course and you don't put a disciplined structure around yourself, you will spend an inordinate amount of your time doing the things you like doing. Many people are good at the operations side of their business but there tends to be weaknesses in the commerce around their core businesses. And it is commerce that pays you. You have to understand that your business is a means to an end and not an end in itself. If you can understand this it is easier to achieve success.

Many of you will have come through from the corporate world. You have been either the victims of, or active participants in, the various types of quality systems operating within that section. Nobody really talks about it anymore – it's a given. In one sense they are a good thing and in another sense they're not.

I was in Vietnam some months ago and when we were driving through Hanoi and Ho Chi Min City, all the big offices and factories had ISO 9001 or 9002 signs all over them. Fifteen years ago we were like that here in Ireland. I remember being involved in some of the first businesses to get ISO accreditation. I remember one of them displaying a big banner declaring this fact in a very prominent place in Dublin for about twelve months. They were so proud of their achievement and used it essentially as a marketing tool. Today they would be embarrassed to put it up. It just goes to show you the way businesses have changed. In reality all those quality standards were good but they were misused completely. They were misused because they were used more as marketing tools and had very little to do with quality rating. They were quality assurance systems, which meant that if things were done in a certain way and certain procedures were followed, at least you would get consistency. They became 'paper mountains' and they were really of very little value to many participant businesses. The standards themselves contained a lot of good aspects of management practice, which often tended to get neutralised by the volume of paperwork. The better businesses have built on this initial experience and moved on to world class standards. All of these interventions are built around the sound logic of the following.

1. Alignment of your Objectives

The base line for any improvement system is alignment of your objectives. The objectives you have for your business must be aligned - you can't have them shouting at each other. If you set an objective to do something that is fighting with another objective, then you have a real problem. Your objectives must be aligned.

2. Customer Focus

You are in business to serve your customers. Is that a true statement?
The answer is, not necessarily. You are in business to optimise your bottom line which has a direct relationship with your customer's perception of your service. You create wealth by serving customers, but you are not in business to service customers. Customers are your means towards the creation of wealth.

3. Organising the Work Place

As you observed in Chapter 9, there is a very strong correlation between organisation and efficiency. Remember the phrase, 'a cluttered desk equals a cluttered mind.'

4. Visible Measurement System

What you measure gets done. What do you measure in your business? How do you know whether you are doing well or badly? When we are looking at finance in the next chapter I'll be trying to focus you in on what you should be measuring, because you need to be very clear about what you decide to measure in your business.

5. Eliminating Waste

Issue Template

A. Identify an issue to be addressed in your business.

B. List three reasons why you haven't addressed this issue before now:
    A.
    B.
    C.

C. Set an objective for addressing this issue.

D. Sketch out your proposed Action Plan.

E. How are you going to monitor progress?

I want you to use this Issue Template to facilitate you in addressing the critical issue of waste in your business. I want you to look at your own business and identify where waste is happening at the moment.

You have the visual waste that you can see on the floor, but doing a job twice is also wasteful. I want you to identify some of the excuses you have used for not addressing your waste issue up to now. I want you to calculate 5% of your turnover for last year. If you had a turnover of €100,000, 5% of that amounts to €5,000. So I want you to find €5,000 of waste in your business. I want you to set that monitory target as your objective. I want you to develop a plan of action to eliminate it and monitor the waste. One of the ways to improve profits in your organisation is by reducing waste in a planned way. A lot of your focus is on making money but one of the ways of actually improving your bottom line is via the planned reduction of waste. It is very unlikely that there is any business that can't find waste. I believe you can find a 5% equivalent of your turnover without having to dig too deeply. When you have 'killed off' that 5% then go back for the next layer and so on. This is a journey not a destination. 'Every great journey starts with the first step.'

Chinese proverb

Some of this potential waste could be failure to generate business. It could be pontificating about what you are going to do and not doing it. That's waste. It could be setting up a meeting or failing to set up a meeting. That's waste. The physical waste you tend to see a bit more. Time can be wasted. Repeating a job can be a waste; making mistakes is waste, having to discount, that's waste. Having to go and deliver twice due to short shipment is waste and panic buying can lead to a number of waste options like a non-competitive purchase price, delayed jobs due to material shortage etc.

6. Team Work and Staff Involvement
'No man is an island' and neither are you in your business. In order to achieve your objectives you need input from many sources both from within and outside of your business. Bonuses and incentives are the 'normal' tools used in order to gain buy-in and commitment from the team. It's a difficult area and an area you have to be quite careful with. We will look at this later, when addressing your human resource issues.

The better companies are trying to move towards continuous improvement. They have action plans under each of these headings. You too should be taking a number of those issues and working on them in your own business. That's one of the reasons I'm suggesting you work this issue template.

Strategy
Is strategy important? If so can you define it? Every time you pick up the paper, listen to television or hear politicians speak, it's all about strategy.

Strategy in the first instance is a military term. Before and during wars, generals are always outlining strategies in order to give them an advantage over the enemy. In the old days it was about taking the high ground or controlling the bridge. They were manoeuvring their army resources to a more advantageous position so that they could enhance their potential competitive advantage and win the battle. The experts say that all wars are won before you go to war.

After the Second World War, a number of the generals came back into industry. They were highly educated and were able to control masses of people, who were now on production lines rather than lying in the trenches. A number of the generals came into senior management positions to more or less control these new armies. That's how the whole terminology of the war and strategy came into industry.

> "A Victorious army wins it's victories, before seeking battle" Sun Tzn

Nature's law of **cause and effect** states that for every effect there is a cause. If you look at your business, the effect you are trying to achieve is the optimisation of your bottom line. In order to achieve that, you have to manage the various inputs of your business.

Strategy is about deciding what effect you want for your business and deciding what causes/inputs you can better manage to give you your desired effect, which is the optimisation of your bottom line. The army general wanted to win the battle. In order to win the battle he or she had to manage the various resources including ammunition and the positioning of the soldiers. All of his/her ducks had to be positioned in line in order to exploit their advantage. It is the same in business.

As a manager you have two dimensions to your role: operational and strategic. Your strategic role is by far the more important. It addresses such issues as: 1) what business are you in and 2) what business should you be in. Once you've decided what business you are in and where you want to strategically position it, then you have to draw up a plan of action to manage the causes or inputs in order to make it happen.

Clarity of Purpose

You are the most important cause or input to your business. You are the equivalent of a general who has to put together all the various bits and pieces to optimise their war effort. You too have to manage the total input mix in order to be successful. Back in your mother's day when she was baking the Christmas cake, she had her own recipe, which was her intellectual property (IP). Based on these recipes, she put the ingredients together so that the resulting cake was unique. In her view it was far superior to Mary's down the road. You being the non-paying customer (and knowing what was good for you), nodded your head in agreement. The only time you probably got excited about it was if the neighbouring children started to brag about their mum's cake. I am sure you rose to this challenge. If you didn't, I would probably advise you to stay on somebody else's payroll. You probably didn't inherit that cutting edge required to make it in the challenging commercial environment.

Managing your business is the same, except on a more serious level. As a manager you are the equivalent of your mother baking the Christmas cake. She was very clear about the cake she wanted. Are you as clear about the business you want? If you manage to do your business based on clarity, quality of service and desired contribution to your customers your business results will reflect this.

Clarity of purpose is the most important issue in relation to your success. It will have a bigger impact on your success or failure than anything else. No one can predict the future with any degree of accuracy, so you must make certain assumptions in relation to the future. It is important that you try to visualise the future. What the mind can conceive, you can achieve.

The quality of the assumptions that you make underpins the whole basis of your business decisions. Then you have to gather the resources to go out and make it happen. Many business people can successfully write a business plan but then fail to implement it. This may be your first exposure to this kind of thinking. It wouldn't be unusual to conclude that it's just theory. However it is most important for you to understand this concept of strategic thinking. If you don't determine where you want to strategically position your business, then all the other things that you are doing with your business are going to be pretty well null and void. Strategy is about the future. Because it is somewhat vague, people tend to get nervous.

So why should you set a strategy? It is about trying to prevent yourself from preparing for the last battle instead of the next one. There is no point in looking backwards. All your future business success depends on what you do from now on.

Where your business is going to be in the future depends very much on the quality of the decisions you make from now on. You have some control over what is going to happen to your business into the future. You have to learn from the past in order not to fall into the same black holes again. The strategic decisions that you make in relation to where you want to position your business will determine whether you are going to become a millionaire or not. You have to decide what problems you are going to develop a solution for; solutions that will be perceived by your target market as being better than those of your likely competitors. That one strategic judgement call is going to be critical for you and will have a far larger impact on your future wealth than all the operational issues you worry about.

Many of you may end up doing something different in the future as a result of these decisions. Trading environments change and you need to reflect these changes in the strategic decisions you make. There are waves of opportunity out there but you cannot go with them all. In surfing terminology, you have to decide which wave you are going to ride. It is a physical impossibility for a jockey to ride two horses at the one time. Imagine the pain if they start to run in non parallel lines. The same applies in your business. Sooner rather than later, you must decide to let one horse off, focus on your chosen horse and go for the winning post.

You may be in a situation where you will have to make a decision from a number of possibilities. You'll have to make a judgement call on something you only have outline knowledge of, based on the assumptions you have made. Do not necessarily identify the ones that seem to have the most potential, but rather identify those with the least potential and eliminate them. That way you're left with the ones with most potential. It's just a different way of achieving the same result. There is also a second point worth noting regarding putting some options on ice for now. Their time might come. Matching the time to the market is very important because you know the old saying, *"be not the first on who the new is tried, nor yet the last to lay the old aside"*. It is often bad strategically to be the first into the market. While many people say it's great because it provides you with the opportunity to create and capture the initial market share, the reality is you probably won't. The people that make the money are the people who are probably second or third into the market. The first into the market generally has to educate the market, and they often run out of resources before they have the market penetrated. The second one in then merely continues and it's the third or fourth who tends to succeed because the market is tuned up at that stage and they come in for the kill. Big companies can succeed by being first in because they have the necessary resources both to influence the early adopters and to wait financially for the next wave of adopters.

I am not suggesting that you shouldn't be innovative, but you should be careful about trying something very new. It's great if you can make it happen, but it also carries the highest risk because it is something untried. If it works somewhere else you have a far better chance that your variation of it will work too. At least then it's a proven formula, but something completely new carries a higher risk. There is an old bit of Kerry advice: *The best place to start is where other people have dropped off*.

What Does R & D Stand For?
Most people will answer that it means Research and Development. For many businesses it really means **R**ob and **D**uplicate.

In reality, there is very little real research and development happening out there. What is going on is a form of rob and duplicate. People are robbing someone else's idea and duplicating it with a slight variation. Going with a completely new idea is very dangerous territory unless you have the resources to be able to stay with it long enough for it to be successful. If you are robbing someone else's idea, a proven idea, and duplicating it but with just a slight difference, at least you know there is a proven formula. If you are taking something that works rather well and you can customise it for your local market, it's a far safer strategy and much more likely to be a successful formula than something that is completely new.

Ireland lacks numbers and there are too many people trying to fish out of the same pond. If you seem to have a successful business formula, others will try and copy you very quickly. The more players that come into your pool, the lower your margins get. This is the reason why you have to try to be meaningfully different, in some sort of a protected way. Issues such as patents and brand image come into play here. It's great if you can become the standard bearer, but it is costly.

Everyone is going to be pinching at you in some shape or form. Usually the market leader tends to control in excess of 30% of the market, the second and third between them probably control about 15% of the market and the rest of the market tends to be spread between everybody else. At the start you may control 100% of the niche but over time the above structure tends to evolve. If you're here in ten years time your market share might have gone from 100% to maybe 30%, but you could be earning a lot more out of this 30%. Smart business people make judgement calls based on the return on investment (ROI) they are going to make from this project, both over the longer term and the shorter term. You have to make the investment before the rewards and that's where the real trick is. Are you courageous enough to make that investment so you can position yourself to get the required return? Some people look for the return before they make the investment and that's why you get a lot of disappointed people. Keep subjecting your investment decision to this formula and it will concentrate your mind. But what if you made a very considerable investment only to find that it wasn't the cleverest move?

There are two things you have to decide: Has it the potential to make the necessary return if you manage it differently? If the answer is no, do you have the confidence to decide to cut and run before the curtains are dropped by the actions of another stakeholder?

I met a lady recently who has a mature business where her margins are continuously being squeezed. She has been forced into very difficult negotiations and my advice to her was that if she doesn't get what she wants out of these she should quit. Of course that's a huge decision for anybody to make. After spending ten or fifteen years with a formula that's just about working, should she spend another five or ten years struggling with the same formula? For her, this is a real strategic decision. Her business is not an attractive one to be in because the entry barriers are too low. Others have come and gone and destroyed the margins as they passed through. If negotiations go well she'll probably have a reasonable outcome, but if they don't go to her liking then my advice to her is to get out now.

• You cannot keep frontloading your business if you are not prepared to off load on the other side.

In her situation, she cannot consider exploiting other opportunities if she doesn't decide to exit this declining business. In other words, to equip herself to frontload a new opportunity, she has to decide to offload this business at the other end. That's a radical and strategic decision. What most people do is **not** make a decision. They grouse and moan and finish up going nowhere. They are the same as people who are in jobs that are going nowhere. Their situations are just about comfortable enough to keep them in their box, but not comfortable enough to satisfy them. What is your situation?

Strategy is about repositioning yourselves in relation to your competitors. Where do you position yourselves in relation to your competitors?

You have to capitalise on your strengths and reduce your weaknesses in relation to your competitors. At the end of the day the customer is king and he will decide who wins and who loses. You need to know your customers' deciding criteria and play that game better than your competitor. You have many strengths and weaknesses and there is a wealth of opportunities out there but you need to exploit them. You can have all the theory, all the paperwork and the best research in the world, but remember it is the market that pays you. Often the more research that companies do, the less action there is at the end of it.

Research is often an excuse for non-action, particularly for those who are not comfortable getting out there and putting their proposition in front of potential customers. They will use every type of excuse so as not to get in touch with customers. They will say we haven't our brochures yet or we need additional information. These are all reasonable excuses that appear rational, but in reality they are just an evasion.

What issues or opportunities have you been standing back from in the last six months?

What excuses have you been using?

Are they rational now, when you look at them and are true to yourself?

The first two to three years of any business is really the market research phase. If you revisit the same businesses three or four years down the line, they are often doing something different to what they originally set out to do. What they are doing is often a variation of what they set out to do and that is good. Being active in the market facilitated them to better understand the changing trends, which they then adjusted to in a professional manner. The best market research in my view is being out there face to face with your customer. Do all the market research you like, but you will learn more by being out there in front of your potential customer trying to get a purchase order. The first time you did most things they were difficult. I want you to record some of the difficulties you encountered the first time you sold something.

First Time Issue/ Activity	Your Experience

It's not easy the first time you do something new but after that initiation it does get easier. The selling scenario can often be difficult if you are not a natural, but you can still be a very effective salesperson. I will address this in more detail in a later chapter.

Planning is defining your desired future and plotting effective ways of bringing it about. It is really a four stepped process of deciding where you have come from, where you are, where you want to be within a particular timeframe and then deciding how best to get there.

Do you have a business plan?
Even if you don't have a written business plan, you have one in your head. I want to encourage you very strongly to put what's in your head down on paper, but in a structured way.

What is the purpose of a business plan?
A lot of business plans are written for the wrong purpose. In many cases they are written because when you go into a bank or a lending agency seeking capital, one of the first things they ask for is your business plan. What a lot of people do is they say to their consultant or accountant: *'Will you stick a plan together for me there; I need it to get money.'* That's a fairly useless exercise. I've discussed it with bank managers over the years and they say that when their potential customers return with their business plan, it's generally in a sealed envelope and they say to the bank manager. *'Have a look at that, sure you would know more about that than I would.'* What kind of a signal are they giving to their bank?

A business plan written by yourself is far better than one written for you by a management consultant or accountant. It might not look as pretty but it is yours. While you may need help with its construction, the guts of it have to come from you. If you put something together you will have ownership of it, which is critical, since you are the person who is going to have to make that business work.

The main use of your business plan is for yourself. It's your roadmap upon which you will drive your business forward. That doesn't mean some of the projections and assumptions you make about your business won't change; they probably will. But it is still better to have it than not to have it. You can use it to monitor your own progress and as a promotional document if you're looking for finance.

The following page contains a fairly standard format for a business plan. If you already have a business plan and it differs from this don't worry, the format is by no means fixed. If you do have an existing business plan perhaps this may be an opportunity to re-visit and upgrade it.

Business Plan Model

While each Plan is unique, the following format is fairly standard.

Cover Page   Business name plus contact name and phone number.

Page 2   Legal status of the business and registration number.

Page 3   Executive Summary: Should summarise what you are proposing to do, how you are going to do it, what you want and how it is going to be financed.

Page 4   Index Page.

Page 5   Information on the team and team structure.

Page 6   Mission Statement.

Page 7   Corporate Objectives.

Page 8   SWOT analysis and conclusions drawn.

Page 9   Manufacturing / Operations Plan.
- *Flow-chart your process.*
  - ❏ *A/c computerised.*
  - ❏ *Licences.*
  - ❏ *Insurance.*
  - ❏ *Patents etc.*

Page 10   Investment Proposal
- *Outline of investment.*
- *Phases of payment.*
- *How it will be financed.*

Page 11   Market Research
- Customer Profiling.
- Competitor Profiling.
- Marketing Strategy to be adopted.
- ■ Management of the marketing mix.
  - ❏ Product / Service analysis and conclusions.
  - ❏ Pricing policy.
  - ❏ Place - channels of distribution to be used.
  - ❏ Promotion plans.

Failing to plan is planning to fail.

Page 12   Financial Data and Projections
                   ❑   P/L/account.
                   ❑   Sales Projections.
                   ❑   'Cost of sales' projections.
                   ❑   Overhead Costs projections.
                   ❑   Balance Sheet.
                   ❑   Cash Flow Statement.

Page 13   Appendix
- Brochures.
- Plans / Planning Permission.
- Certificate of Incorporation.
- Price lists.
- Specification Sheets etc.
- Photographs.
- Qualification Certificates.
- Others.

How well you complete your business plan will vary from person to person. For each SMART business objective, you need to formulate and implement an action plan to make it happen. These individual action plans will combine into an integrated overall plan, for the short and the longer term. Putting your business plan on paper challenges you to think through the strategies, which must be aligned, so that all your business objectives can be achieved.

The process allows you to plan on paper before you commit any tangible investment. It gives you a roadmap to guide you on your commercial journey, from the point where your business is currently at to the point where you want it to be, within a certain timeframe. It also helps to communicate your proposition to the various stakeholders whose support will be vital at critical points along the journey. By involving the various stakeholders in its formulation, you are helping to empower them. There is truth in the saying, *'One tends to support what one helps to create.'* This team approach is a useful tactic to employ in working towards the successful implementation of your plan.

Hierarchy of Business Planning
The two basic dimensions are:
Planning at the **strategic level** and
Planning at the **operational level**
Both are part of the whole, but in a way which is aimed at people at different levels of your organisation.

The diagram on the following page illustrates this planning process as an integrated model from top to bottom and from bottom to top.

I have presented this integrated planning model as an inverted cone, which becomes more constricted as you look down through the model. Everything starts with your *Vision*. What mental picture of your business are you carrying around in your head? The normal timeframe here would be about five years hence.

The next step in your planning model is formulating your **Mission Statement.** As you can see this is forcing you to start to put some boundaries on your vision. The normal planning timeframe for this is two to three years.

The next planning step is setting your **Annual SMART Objectives.** This is bringing your mission statement down to measurable objectives which need to be achieved within the twelve month timeframe.

Following this you need to break the yearly SMART objectives down to **Monthly SMART Objectives,** divided out to either various profit centres or different product lines. The final step of the planning model represents setting **Individual Targets** for your employees.

What often happens in business is that the people at the coal face have very little comprehension of where you are driving your business. Their planning horizon is the next pay day. Many people don't plan ahead much further than that. You have to understand that that is the mindset they are in. If you agree that this is reality, then you must work the objectives for them within the mental timeframes they have in their heads. The double arrowed line running up and down the model indicates that each level is integrated. There is a direct link between the vision you have for your business and what your people are producing tomorrow for your business. Tomorrow is day one of your journey towards energising your mission and ultimately your dream. So the trick is, you have to cascade your vision down through the ever constricting stage of the planning model to individual daily/hourly production targets.

The better companies have this integrated model well worked out. There is a direct link between their vision and what their staff are doing on a daily or weekly basis. However, there is often poor communication between the top and what is actually happening on the ground. This is where the value of appropriate planning at the various levels comes into effect. It isn't enough just to scale the big picture down to an individual level and a format and language that they understand. If you want to be successful, you need to take it down to those individual layers. *What's happening on the ground is often shouting rather than supporting what's planned at higher levels.*

So if you really want to get the value out of understanding this model you have to cascade it down to the appropriate level. Of all the exercises I am challenging you to do as you work your way through this book, if you could actually get this model working for you, so that your daily, weekly and monthly performance objectives are being met and monitored, they will build up to the achievement of your yearly SMART objectives and these in turn will energise your mission statement. You are then well on the road towards energising your vision.

Sometimes people get lost in this kind of thinking. If you look at your business plan, you already have this framework in your financial projections. You have your sales, your cost of sales and overheads broken down by month. You can break it down further into weekly, daily or hourly targets. This is not complicated by any means, but it is a very vital exercise. *If you want a road map to keep you focused, this is it.*

Your business meetings with your team should focus on this model. You will be judging last month's performance against the objectives set and agreeing an action plan so that the whole team performs against the objectives for the next period. You are monitoring what has happened and you are planning for what has to happen over the next period. It is a very important exercise and it's up to you to do it. If you don't, it's a missed opportunity.

The broader top part of the cone is the strategic level. This is really a statement of your business intent. It plots the overall direction in which you intend to drive your business into the future. It allows you to define your business's grand purpose, what you ultimately want to achieve and indicates the broad sweep strategies you will use to realise this vision/mission.

What is the grand purpose of your business? What do you boast about within your business over a few 'jars'? Bill Gates had the vision that he could see a computer in every household. That was his Big Vision.

What is your Big Vision for you and your business five to ten years hence?

Your **Mission Statement** is the next level of planning. It's a broad statement of intent about the proposed positioning of your business. It should give some signal about your business. To focus your mind, answer the following three critical questions:

1. Who is your target customer(s)?
2. What value are you proposing to bring to them?
3. How do you propose to do this?

When you have teased out your answers to these fundamental questions, you should summarise your answers in the form of a broad statement of intent, which is your Mission Statement. Its purpose is to give you broad focus so that you can better decide which opportunities you should grasp and which ones you must say no to. It is really your overarching statement. Any opportunity falling outside this diameter is not within your business definition.

Having decided the direction, you must put together a strategy to gather the necessary resources and capacity to energise it so that the various staging posts along the way can be reached. As you come down through the planning cone your timeframes shorten and you get into more measurable details. Having agreed the strategic direction, the focus at the operational level is on day-to-day management. This is where you communicate with your line managers, charge hands, right down to the measurable output of the individual operation jobs. Here you are working with SMART objectives, detailed budgets and timetables.

As you can see from the steps of the process, there is nothing in there that you can't tackle. You may need some help with aspects such as financial projections, but the major part of it should be your own thinking and decision making.

As per the template, the first page of your business plan just records the business name, contact name and telephone number.

The second page covers the legal status of the business and its registration number. This may not seem particularly important. However a banker or investor needs to know what legal entity he is was dealing with. You should anticipate their questions and answer them before you are asked.

The next page is the executive summary, which is a summary of your total proposition. It should probably be three quarters of a page at the most. It is however one of the most critical pages of your business plan. If you are presenting your plan to a bank, development agency or investor, the first thing they will read is the executive summary. If they don't get the essence of what your business is about in the executive summary, the chances of them reading the rest of your business plan are pretty small. They are busy people. It is easier for them to say **no** to you rather than yes. You have to help them to say YES. No bank executive was ever fired for saying no, but they must be selective when saying yes. The executive summary should state clearly what you are proposing to do, how you are going to do it, what external assistance you require and how it is going to be financed. It makes a great deal of sense not to finalise the executive summary until you have the plan completed. Then insert it as Page 3, so that the reader can cut to it immediately.

The next page is an index page. You don't have to have an index page but it makes reading the whole plan easier.

The following page gives information on the team. Do you remember I told you about the guy we came across during our survey with the banks? He inserted a full organisational chart, with each function fleshed out for the team he planned to build, in order to develop his business in an incremental way. At that particular stage, he was a one person operation, but he was giving a very professional signal about the business he was planning to build. You should do the same thing in relation to this section of your business plan. If sub contractors are a critical element of your business, you should profile these and show were they fit within your proposed delivery team You should also include your professional advisors, such as your accountants, legal advisors and consultants. The perceived quality of those professionals is important, as their involvement gives you credibility and gives banks and investors some degree of comfort.

The best plans are sharp, snappy and about ten to twelve pages long. It is more difficult to write a sharp snappy plan than one which waffles on. You can use the appendix section to put forward your supporting documentation, such as specification sheets, brochures, research reports and other additional information.

The issues listed under the other pages of the business plan template I will address during the following chapters.

Many people are afraid of business plans because they have never written one before. If you have never done something, you tend to be afraid of it. Rest assured that there is nothing in this plan that you can't do. A lot of people don't like writing, but the discipline of writing facilitates you to crystallise your thoughts.

Do you doodle?

Doodling is associated with the creative aspect of your brain and helps you to tease out your thoughts and intuition. It is just another form of writing, where you are using symbols instead of letters. Think of your plan as doodling in a structured way so that both you and others can clearly understand it.

Strategy

Your business plan is really your action plan. It will guide you in implementing your plans for driving your business forward in your chosen direction. Let's focus in on what strategy is about.

No man is an island and neither is your business. It has to exist and succeed by successfully managing a series of both external and internal factors. Your business has to manage its relationships with external players such as your customers, suppliers, competitors and regulatory bodies. Although external, all of these players are critical to your business. The operational aspects of your business operate within your business. There is a direct relationship between this internal/external model: the 80/20 rule and the concept of effectiveness and efficiency.

Is there a difference between efficiency and effectiveness or are they the same?

_____

_____

Yes, there is a link between them, but they are different. You often hear politicians taking about efficiency and effectiveness. Do they know what they're talking about?

Yes_____   No_____

Efficiency is about being good at doing things right. Effectiveness is about doing the right thing. About **80%** of your business success depends on how good you are at managing the **external forces** like your customers, suppliers, competitors and regulatory bodies. Only **20%** of your success comes from how good you are at the **operational side** of your business, which is what happens within your business structure. The strategic part of your business is everything that happens outside your business. If you go to any management course or read most management books, much of the focus tends to be on the operational side of your business, but in reality you are only pitching for 20 % of your success that way.

Far more important from your business perspective are the following three questions:

- Are you in the right business?
- Are you in the right niche?
- Are you presenting your business properly to your customers in that niche?

These are the fundamental questions you have to answer and your decisions here will really determine up to 80% of your success potential. Having decided where you are strategically positioning your business and upon what basis are your going to build your advantage, you can then become as efficient at the operational level. There are many very efficient companies out there but they are not necessarily effective.

One company crosses my mind every time I talk about this subject. Of all the companies I've visited over the last twelve years, I would say that this company is the most efficient business that I've ever been in. Conversely, they are also one of *the least effective businesses I have seen in action. If I was marking them I'd give them 20 out of 20 in relation to efficiency but I'd only give them about 10 out of 80 in relation to effectiveness. They just happened initially to drift into a nice niche of the market, but they are so clinical and miserly about everything that they are afraid to optimise their potential.*

I remember being at a management meeting in their offices when a call came through in relation to a potential contract. After discussing it for about two hours they decided not to send an engineer because they weren't certain that they would get the business. They are too focused on the efficiency of every penny, rather than looking at the effectiveness possibilities, which require some risks, but possible remarkable returns. You can be too mean to grow your business, and these boys, in my view, are too mean. There wouldn't be a penny or a sheet of paper wrong in that place; it's clinical, it's like a hospital, but they are losing out. You have to break a few eggs in order to make an omelette.

Effectiveness is about how you can play this game and is not a black and white scenario.

What niche of the market are you after?

How do you position yourself in relation to that niche?

Who are your competitors?

Where is your competitive advantage in relation to your competitors?

Where is your competitor's soft underbelly and how can you gain a competitive advantage over them?

How can you present that differentiation to the market?

Not only does it take time but it takes guts and resources to differentiate your offering.

What is meant by positioning?
When we use the words 'positioning and strategy' we are talking about manoeuvring your business or positioning your business in such a way that it gives you an advantage as you interplay with your business's external forces, such as your customers, suppliers, competitors and the regulatory bodies. How you position yourself in your dealing with those external forces will determine what degree of success you will get from these interactions.

In your business much of your focus should be on external factors. However it is more difficult to do this in a small business, since you have to get more involved in the operational side of things. It is essential however that you don't lose focus on managing these external relationships. Can you delegate some of the operational tasks to release some of your own resources to allow you to play the external game a bit better? You have to look at each external grouping and decide how are you going to manage your customer base better and how are you going to manage your whole supply situation better. Supply is not just the supply of raw materials, but also employees, capital and technology. How are you planning to gain an advantage over your competitors in these areas? How are going to operate within the regulatory regime etc. This is really playing the 80% issues and thus managing effectively.

Should I stick with my own formula irrespective? If it worked before surely it will work again?
Opportunities and threats continue to evolve and if you don't reflect these changes in your business strategy and tactics, then your business can get sidelined over time. Sticking doggedly to your formula is foolish. Family businesses for example often stick with the formula that created their initial success (my father always did it this way). This approach is often inappropriate for the evolving environment.

While it is very important to get the operational side of your business right, just having the engine right is of no use if you don't have a pay load to transport. A lot of people who start a small business come from the operational side. They tend to spend more time at the operational end of things as that tends to be their comfort zone. *Your focus should be on creating the pennies; you will always get somebody to count them.*

The first step is knowing where your business has come from. Where did it evolve from and what are its fundamentals. The second is determining where your business is now. You need to analyse what are its strengths and weaknesses. What makes it tick? Where is it good? Where is its potential? What is the current profile of the business in relation to the identified needs of your chosen market niche?

The third step focuses on where you want to drive your business into the future. Discussion and decisions around that issue are critical to the future of your business. The final step is deciding on a plan of action to reposition your business based on the above process. What resources do you want, including such issues as finance, staffing and facilities? You need to get all of this lined up if you are to successfully energise your action plan.

These are the questions you need to answer if you are going to write a strategic plan for your business, which will underpin your business plan. On paper they look like easy steps but in practice you really need to get down to the basics of the businesses to understand what is behind them.

Emotion versus Passion

In business there is little room for emotion, but passion is essential. I heard Bill Cullen being interviewed recently. As you probably know, Bill is a natural sales-person. During the interview he was talking passionately about the passion he feels for his business. Are you passionate about your business?

My angle here is to get you to focus in on your business and in particular on the commerce of your business. I know many people who are passionate about their core product/offering but they are a disaster when it comes to the commerce of their business. Artistic people tend to be like this. They are passionate about their art or product, but generally they are a disaster at the commercial level.

You are the one who will decide what your definition of success is. You need to become more passionate about the commercial success of your business or career. You need to move beyond the stage of wishing and hoping that it will happen.

What is a Mission Statement?

Professional consultants have a lot to answer for in relation to Mission Statements. The purpose of a Mission Statement is not the statement itself; it's the actual thinking that goes on behind it that is important. Many companies don't go through that process. I suspect a lot of the Mission Statements you see are the result of some consultant being brought in for half a day and being asked to put something together for the company. It might sound impressive but it is next to useless. The real value is to be had from the process of brainstorming the critical issues with all the stakeholders and coming to a consensus about the future direction of the business. The Statement is the end result of that thinking, and clarification in relation to where your business is, what it is about and where you are heading.

We in MRI often go away with companies to facilitate a strategy weekend for them. Our clients invest a lot of money in the process through the payment of hotel expenses, the cost of their own people being there and of course our professional fees. At the end of the weekend's work we may end up with a two line Statement and one could say: that's a poor result for two days work, a two line Statement!

If you were looking for a return on your investment, would a two line Statement be acceptable?

Why?

I'll give you an example to show you how sensitive this process can be sometimes.

I remember facilitating a weekend workshop for a large organisation about three years ago. A new chief executive had been appointed to the organisation some six months prior to the workshop. After reviewing the organisation's situation, he decided he wanted to drive the business in a different direction so as to exploit new opportunities and avoid emerging threats. He was sensible enough not to impose his vision in a unilateral way. He wanted to empower his people rather than impose his new vision on them. So he decided to have a strategy workshop with them. As consultants we knew where he wanted to finish up, so we had our riding instructions about the finishing line. On the Sunday morning, it became very obvious that the company was going to be driven strategically in quite a different direction than it had been; there was one particular section of the business that was going to become the new star and the traditional core business was to be sized downwards. The whole senior management team of nine were all seated around the big boardroom table, displaying varying degrees of smugness and fear.

Eventually the penny dropped for the guy that was heading up the traditional core business. He suddenly realised he was finished. He jumped up and caught the guy heading up the emerging star business section by the throat. That's how emotional some of these processes can get. The reason for this is that there will always be both winners and losers when a decision is made to drive your business in a different direction.

The intervention was left for a couple of months and eventually we started to work individually with various participants. In order to satisfy the loser, we agreed to change just one word of the Mission Statement. It was irrelevant in the overall context, but he wanted to put his stamp on it and he felt that was his pay back. He exited the business fairly soon after that. The thinking underpinning the decisions that were made that weekend was invaluable. This business has travelled on at a pace with great success. They got an extraordinary return on their investment in this strategic change process. The two lines was not the issue, it was the thinking and the process behind it.

It's very empowering to meaningfully include your relevant people to try and get a consensus on your Mission Statement. You are empowering them to be part of it.

Now, I want you all to write a Mission Statement for your business in this space. I'll give you a formula later, but I want you to have a go first.

Mission Statement

How did you get on?

Re-read what you have written and decide whether it conveys what your business is about.

There is no such thing as a right or wrong Mission Statement. Your Mission Statement should answer the following three questions about your future business direction:

1. Who is your targeted market?
2. What are you proposing to do for them?
3. How are you proposing to do it?

The first dimension is **who.** In other words, who are you going to service or who has the problem that you are going to solve? Your Mission needs to reflect this niche type, without being too specific.

The second dimension is **what** solution you are proposing to bring to them. What do you want to do for those people or why would they want to write a cheque for you?

The third dimension is **how.** What is your action plan that will enable you to deliver your proposed solution to your identified market niche?

If you look at the Mission Statement you have just written and subject it to this formula, does it answer those three basic questions?

These are the three fundamental questions you have to ask in relation to your business. What niche of the market are you focused on? What problems/ issues are you proposing to provide solutions for, and how do you envisage going about it? Now rewrite your Mission Statement as an answer to these three questions. Don't worry about the language at this stage. You can refine it later. It's really about being clear in your mind about the fundamentals of your business.

Your Revised Mission Statement

Those three questions are easy questions to ask but difficult ones to answer. As a manager, you are struggling with those three questions every day. All great organisations sprung from someone's initial vision about what was possible against the odds. As we indicated earlier, every business needs a visionary person, a business person and a son of a you-know-what. Individually they are of little use.

Take the birth of Kerry Foods from its very humble beginnings. A small team had a vision, a strategy and the commitment to make it happen against all the odds. A vision without the resources would be useless. This is where their formula to change from the capital restricted co-operative structure to a public listed company (Plc) was critical. This provided them with the capital to fund their aggressive forward movement in a very clearly defined food ingredient route. They were actually working the model before the model was printed. You need to learn from that success formula.

You too have to have a vision as to where you are going. You have to be realistic about what resources you need.

Two words accurately describe what business you are in (regardless of the type of business). You are all in the **solution business.** If you are not providing a solution to somebody else's problem then you are not in business. The only reason someone will write a cheque for you is that you have a solution to his problem or need. You have to ask yourself what solution you are bringing to the market. You need to understand you are in the solution business. You have to ask: *'Who has the pain? What tablet or solution can I provide that's going to ease that pain?'*

When you look at your business and define it from a solution perspective it gives you an insight into possibilities. You identify someone else's need and determine how you can come up with a solution to that need.

Back in the period from 1999 to 2002 there were a lot of IT people supposedly creating solutions. They were often focused on non-existent problems that were a puff of smoke. That's why the whole IT thing blew up. Anyone who survived it was actually providing a solution.

One tends to defend what one has created. However no one has a monopoly on good ideas, not even you. You should open the challenge to your people and encourage them to take ownership of the process and the outcome. This is real empowerment. I have seen the most wonderful ideas come from the most unusual places in businesses. People love to be asked; there is probably a lot of latent talent in your business and you've got to give employees a chance. Bouncing ideas around challenges you to crystallise your thoughts. Of course it is often more difficult in a small business where there are fewer employees or maybe none to confer with. In this scenario an outside consult is very useful.

A word on leadership here: You cannot do everything but you must lead the process. A leader might be described as somebody who has the map and brings his or her followers down a charted route. He needs to keep making sure that the people are following on behind. If you lead faster than the troops there will be a space that is not manned and this is dangerous.

As consultants our Mission Statement is:

'To initially <u>understand</u> and then challenge and empower our existing and potential clients to significantly increase their performance capabilities so that their continuing agreed objectives can be achieved.'

A consultant cannot help unless he <u>understands</u> what his client's needs are. The second part is: *'to challenge and empower our clients'*. I'm trying to challenge you to understand yourself better. I'm also trying to encourage you to have a go. And finally, *'to significantly increase your performance capability...'*. Here I am trying to encourage and empower you to increase your capability to be more successful. It is your business and you alone can do it. All I can do is give you the confidence and some of the tools *so that your continuing agreed objectives can be achieved.*

As you reflect on the learning points, does the above Mission Statement capture what I'm trying to convey?

I continuously challenge clients' beliefs by asking them the basis for their assumptions. If you are telling me that your performance is at a certain level, I might say to you that I know somebody down the road who has performed better. Because of my confidential access to such a wide range of businesses, I can act as a conduit for a great deal of benchmarking data. Invariably I will have come across a better performance elsewhere. The disparity between your performance and what is being achieved elsewhere acts as the challenge for you to come up with an action plan to close the gap.

Challenging is one thing, but empowering people is very important: *'Give a man a fish and feed him for a day; teach him how to fish and you feed him for life.'* You can challenge people all their lives, but if you don't encourage them to step over the line it will not achieve the desired result. In a small business, it's a lonesome game and you don't have many opportunities of really being honest with yourself. There are not that many people you would be comfortable in being open with, hence the importance of the benchmarking exercise I suggested earlier.

Throughout this book, I am challenging you through exercises and questions to internalise the issues I am addressing. You will notice that I strive not to give you a listing of pat answers. If you work out your own answer you will learn a lot from it whereas if I give you an answer to a question you might or might not think about it again.

Business Objectives

Earlier in the chapter we talked about your Vision and your Mission Statement which helps you to look at your business from an overall or global perspective. Here I wish to focus on the next level of planning, which is setting your SMART business objectives.

I want you now to write your own business objectives in this space. Write down a maximum of five business/career objectives.

	Your Business Objectives
1	
2	
3	
4	
5	

The following gives you a flavour of the first attempt by others who participated in this exercise.

- Market more effectively.
- Widen my client base.
- Offer creative, innovative solutions to potential customers.
- Improve reporting back.
- Provide cleansing solutions.
- Provide enough opportunities to increase revenue per hour.
- Make me wealthy.
- Help people in emergency situations.
- Re-establish commercial travel.
- Try and get a direct agent / supplier.
- Double turnover year on year for the next two years.
- Operate cost effectiveness for the customers.
- Grow the business to at least € 1M plus by organic or acquisition means.
- Inform the market about my product.
- Build a self-sufficient and easily evolving company that can handle industry changes.

What gets Measured gets Done
The above represents a nice range of different aspirations but they are not real business objectives. Most of them are more like wishful thinking than objectives.

To be useful, your business objectives need to satisfy the SMART formula. They need to be:

SPECIFIC
MEASURABLE
ACHIEVEABLE
REALISTIC
TIMED

If you look at the 'supposed' business objectives above, most of them would not conform to that formula. An objective is an exact statement about WHAT you want your business to achieve within a stated timeframe. It answers the WHAT question. Having agreed the WHAT, you then need to formulate the appropriate Action Plans to energise these SMART business objectives. This step represents the HOW part.

If you set unclear, woolly business objectives you are going to have a woolly result. There has to be measurement in there somewhere. If you can't measure something the chances of it being achieved are negligible. It needs to be achievable and it needs to happen within a timeframe. If somebody says to me 'I want to double my profits', that's not an objective, it's an aspiration. Do you want to double them next year or over the next two years or twenty years or when? If somebody tells me 'I want to double my net profits in the next three years', then that's a completely different challenge. One is open ended, the other is specific. If I was working for a boss who gave me woolly, open ended objectives I could never be accused of under performing.

In your business plan this page is the most important page. In it you are stating **what** you want your business to achieve. You are setting out your stall and the rest of your plan is about **how** you're going to achieve it. If you are not clear about **what** you want out of your plan, then precisely what is your plan about?
How did your first effort at writing your own business objectives compare?

You should now rewrite your five most important objectives via the SMART formula.

1	
2	
3	
4	
5	

We are often asked by banks to read customers business plans in order to give them a second opinion. When I open a business plan I read the executive summary and I read the business objectives. If I don't get the essence of what the business is about from those pages, I probably won't read the rest. There's no point in having a plan if you are not clear about what you want to achieve. If the WHAT is not clear, then what's the plan about?

I'm focusing on the commercial dimension of your business. Everything you do in relation to your business eventually washes out into your bottom line. You are an expert in your own area, so my focus here is to facilitate you in looking at your commercial business model in relation to what you are doing for your customers.

It is very important that you have alignment between your SMART business objectives and your own personal goals. If they are out of sync, then this will cause stress - and ultimately health problems - both in yourself and your business. Your personal goals will tend to be more qualitative, whereas your business goals should be more quantitative.

The other very important issue is the timeframe you are deciding to deliver the objective within. We addressed the issue of imposed deadlines by external forces in the last chapter. You shouldn't always be dancing to other people's tunes. You must become disciplined enough to set your own time deadlines and start to dance to your own tune. I'll give you an example of a company I'm very familiar with.

All this company's contracts have externally imposed deadlines. In order to take the panic out of finishing contracts and to put themselves more in control, the company impose their own deadline some two weeks prior to the externally imposed deadline. By following this tactic they are managing their business proactively rather than reactively to external forces.

Realistic

You have to be realistic. There is no point in setting an objective that you know and everybody else knows is completely unrealistic. What happens then is that you eventually lose heart and just throw it away. Remember the elastic band concept we discussed earlier? Your objectives should be as flexible as that. Everyone will have different tolerance levels for pain, but you do need to stretch. If you are not stretching your experiences, you are not growing.

Set realistic goals for yourself. Remember what is realistic for you could be totally unrealistic for somebody else. This is your business plan. You have to look at it from where you're sitting. It has to be realistic from your point of view. Something can be realistic and very comfortable but may not stretch you enough.

Timeframe

Your timeframe is also critical. You may be able to set goals that are realistic over a twenty year timeframe but this is not acceptable. It is impossible to maintain a burst of energy over that period. What you need to do is to break the timeframes into steps and set mini SMART objectives for each step. Once you have one step killed off then move on to the next SMART objective. This week, or this year, is the first step of that journey. It is important to revisit your objectives to ensure that you are meeting them. This will ensure that the time you are investing is productive.

The purpose is to create a road map for yourself against which you can judge your performance. The identified gaps between what you have planned and your actual performance will create the challenge for you to have an action plan to make it happen. There is something in our psyche that loves a challenge. You can't predict the future with any certainty. You have to make certain assumptions about the future based on your experience and any research you might have completed. Planning is not about setting things in stone; it's about being ready and flexible, it's about grabbing an opportunity and avoiding threats.

SWOT Analysis

Having set out WHAT you want your business to achieve within the particular timeframes, as recorded in your Mission Statement and your SMART business objectives, you next need to tease out the forces which will both enable and hinder you in achieving same.

In order to give yourself some structure in doing this analysis, you can utilise a number of 'tools'. The simplest one is known as 'SWOT Analysis'. It is a convenient model that helps you to identify the strengths and opportunities that will enable you to achieve your SMART business objectives. It also helps you to identify the weaknesses and threats which may threaten to hinder your efforts to successfully achieve these objectives.

Strengths	**Weaknesses**
Opportunities	**Threats**

Just do the strengths and the weaknesses first. Look at your business in terms of the future, not necessarily where it is today. Visualise how it might look under a number of critical parameters. Jot down in bullet points what you consider are the good and not so good aspects of your business.

This first part of the analysis is focused on your business internally.

Now look again at your business going forward from today. What are the opportunities for it? Where are the attractive niches that you should be focussing in on? What threats are being pointed in your direction which could negatively affect your business?

The purpose of this SWOT analysis exercise is to give you a structured approach to identifying the critical issues that you need to be better prepared for. If you look at your analysis, I suspect you will have about twenty issues between the four squares. I want you to identify the five you consider to be the most critical. List them separately.

	Critical Issues for your business
1	
2	
3	
4	
5	

You may find it difficult to decide if a particular issue is a threat or just bad management. For example, you might say that you are powerless to do anything about rising interest rates. However you can look at the totality of your borrowings and the better management of your debtors so that you have less on overdraft. You could renegotiate with your banks on the margins they are charging you. So there is always some action you can take.

In your business there are probably a hundred and one things you need to improve on, but within that hundred and one there are four or five that are critical. If you could have an action plan in place to address each of these critical issues, you are starting on the right road. Put SMART objectives behind each of them and formulate mini action plans to show how you are going to achieve these documented objectives.

I'm not saying forget about the rest of the issues. It's going back to the time tactics I gave you earlier, when speaking about your diary usage. Pick out the real important issues and let the other issues float around them. If you write them down, it will help you to crystallise them in your mind and they will eventually get done, provided they are worth doing.

It is very difficult to sustain working on long-term issues. What you must do is break them into a series of shorter term time slots and set SMART objectives and mini action plans for each of these. The accumulation of these in sequence will ensure that your longer term objectives are achieved.

I'm trying to get you to think about your business and its key issues a bit differently.

I have a client who is part owner of an attractive business. While teasing out the importance of these business objectives, he stated that his higher level objective was to get the maximum out of this business for the least effort on his part. In a way he is right; he is being totally honest. We teased out what the maximum output was, because he is looking for serious value out of the business and he wants to put in the least effort in order to achieve it.

That's a good vision for him to have. We agreed SMART objectives and an action plan to enable him to achieve his vision.
What objectives are you going to set for your business? You need to cascade them down to individual staff targets with relevant timeframes and in a language your people can work with. Have a monitoring system in place that will ensure that this happens consistently.

As you develop your business, you have two extreme strategic options from which to choose. These are shown in the continuum below as cost leadership at one extreme and differentiation at the other.

Cost Leadership · Differentiation

Cost leadership means that you are the lowest **unit cost** producer in your niche. You may not have the absolute lowest cost base but on a per unit basis, you are the lowest.

Differentiation means that your product/offering is meaningfully different from your competitors offering **as perceived by your target customers.** You can decide to position your business at either of these extreme points, or any point in between, such as point X. You must play the appropriate game suitable for the point you have chosen to position your business at. If you decide to position your business at X, then that's okay provided you play the game that is appropriate for that positioning. What often happens with weaker businesses is that they decide to position somewhere like X and incur the cost to gear their operation for that position. When the competitive pressure hits them, they are not strong enough to fight the price war and they finish up selling at prices appropriate for the cost leader. This is a very weak position to be in because you have incurred the extra cost of playing the game at X, but are selling at Y. To be able to sell profitably at point Y, you need to adopt the 'Michael O'Leary model'. Are you strong enough, in every way, to be the Michael O'Leary of your niche?

If you are not then you must differentiate your offering in a meaningful way, as perceived by your targeted market and then charge the appropriate premium price. Moving up and down this continuum without anchorage will lead you eventually into an untenable position.

Through good management, Michael O'Leary of Ryanair has positioned his business at the cost leadership point of this continuum. Aer Lingus were very much at the other extreme, but are now striving hard to come into a cost leadership position. They will always struggle to make their unit costs competitive with Ryanair because of the many restrictions of where they set out from. Ryanair established their competitive advantage by becoming the lowest cost operator in the market. They achieved this by putting more passengers through per employee than their rivals. Because of their efficiency, each passenger has to carry a lower fixed cost than their rivals. With the numbers going through, every cent either saved or earned by peripheral sales translates into serious money. Being the lowest unit cost carriers facilitates them in giving the lowest price, and that is their differentiation factor.

Take the supermarket business as another example. The old Dunnes Stores philosophy was very much at the cost leadership point: stack them high and cheap. This worked very well for them. Then look at the Fergal Quinn model which was positioned way up at the other end. He was into customer service and good quality because he was hitting the higher net worth type customer. They were both in the supermarket business but both taking completely different views of it. Over the last six to ten years, Dunnes Stores has repositioned up along this continuum; they have moved upmarket. In doing this they left a vacuum which is now being filled by the German discount supermarkets.

The nature of business is that a vacuum will always be filled. Now what are the implications for you in your business from this type of thinking?
I don't think I have ever seen a small company capable of adopting a cost leadership strategy successfully. I've seen many a small business aiming to position up beyond X but then selling at Y. That's a disaster. Smaller business must focus instead on establishing their competitive advantage via meaningful differentiation. Have a look at your own business and challenge yourself to identify where the meaningful differentiation possibilities are for your business.

Management is about making these positioning calls after considering the relevant facts. If you decide that your business is positioned incorrectly, then you owe it both to yourself and the other stakeholders to admit to this fact and to put in place an action plan to reposition to your targeted point. Don't adopt the ostrich strategy.

In a family business mediation case I was facilitating recently, the parties in dispute were fighting about symptoms of far deeper issues which had been in existence for ten years but hadn't been addressed. They had all been shadow boxing around these sensitive fundamental issues for years. They had also adopted the ostrich strategy about the fundamental issues. Now that all the issues are on the table they are being solved. You can't solve a problem if it is not brought out in the open. It is very unlikely that you are going to face an issue that hasn't been faced a thousand times before. Just put it on the table and try and sort it out.

There are a number of strategic options you can follow if you want to grow your business into the future. One option is to drive your business to gain a higher market share with your current 'package'. If you have saturated your current market position and you still want to grow your business, you could adopt one of the following three strategic options or some combination of them.

1. Stay with your existing market but come up with a new product or service.

2. Stick with your current offerings but go to another geographic area.

3. Establish a new package of offerings and take it to a new market.

Number 3 above is the highest risk option because you are going into a new market with a new offering. Following this strategy involves managing two new fundamental variables: the new package and the new market. Having to manage two variables is obviously more risky than having to manage just one. Risk and reward tend to hold their inverse relationship over time. Generally the higher the risk, the higher the reward, provided you manage it correctly.

As you develop your business over the next three years, which strategic option will you adopt?

If you have a number of products/services, then you may decide to adopt different strategic options for each.

The strategic decisions which I am encouraging you to make are fundamental to your business success. You know the 80/20 rule? Decisions you make here are the 20 percent of effort that's going to give you the 80 percent of return. They are all linked in different ways.

When you look at your business from this global strategic perspective it makes your business look a lot more interesting.

I use this type of thinking to help client companies to see where they are going strategically. Try and work out its implications for your business. Just reflect on the strategic angles I have addressed in this chapter; think about them for a while and keep challenging yourself and debating it in your own head. The principles are right but you have to interpret them to suit your particular situation.

If you use this knowledge, you will see results and you will succeed. They do work.

Summary

1. Understand the difference between effectiveness and efficiency.
2. Strategic decisions are focused in on the 20% effort which gives you the 80% response.
3. Strategy is about the big decisions you make about your business. Where do you want to position your business within the ever changing forces operating outside the walls of your business?
4. Clarity about the direction you should be driving your business is critical. Defining the WHO, the WHAT and the HOW help you to get that clarification as articulated in your Mission Statement.
5. Understand that the hierarchy of planning within your business represents an integrated model.

6. Where do you want to position your business between the two extreme points of Low Cost and Differentiation?
7. How can you differentiate your 'offering' in a meaningful way, as perceived by your targeted customers, so that you can charge premium prices?

Chapter **11**

Health Checking Your Business

In this chapter we will look at finance. Finance may be a dull subject but it is a very necessary one. I will try and make it as simple and interesting as I can. I am not going to try and make an accountant out of you; I am not even going to try and make a bookkeeper out of you but I do want you to understand what your financial accounts are about. This information will equip you to make better management decisions.

As you work your way through this chapter I would encourage you to look at your own set of financial accounts. This will help you to see the relevance of what I am talking about. If you are comfortable with you own financial accounts you will be a better manager. It's as simple as that. Everything you do in your business washes out into your financial accounts.

Do you go for an annual health check up?

Do you take your car for an NCT test?

Would you take it if it wasn't a legal requirement?

If you are driving down the road in your car and a red light starts flashing on your dashboard, what do you do?

It's amazing what different people will do. Some will drive faster in order to get home quicker. Others will pull aside and ring a mechanic. People adopt different strategies. A friend of mine got so annoyed with the flashing light that he just pulled out the dashboard and disconnected the wire to stop it annoying him. Four or five miles down the road his engine's head gasket blew.

If the red light is coming on, there's a reason for it. It's the same in relation to your business. There are lots of warning lights in your business. Not just red lights but amber and green ones too. You need to be able to understand what they're saying to you but you need to be able to recognise them first.

Your business lights flash in the same way as the lights on your car dashboard but how do you react? Do you adopt the ostrich strategy: put your head in the sand and drive on in the hope it will go away? Just like my friend and his car, if you don't deal with the danger signals the whole thing will blow up at some stage along the way. You should be mindful of these flashing lights and understand why they are appearing and what message they are flashing at you. It is often too late when the red light flashes. Things may have gone very wrong at that stage. Before the red light stage, the amber light tends to flash. It's an early warning signal indicating that something might be amiss down the line. There are also green lights in your business indicating emerging opportunities that you must consider exploiting.

There is a lot of information in your accounts which you need to understand and be able to extract in a format that you can use during your decision process. You need to be able to identify factually what is working well and what is not. This information needs to be accurate and timely. You need to recognise the 20% that's giving you the 80% of your success. If you are not using this financial information in a value added way, then it's a missed opportunity.

Few businesses go bust in a flash, unless there is a domino effect as a result of a large debtor going belly up, which you did not have prior warning about. Even in that situation, there are always symptoms beforehand. In most situations, the signs (or amber lights) have been flashing. You either didn't want to see them or just didn't understand the message. Having sat with directors of businesses which had recently gone bust, it is evident that they didn't see the amber lights changing to red, or maybe they were just in denial and hoping it wouldn't happen. Often they are too focused at pointing the finger at others and not professional enough to look at the three fingers pointing back at themselves and their inaction as the flashing lights changed from amber to red.

Often all the symptoms were there for two or three years but nobody was doing anything about it. I will point out these lights to you through the remainder of this chapter. You need to be able to recognise the three coloured flashing lights so that you can put in place the appropriate action plans in time.

Two figures in your profit and loss account that you really need to look at are your gross profit percentage and your net profit percentage.

If you say to me 'our profits are up this year', that means nothing to me for a number of reasons. First of all what do you mean by profit? Are you talking about gross profit or are you talking about net profit? Are you talking about profit before or after tax? You have to be precise and know what you're comparing with. Secondly, if you're only comparing yourself with yourself it may not be a good benchmark, since your performance last year might have been awful. An improvement on awful is still a poor performance. This is where benchmarking with an appropriate partner is so important. Remember my advice to you earlier in the book? If you find that someone else's gross margins are a lot better than yours this will challenge you to go and find the causes. Let's assume your gross profit percentage dropped from 59% down to 56%. You could say it's only a small bit of a drop and you shouldn't be too worried about it. Maybe a red light is flashing?

What are the variables involved here? Where should you go looking for answers? You'll see it better if you have your own profit and loss (P/L) account in front of you. There are only three major variables that make up your gross profit figure. One is your pricing, the second is your purchasing and the third is wastage. The 3% drop could be in any of those three areas, but there is likely to be a bit in each of them. Your gross profit is calculated by subtracting your cost of sales from your sales figure. Your cost of sales is an accounting term and accountants like all professions tend to use language to confuse poor souls like you and me. They often use terminology to confuse as much as to elucidate. This is their differentiating angle, which in turn allows them to charge top dollar for fairly basic services. Your supposed financial ignorance allows this to prosper.

Cost of sales really is the cost of the material that you use to manufacture or produce your goods. In order to reduce your material costs, good purchasing and stock management is critical. Shrinkage or pilferage will obviously raise your material costs and thus reduce your gross profit. Statistically there is a lot more shrinkage in companies by overpayments than anything physically walking out the door. Overpayments can take different forms, such as paying for products that were never delivered or incorrect checking of invoices for both quantity and prices. I have seen people passing invoices in a company with their eyes closed in order to meet the cheque run-time deadline imposed by accounts.

The reason is usually a combination of inane mistakes and organised fraud. There is a lot of trickery going on that may negatively impact on your gross profit if your system is not robust enough. You might say that it would never happen to you because you are running a small business where you are checking everything. As you grow your business, you won't be able to supervise everything. Your procedures and systems will then need to be robust enough to keep your business honest. If you are in a service type industry you wouldn't necessarily have a cost of sale figure, since you wouldn't be using a raw material.

Different accountants will present your P/L account in varying ways, depending on your business type. Some will bring labour/sub-contract costs above the line, thus it is included in the calculation of your gross profit figure.

It is vitally important that there is consistency in the way your accounts are presented from one financial period to the next, in order to facilitate comparison and gap analysis. When you are benchmarking your performance with your benchmarking partner, you need to be careful to ensure that both sets of accounts are presented in the same format, so that you are comparing like with like.

That 3% drop in gross profit is a flashing red light. You have to investigate and see what is causing the red light to flash. You can ignore it and drive on, or you can say this is serious and if I don't do something about it my head gasket might blow and I won't have an engine.

Your net profit figure is calculated by subtracting all your operating costs from your gross profit figure. The trend in this figure will represent a green, amber or red flashing light. Again you must use gap analysis to identify the causes and decide the appropriate action plan to address or exploit same.

There is a lot of valuable management information contained within the P/L account. You can use a technique known as ratio analysis to help you to identify more meaningful management information. The technique works by expressing each cost item, such as wages, transport etc. as a percentage of your sales. Again, it is the trend in these ratios over time or against either your budgets or benchmarking partner's figures, which will help you to define the performance gaps. Once defined, you can then put in place the appropriate action plans to optimise your business under these various headings. Remember the previous example of the client company who eventually increased their net profit percentage from 2% to 12%, driven by the tension of the identified gap between their performance and that of a keen competitor? There is always more to be squeezed out of our performance.

Again, to quote Henry Ford: 'if you believe you can or you believe you can't, you're right.' The advantage of gap analysis works off this type of thinking.

Where can you get figures to compare with?

If you identify and court a benchmarking partner you will be able to make comparisons. If you don't benchmark, your accountant is very likely to have another similar business. He or she won't break confidentiality but they should be able to give you some guidance. If they haven't got a business like yours on their books they should be able to get figures from a colleague. If your competitor is operating as a limited company, you could download abridged sets of their accounts from the company's registration office (CRO) and do the analysis to extract the relevant information.

Another red light is your bad debt profile. Look at the age trend of your debtors. Is the percentage of your debt in the ninety day column increasing or decreasing? There are a couple of problems here for your business. The first problem is that your money is in their bank account and not in yours. That is the most obvious problem. Secondly, there are some outstanding issues which may be real or contrived. Either way they will be used as an excuse to keep your money in their bank. As a manager you must hit these outstanding issues up front. What often happens is that people get so busy and they mumble and moan about their debtors but do very little about them. Eventually it leads to cash flow problems and the eventual write off of the debt.

I can recall a case where we were asked by the bank to review a business which they were considering putting into liquidation because of their continuing severe cash flow problems. When we examined the issues we found that their debtors had really slipped completely out of order. At that particular time they had eighteen unfinished contracts. I remember one contract in particular, where there was € 80,000 outstanding. The client was refusing to pay because there was a day's snagging needed. The other seventeen outstanding and near completed contracts had much the same profile. When I tackled the directors about the problem, I was told that they were too busy with the new contracts and didn't have time to do the snagging. This was a business which was within seven days of receivership over money owed to the bank and in their own mind, they didn't have time to get the snagging done and their money collected. I don't think that's unusual. People rush on to the next job without finalising the job that's nearly finished. That's just creating excuses for customers not to pay you.

Another small business owner has a core staff of forty plus contract workers. He is still owed € 130,000 for a contract he finished fourteen months ago. I also know of two other subcontractors who are owed in excess of € 200,000 each from the same client. This client is well known nationally and is not averse to giving advice to people on how to run their businesses. They will eventually get a discounted payment, but in the meantime their money is not in their bank accounts. This working capital is critical for these small businesses to survive and grow.

The golden rule regarding funds is that **they can't be in two places at the same time.** Your debtors appear as a current asset in your balance sheet, but money owed to you doesn't appear as a credit in your bank account and that is the real game.

Another red light is stock turnover. For those of you with stock, how many times a year do you turn it over - four, five times? How often did you turn it last year?

Is that going up or is it going down?

How does this compare with your competitors, or do you know?

If you are turning your stock four times a year and your competitor down the road is turning his stock six times a year, he has a big advantage over you because he needs a lot less stock than you do in order to support a given level of sales. You need an accurate stock figure for your accounts. If you are not absolutely familiar with these figures the danger is that you will be making decisions based on false information. The market will adjudicate on your stewardship at the end. The audited accounts are supposed to be a full and accurate representation of the company. How can this be if your stock figure is not accurate?

Complaints from customers could be another amber light flashing. If you have been involved in any of the quality assurance systems, one of their anchors is to have a procedure for handling customer complaints. The customer who is complaining is doing you a favour. You might not like it but they are actually helping you. If they complain behind your back that is a bigger problem. We are not very good at handling complaints; we're not very good at recording complaints and we're generally poor at tracking complaints. Do you have a positive procedure for handling customer complaints?

Can you describe it?

Staff turnover is another flashing light. The particular colour depends on your business circumstance at any particular time. If you have a very high staff turnover, it indicates a weakness in either your recruitment or your local management practices. If your staff turnover is very low this too could indicate a level of comfort zone security, where there is no stretching happening. Again it's about tracking these issues and deciding what are the emerging management messages.

Repeat business is another flashing light. What colour is this light in your business?

What percentage of your business do you get from new customers?

What would be a good figure for your type of business?

How do you know if your figure is good or bad?

You might say that eighty to ninety percent of your business is repeat business. In one sense you could say that's very good because it is an indicator of very high customer satisfaction. However, if a very small percentage of your business is coming in from new customers it could mean that you are not very aggressive in the market. In a new business every one of your customers will be a new customer until you start to build in repeatability. Eventually you will find that some of your customers will start to become referred customers. This is the real trick, if you can start working the two **R's: repeat and referred strategy.** You should be setting a SMART objective for the next three years about the percentage of your business you plan to come from both repeat and referred customers.

Year	SMART Objectives	
	Repeat	Referred
1		
2		
3		

Calls from your bank manager are another form of flashing light. The colour is green if he is inviting you to lunch or to play golf. The colour is amber and going towards red if he wants to know when you are making your next lodgement.

There are two types of financers: lenders and investors. While they are basically in the same field they have two different agendas. Lenders or banks are really purchasing money from depositors or on the money market and selling it to you at the highest margin possible and at the least risk. Investors make a judgement call on your proposition and are looking for capital gain within designated timeframes of probably five years at most. Even if things are going very well, they still want out of it when that time span expires. They want to roll their funds into something else. Neither lenders nor investors are fools. They are looking at you firstly to see how good a jockey you are. This is most important, because a good jockey even on an average horse has a better chance of winning the race than a poor jockey on a good horse. Then they will look at your business, which is the equivalent to the horse and decide how much capacity it has to develop. Banks are looking at the collateral as a form of security against their planned exposure. They need to know how much you want and what you plan to do with it and its anticipated return. Be careful of the following question: *'How do you know this amount is enough or could you do with half?'*

How would you react if you were asked that question?

You should say no. The reason is that your proposition should be correct from day one and believe me you will be asked that kind of question. Part of the reason is that historically bankers were used to people asking for more and hoping they would get half of it. That is a very amateurish way of doing business. You should put your proposition across factually and back up what you are doing.

One thing you can't have in relation to your business is half of the capital you need. You are actually better off with nothing. Half of what you need is no good to you.

It is very tempting in a business situation to take whatever is thrown at you, but be professional enough not to take half.

Your bank will be observing the following red lights in your business:
- Your trend in exceeding your credit limit.
- Declining activity in your current account.
- Payments passing through your account to other financial institutions.
- Unusual number of enquiries about you credit worthiness from other financial institutions.
- Customers placing stops on cheques without explanation.

Banks love security. If they are holding security to the value of €500,000 and you have borrowings of €100,000, then they are holding €400,000 excess security on you. This represents an asset which you are getting no leverage from. Depending on your risk profile, this represents a potential missed opportunity to optimise your return on your assets.

If you look at your balance sheet, the long-term funds in your balance sheet appear as equity and reserves. Equity is the money you and possibly others invested into your business. Reserves are the profits that you haven't taken out of the business, but the business owes it to you and the other shareholders. It appears in your Balance Sheet as a long term liability, because the company owes that balance to you and your fellow shareholders. Your overdraft balance appears as a current liability in your Balance Sheet because in theory it should only be used for very short term financing and should be capable of being paid off within the twelve month period. There are lots of small companies using overdrafts as their main source of finance. This is wrong. It is too expensive and the wrong structure of financing.

Many bank customers really don't understand the true cost of funding to them.

Are you on top of your own accounts?

Have you identified any bad trend and what was its nature?

Other current liabilities in your Balance Sheet are your creditors. Generally they are the suppliers you owe money to. Money owed to the Revenue also appears as a current liability. Don't use delayed payments to the Revenue to finance your tight working capital. It is too expensive and it's a perilous method of balancing your business.

Working Capital

Working capital is an accounting term which basically refers to the funds that you need within your company on a day to day basis in order to keep it going. I want to show you how the funds flow through your business, because if you can't keep the funds flowing then you won't have a business. As you stand or sit there your blood is being pumped through your body by your heart. If this pump stops working what happens? You fall over. The very same thing happens in your business. If the funds (which are the equivalent of the blood in your body) stopped running then your business tilts over.

In 2007 there were probably about seven hundred businesses going into receivership in Ireland. At least five hundred of them went not because they didn't have enough business, not because their product was wrong, but because they ran out of funds. It is by far the biggest reason why companies go bust. How often do you hear in the media that company X was put into receivership today although their sales book was full? People will question how that can happen. It can happen very easily and strangely enough, more businesses go bust because they grow fast rather than slow.

I want to illustrate to you here how that happens.

Management Resource Institute
Basis of Cash - Flow

Take as an example the water tank in your house attic. It is full of water and its level is regulated by the ball cock which leaves in the same volume of water as that which is drawn away through the system. This water tank is equivalent to the cash tank in your business. You have to initially fill it with funds and then keep it topped up in a balanced way. If you have cash sales, that's cash into the tank. If you borrow from the banks, that's cash into the tank. Share capital or any investment you make in the business is cash in. Any grants that you might get from Enterprise Ireland or the Enterprise Board is cash into the tank. I am showing dividend with a double arrow. The reason is, if your business receives a dividend, that's cash into the tank. If you're paying yourself dividends out of the business, that's cash out of the tank. When you purchase goods for cash, obviously that's money out of the cash tank. The operating expenses that you have in your business, such as wages, rent, transport, and interest have to be paid for and represent funds out of your cash tank. Most people can understand that part of cash flow reasonably well.

People sometimes have a problem understanding the concept of working capital in their business. The working capital is the guts of what your business is about. This diagram represents a manufacturing type of business. In order to have a finished product to sell, it has to purchase raw material, put it through the manufacturing process and finish up with the final product to sell. At any point in time within the system it will have raw material, work in progress (WIP) and finished product, all of which have to be funded. The finished product is then sold, probably via a credit sale, thus creating debtors. Eventually these debtors will pay for their purchases representing a flow of funds into your cash tank.

It's nice and neat when you see it on a diagram, but the problem is keeping the fund level in the cash tank consistently above the danger level point.

If the ball cock in your tank was stuck and didn't allow water in, as the level of water reduced what would happen? It would eventually blow up. The very same thing happens in your business. If that tank of cash goes below a certain level then you have the very same problem, your system is dry and it will burn out eventually.

The balloon cycle represents your working capital, where you are buying in raw materials, doing something with the raw material and then selling it on, creating a debtor and eventually getting paid. It is the length of this cycle which is critical. The longer the period from purchase of raw material to eventual payment for your final product, the more funds you need in your cash tank. The quicker you grow your sales, the larger this working capital balloon gets and the more funds you need in your cash tank to support this enhanced level of commercial activity. As the business grows quickly, so does the balloon.

If for instance you are going to grow your business by 25% next year, instead of it being fantastic it could actually destroy you if you don't understand the dynamic of what's going on. You will need 25% more stock, 25% more work in progress and certainly you will have in excess of 25% more debtors. This all requires more money. Creditors and/or suppliers will probably finance some of it, but where will the rest of the finance come from? The quicker you grow your business, the more likely your stock control is to go out of order because you haven't the time to set up a system. Some stock will get damaged. You will have more work in progress because everybody is shouting to get that job done, so rather than disappoint people you will keep starting jobs but you won't finish them. If you have a lot of work in progress it means you can't invoice anybody so you can't even create a debtor. You only create a debtor when you issue an invoice. Eventually when you do issue an invoice and create a debtor you will probably then be too busy to follow up and collect your money. What happens is this balloon gets bigger and bigger until it reaches beyond its resistance point and bursts. Then the receiver comes in to try and clean up the mess on behalf of the secured creditor, which is normally the bank. Even if you are a service business and don't have a product you still have a working capital cycle to fund, but it is less exacting.

It's very difficult to go wrong in a cash business because you are converting your stock or services into cash straight away and by-passing this debtor's black hole. There are a lot of businesses today taking on big contracts and they don't have enough working capital to fund the delayed payment culture within their particular industry niches. It is bad enough that they are tight margin type businesses, but it is the delayed payment schedules that eventually siphon the funds from the cash tank to below the danger level point.

There is sometimes a temptation to use cash flow to fund the purchase of fixed assets such as machines or factory fit-outs. This can be a disaster particularly if you are growing your business at a pace. You will need these funds to support your expanding working capital. The golden rule in finance is to match the funding for a purchase with the expected life of that purchase. If you are purchasing a machine that will last five years, then you should secure five year funding. It is always easier to get funding for the purchase of an asset rather than for working capital. There is no point in having a new machine if you cannot afford to purchase the raw material to work it. Why should one year carry all the liabilities for something that you are going to have for five years? I'll give you an example which demonstrates this message.

Seamus is the owner of a very successful business. He was a great man to go to trade shows and see what was happening around the world. This strategy was part of the reason he was so successful. He had his eye on a machine which at that stage was beyond his reach. A few years ago he was at a particular trade show on the continent where this machine was on display. The manufacturers decided to sell the machine off as a demonstration model at the end of the show. It was thus good value at the discounted price of €600,000. I happened to be in his factory when Seamus rang the financial controller and asked: 'How much money do we have in the account?' At the time they had €360,000 in the account, so he said, 'I'm going to buy this machine, so transfer across a deposit of €300,000, the balance to be paid when the machine arrives at the factory, less a 10% retention for three months.' He bought the machine and the plan was that the machine was to come straight from the show into the factory and technicians from the manufactures were to come and set it up. It was anticipated that it would be in full production within four weeks.

First of all the machine was damaged in transit. Parts were required and it took six months before it was actually working. Now, instead of generating funds after four weeks, there was shrinkage of funds due to the delay in commissioning. Because he bought it at the show the manufacturers weren't responsible for its transport; they were responsible for the commissioning of it but not the transport. He got to a point where they were very tight on working capital, since €540,000 of it was sunk into a non-producing machine and was thus not available for normal trading activity. Their bank got seriously worried about them and they were threatening at one stage to actually bounce cheques on them.

What was the problem and what were the possible solutions?

Of course, they should not have funded it from their cash tank. They should have obtained outside funding for it which they eventually had to do. They had to go back and refinance the machine. Luckily enough they were able to do that but it shows that even though they had €360,000 in the bank at one stage, that company could easily have gone under. They tied up all their working capital in a machine that was supposed to be generating funds within a month but it was nine months before it produced any cash flow.

If you don't have enough funds flowing through your business then you don't have a business, irrespective of how many customers you have out there.

If you can't keep your cash tank full beyond the danger level, then you have a real problem. You have to pay the wages every week; you have to pay the electricity, telephones and all the other operating costs. If you are not able to keep your creditors paid, they will eventually stop supplying you and ultimately your business goes.

It is important to note that when I am speaking about cash, I am not talking about 'hot money'. I am talking about the funds flowing through your business.

Cash can't be in two places at the one time

You might say I know that, but do you really understand it in a practical way? Funds can't be in your bank account and in somebody else's bank account at the same time. They can't be in your bank account and up on your shelves as stock at the same time. They can't be in your bank account and down on the factory floor at the same time. There are people who expect the same block of funds to be in about two or three different places at the same time. They are not managers, they're magicians! They are failed magicians because it's an impossible situation. If you just understand that cash can't be in your bank account and somewhere else at the same time you will have learned a valuable lesson

I have outlined the following important learning points:

- Cash can't be in two places at the one time.
- The faster you grow your business the more working capital you require. The reason you need more working capital when you grow your business faster is that you will need more stock, you will have more work in progress and more debtors.

Do you understand the difference between cash and profits?

Write down your understanding of the difference.

_____

_____

_____

_____

_____

Cash is King

If you look at your P/L account, the sales figure doesn't distinguish whether it is a cash sale or a credit sale. Your profits are calculated from this sales figure. Therefore you could be showing a paper profit, but still have no funds because you haven't been paid. Commentators talk about profit, but it's not necessarily the most important measurement. **The most important measurement is your cash situation.** The mental measurement in your head is most important because this is where your focus will be. *What gets measured tend to get done.* What is not measured tends not to get done.

Your debtors are the people who owe you money. They appear as a current asset in your balance sheet and they are included in your sales figure in your P/L account. In your cash flow statement, your debtor is only potential cash. So your debtors appear in three different ways in your set of accounts.

Stock appears as a current asset in your balance sheet and as an outflow of funds when you pay for it in your cash flow statement. It is critical for you to do a forward cash flow statement for your business and then to measure it against this benchmark. It will show you when you have surplus or when you are likely to be in deficit, so you can take action in time. There is no point in you getting a call from the bank manager saying there are no funds here to cover that cheque. They shouldn't have to ring you, you should know that and you should have known that weeks ahead because you need to manage that cycle well ahead. If you had done so you could see the balance ahead, which should force you to take timely action.

The only way you can do this is to press your debtors, tighten your stock and negotiate a delay in your payments to creditors. Keep talking to your bank manager. They don't like surprises. If your business is in a tight cash situation with the bank make more frequent lodgements in order to keep the account alive.

'Should I put more funds into my business?' That is a question I've often been asked by companies who are in a tight situation. It's a very awkward question and there is no easy answer to it but the answer is generally no. Why? Because it would make you look elsewhere for relief. Remember the analogy of the leaking bucket. There were two tactics available to keep it full. One was to mend the leaking holes and the other was to keep topping it up with water. Many businesses tend to go for the second option. Putting more funds into a business that is in a tight situation is the equivalent of putting more water into a costly leaking bucket. You need to address why and where your 'bucket' is leaking and to what extent.

I spoke above about the flashing lights in your business and the necessity for you to identify these and what they are indicating about the management decisions you need to take. If cash is a problem in your business you have a major red light flashing and you must do something about it.

There could be very good and justifiable reasons for the cash problem. You might be carrying extra stock, extra work in progress and extra debtors to support your enhanced sales level, but it still sucks up funds. This scenario might justify refinancing. If the fund shortage is because of shrinkage in all its guises, then you cannot put more funds in because they will just continue to leak. If the business has a cash flow problem then you have to identify the root cause. You shouldn't adopt the ostrich strategy and ignore the glare of the red flashing light. You might ignore the glare, but the cause is still there.

How you manage your credit procedures will have a big impact on your cash flow health. The better businesses constantly review their debtors' limits. Do you?

Another critical issue is the timing of your invoices. On average you will shorten your debtor's cycle by fifteen days if you invoice at the end of the job rather than the end of the month.

Clearing up queries and avoiding part deliveries will all help to eliminate the normal excuses your debtors will use in order to avoid making payment. Don't blame them, take the responsibility yourself. Of course there is no guarantee that they won't be very inventive and come up with other excuses.

The following tips for collecting cash may be helpful to you:
Check that the agreed credit notes have been issued before you call to collect your cheque; otherwise you are wasting resources going as you have left your door open.

Be very careful about your procedure in issuing credit notes and who has authority to sign then off. I have often seen businesses where they are very tight in relation to the authority to sign cheques but you may see credit note books thrown around the place. They are just as lethal for both your cash flow and margins. Every time you write a credit note it has the same effect on funds as writing a cheque.

It is better to inform people that you are going to call to collect the cheque. If you call unannounced it is too easy for them to say that there is nobody there to sign a cheque.

Do any of your staff come and apologise for collecting their pay cheque every Friday? Of course not, and they shouldn't as it's their money. Then why should you be going cap in hand looking for your money? It's your money but it happens to be in the wrong bank account and will remain there if you are not resilient and structured in relation to your credit policy. It's also better to get a post-dated cheque than no cheque. In this case your debtor is at least acknowledging the debt.

Some businesses who are operating their VAT returns on an invoiced basis and are involved in ongoing contracts issue a VAT invoice at the end of the contract and make a number of 'claims' during the contract. They are only paying the VAT at the end when they issue the full invoice and thus enhancing their cash flow in the interim period. If you are on a cash receipt basis for VAT you should pay in the VAT period that it comes in.

My advice to you is to do a projected cash flow statement for your business (which records your projected inflow and outflow of funds, including VAT and other forms of tax) by period, to give you the net flow. When you either add or subtract that from your opening balance, you get your closing balance. This closing balance then becomes your opening balance for the following period. I would suggest that you might consider using either a three month or ten week floating cash flow statement format. When the front period is finished you add another period to the end. This ensures that you always have the designated number of periods ahead of you.

Anne Marie is the financial controller of a client company and had been using this floating system for the last year or so. She recently came to me and said that they had become very accurate at predicting their cash flow. She went off and got the excel spreadsheet they use. 'Look at this' she said, 'it shows you how accurate we have become.' I challenged her and we teased it out a bit. The net result of this encounter was that they really hadn't become more accurate at predicting their cash flow but they had developed the discipline of doing what they had predicted.

This is a critical management message.

With start up capital of € 50,000 Widget Company Limited were close to having their product ready for the market. The owner leased a premises and the necessary equipment to move from his own mini garage to scale up for the anticipated market demand. He purchased the raw material (had to pay because he couldn't yet secure credit), hired operatives (who had to get paid every Friday) and had all the other start up costs, such as electricity, telephones, insurance and fit-out. All of these were draining from his initial € 50,000. They produced the widgets and sold them on credit to a range of customers. In order to encourage customers to stock the widgets, he had to agree to sixty days credit terms. On paper he was making his budgeted 15% margin. The reputation of the widgets spread and the orders built up so that they had to work overtime to fill the increased orders. During this period, there was an increased drain on the € 50,000 but only a trickle of funds was coming in from the initial sales. Some of the initial customers didn't pay as per the agreed credit terms.

On the other side, he was finding it difficult to get credit from his raw material suppliers and now he had little of the € 50,000 left. It had been used to pay the day-to-day operating expenses and he hadn't even paid himself. He now couldn't pay for more raw materials and his production ceased over the following few weeks. In turn his customers became very annoyed with the short shipments and used the only leverage they had, which was to delay payments. Now the vicious cycle had really kicked in and the business has just folded, even though it had developed a market led product. The business just ran out of cash.

The problem here wasn't profit; it was converting that profit into cash on time. They could have borrowed more funds if they could have got their hands on it, or used invoice discounting or factoring. In business scenarios such as these be careful that you are hitting the disease and not just the symptoms.

Businesses generally start with some cash (mostly too little). The business proposition is to turn this initial cash into trading assets, which in turn can eventually be turned into more cash than the total cost of production and delivery. This cycle should continue indefinitely and simultaneously over the business cycle. As you build your business's credibility you will be able to leverage more credit from your suppliers which will contribute to your working capital, upon which you grow your business at the appropriate pace. This creditor's leverage is generally not available to you when you are at the most vulnerable first stage of your business cycle. Everything is against you at that stage. This is often the stage that separates the 'grain from the straw'.

Everything you do in relation to your business washes out into your accounts in some shape or form. Therefore, if you really want to judge yourself, or be judged, you have to get a workable understanding of your accounts because that is how your business is seen by others. You don't need to be an accountant to understand them.

Data is sterile, information is fertile: You have to redefine this data in your financial accounts into a format that is meaningful to you in your own head. There is a lot of data in your business but you don't know how to use it. It is worse than sterile as it costs you to put it there.

If you have a good set of accounts you are considered a good manager. If you have a bad set of accounts you are considered a bad manager. When you are judged like this you might say that you're in a bad market niche but in reality, if you're a good manager you should be able to be top of the class within that niche. You arc still a manager making decisions which will wash out in your accounts.

One of the key performance indicators (KPI) you should comfortably extract from your P/L account is how to calculate your 'key money.' What does it cost you to put your key in your business door each morning? Do you know what it costs you to insert that key every morning?

You can calculate it by dividing your total operating costs (from your P/L account) by the number of working days in your business year. It can be a frightening figure but it is better to be frightened about it than not to know it. If you know your daily key money figure you can work out what daily sales you need to generate just to cover the cost of opening your business door. You do that by dividing your daily key money by your gross profit percentage, which again you have in your P/L account. I am challenging you now to do these two calculations using your own P/L account. Having these two figures in front of you will focus your mind every morning to deliver paying output rather than just being busy for business sake. Remember the old saying, 'the hangman's rope concentrates the mind'? These two figures will offer the same positive mental challenge to you in managing your business.

What daily sales do you need in order to cover your key money?

What you need to understand is that these two figures represent your break-even point. Whatever profit you want to make in your business has to come from over and above this break-even point. You can't make money in your business if you don't first cover the costs of opening your business door. The gross profit you earn on any sales over this point almost goes straight to your bottom line as net profit, since you have already covered your overheads. If you have to stay open until 4 pm to break even, it's the sales between 4pm and 6pm that are crucial for you to make money. While many business owners may own their businesses, they are still working for somebody else for most of the week. They have to pay their staff, suppliers, overheads and other creditors before they have something for themselves. Many are lucky if they have the takings for part of Friday for themselves.

For what percentage of the week are you really working for yourself?

Are you happy with this?

Has this percentage been increasing or decreasing?

What are you going to do in order to ensure that a larger percentage of your week's takings are for you?

My challenge to you is look at this in a simplistic way and plan to cover all of your costs within three days, which will allow you to have two days takings for yourself.

I came across a company recently which has been up and running for four years. The person who started this company is a highly qualified man with a wealth of relevant experience within his particular niche. He had an offer of €6.5m for his business some months ago. He has about €100,000 investment in equipment, but the real value is his intellectual property (IP). He is about three years more advanced in the specialist niche than the proposed purchasing company. They can develop this technology themselves, but it's more economical for them to drastically reduce the development timeframe by purchasing this business. If you were to apply a multiple formula in trying to value this business, it would run into the thousands of either his sales or net profit. He has decided not to sell at the moment, which I believe is a good decision. So IP protection is vital, provided you have something worthwhile to protect. However, it is frightening how low the percentage of protected products which actually make it successfully onto the commercial market is.

You must decide what your key performance indicators (KPI) should be for your business and lay them out on a spreadsheet and track them over the years. The trends here will be very informative for you as you make your future business decisions. The following table gives you a suggested list of the KPIs, but you can do your own.

Sales		Your Performance (Last Year)	Your Performance (This Year)	Benchmark Partner
	Total Sales Volume			
Margin	Gross %			
	Net %			
Cost Control	Total Operating Costs%			
	Facilities Cost %			
	Carriage %			
Stock Management				
	Stock turn (days)			
	Stock loss %			
People	Number Employed			
	Number added this period			
	Number left this period			
	Number evaluated			
Operating Efficiency				
	Total sales costs per sale			
	Sales call per rep			

Management Information System (MIS)

I strongly suggest that you should do a profit and loss for your own business on a monthly basis and if you are involved in larger projects, then you should do a profit and loss for each project. You do this by allocating all the direct cost to the particular project and allocate a percentage of the overheads, so that you can calculate a net profit per project. Compare that with your budgeted figures and learn from the resultant positive or negative gap. Business success doesn't come from sweat; it comes from using your head. Go back to my basic definition of what a manager's job is: *someone who decides what is to be done, causes it to be done and monitors what is done.* If you build yourself based on this definition you won't go too far wrong.

Most people have a reasonable understanding of their profit and loss account but get very confused when they look at their balance sheet and what it is supposed to say to them. I will give you a very simple explanation of what it is and its value to you as you strive to make better management decisions.

Your **balance sheet** is like taking a photograph of your business at a particular point in time. It records the assets and the liabilities of your business at that particular point in time. Your profit and loss records all your business activities between two balance sheets' time points. Your business assets are broken up into fixed assets and currents assets. The capital tends to be the long term capital in the business. The currents liabilities record the short term financing of your business.

The term 'current' in your balance sheet refers to items which should be capable of being liquidated within a twelve month period. Thus your current assets include such items as cash, stock, work in progress, prepayments and debtors. Your current liabilities include such items as your trade creditors, other creditors, accruals, bank overdraft, current part of term loans etc.

Accruals are really a buffer account against which anticipated bills can be written off when they come in after the accounting period. It's a bit like in the old days in the country, when your granny had money stacked in bottles, jugs, and other places for various events that she expected might happen. In a way these people were great book keepers. They were building buffers or accruals as a contingency in the event that a fire or a funeral or some other unexpected expense might occur. They had a buffer fund they could draw from. Your business accounts are just the same, but with different terminology. You should look for a schedule of the accruals from your accountant and examine the buffers he/she is building in.

Please note that the book value of your fixed assets in your balance sheet may bear little relationship to their market value. The value in your balance sheet is the depreciated value. The depreciation written down in any year appears as a cost in your profit and loss account, thus increasing your operating costs, which in turn reduces your profits. Thus you are paying tax based on a reduced net profit figure. This is the Revenue's methodology to facilitate you in writing the cost of the asset off over a period of time. If you are about to start your new business keep a good record of all your pre start-up expenses so that they can be brought into your first set of accounts. Pre start-up expenses could include such activities as market research, developing prototypes etc.

For many of you, the more important part of your balance sheet is the current section. Here you have your current assets and currents liabilities. If your current assets are greater than your current liabilities then you have a positive net current asset. What this means is that your business is liquid in the shorter term. If your current liabilities are greater than your current assets, then your business has a working capital shortage in the shorter term. It is the trend in this net current asset/liability figure from one balance sheet to the next which you need to observe. It is the colour of this flashing light which should give you guidance for the management decisions you need to take. You can do various ratio analysis calculations to indicate how often you turn your stock, how many days your debtors and creditors are outstanding etc. It is the trends in these which are important. If the trends are going against you then your working capital balloon is going to get more stretched and without smart action it will eventually burst.

If your business can't pay its way on an ongoing basis it won't stay in business for long. If your current liabilities are growing faster than your current assets, then watch out and use your head. If your balance sheet is showing net current liabilities you should examine the current liability figures and see if there are some long term liabilities in there, such as the total of your term loan or director loans. In a tight cash situation, your director loans are more likely to be long term and should appear below the line. Similarly in relation to term loans, only the current year's liability should appear under current liability and the balance should be below the line. If your balance sheet is re-presented in this way it will appear far more liquid if the above scenario exists.

The main message I want to get across to you in this section is that the trend in the net current assets of your balance sheet is critical. This is really the statement of your working capital trends.

The longer term liabilities in your balance sheet are your shareholders' equity, reserves and long term borrowings. Many businesses are built like mushrooms. They have very little initial equity to support the growth. When a financial wind comes, they are more likely to topple over because of this narrow supporting equity stem. Over time if the business trades profitably and the shareholders reinvest a high proportion of the trading surpluses, then these appear in your balance sheet as reserves and they provide a second supporting stem to balance the head of your business mushroom. The reserves appear in your balance sheet as a liability. The reason for this is that your company is a separate legal entity to yourself and the company owes this to you and your fellow shareholders.

How do you value your business?

The net worth figure in your balance sheet indicates the book value of your business. This may be either an overstatement or an understatement of the market value of your business. It really depends on how badly someone wants to buy your business or how badly you want to sell it.

Have you ever been to a cattle fair?

For those of you who have never been to a cattle fair and stood behind a bullock to sell him, you are missing something. Everything you ever wanted to know about business you could learn at one of these fairs. The very same games are used when you are buying or selling your business. You have a buyer on one side and a seller on the other side and a tangler in between. Nowadays, the tangler comes with a collar and tie and a brief case. In the old days, the tangler was the guy who moved around in the shadow sensing where the weakness might be and then moved in to bring the parties together and negotiate the deal. The deal was confirmed by the spit on the hand and the 'luck penny'. There was no signing of papers. It was all finalised over pints in the local pub later, with the tangler getting his cut - often from both parties to the deal.

There are many different formulae you can use as an aid to valuing your business but it boils down to how badly someone wants to buy and how badly you want to sell. Intangible assets such as brands, goodwill etc. are more difficult to value but they may be the real value of your business. Other formulae you could use to get an indicated value would be some acceptable multiples of such figures as sales, gross profit or net profit.

Business Cycle

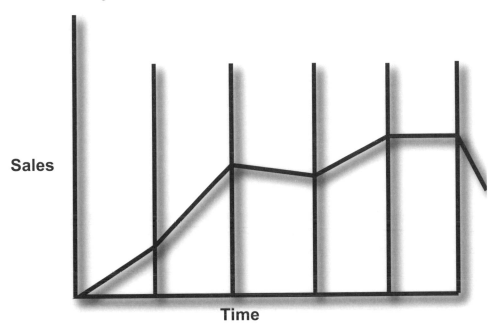

Sales

Time

Every business has a legal right to indefinite life, but the dynamics of commerce may dictate otherwise. Your business needs successive periods of renewal, rebirth and redefinition. Your ability to anticipate the waves of change and to redefine how you are going to strategically reposition yourself will determine this. Some aspects of your business must stay stable while the trading aspects must ride the changes. Financial accounting is one aspect that must remain stable. This is what gives it credibility in the eyes of the various stakeholders. These financial statements must be accurate, relevant and timely. This allows comparisons to be made with confidence both over time and between different businesses. This process is known as benchmarking your businesses performance either against others or against your own historical or budgeted performance.

I recently came across an interesting example in a client company which shows the value of understanding your accounts. This is a manufacturing business operating in a very competitive market, selling exclusively via professional buyers. They have tried a number of initiatives to try and improve their efficiency levels, often without too much real success. We started to dissect their financial accounts and broke the global figures back down to their component parts, in order to try and identify the bottlenecks in their system. We felt that if we could identify the critical bottlenecks and put in place an action plan to reduce their negative impact, then they would make the necessary improvements in efficiency to keep them competitive. After much analysis it was decided that the two key drivers in their particular business model were raw material costs and the number of 'widgets' invoiced out per employee per day. We worked the figures from the annual audited financial accounts to a monthly situation, then back to a weekly situation, back to a daily situation, back to each employee basis, back to a per hour per employee basis. All the figures were there in their audited accounts. It was just a matter of dissecting them out in their component parts and identifying both the drivers and blockages within their business model. We used the law of cause and effect earlier, where we said that for every effect there are a number of causes. In this company, the effect was their production efficiency level, and the causes were the various variables feeding into it. As mentioned above, in this case the two critical causes which had most leverage were raw material costs and the number of 'widgets' invoiced out per employee per day. There was a direct relationship between their financial performance and the hourly production per employee, since the marketing of these 'widgets' was not a limiting factor. They could sell as many as they could produce, provided both the quality and price were right.

The tactic they came up with was a very simple one. They put up a white board on the factory wall and drew a thick line across the middle and wrote the number thirty six in broad print on this line. That figure represented the break-even point plus budgeted unit profits. Every production employee needed to produce thirty six widgets per hour over seven hours, every working day, before they were meeting their target. The production of 'widgets' was tracked and recorded on this board on a daily basis from the employees' individual time sheets. The figures put up were their individual performance 'week to date' figures. This allowed an averaging out and if someone hit a bad patch one day they were able to make it up later within the week. On a separate column, they recorded the individual's 'year to date' performance. Every operator that was operating above thirty six units per hour was recorded above the line and anybody operating at less than thirty six was recorded below the line.

The second tactic they used was that each employee had a clipboard with a production / time sheet on it. Using this they tracked their own production on a per hour basis. It really worked because they soon found out that there was no place to hide and performance was based on measured output, not on how busy someone appeared to be. Nobody really wants to be below this line. If somebody is below the line, they don't have a job anyway. It is so simple and it works so much better than some of the more sophisticated, expensive systems they tried over the years.

The management learning points to be extracted from their experience are:

First of all, that figure thirty six was capable of being calculated from the set of accounts. Having got that figure, they used it. They have now taken off the three supervisors and saved themselves their costs since the process is monitored in the most transparent way by the operators themselves. This has created a much healthier working environment and an element of competition. When the MD walks through the factory he will pick up a clipboard on a random basis and discuss the progress with that operator. This random contact is crucial to its success. The quality of the widgets is not affected as each operator's output is labelled and tracked right through to the final customer. If there are any reworks or rejects they are deducted from the individuals current output. They are working to world class manufacturing standards.

What about morale?

They haven't paid any bonus on this. When the weekly production quota is achieved then the week stops, so that's the goal. It has shown up three people already who just couldn't make it. They struggled to get above the line but couldn't and they have gone.

Now that they have established a credible measurable base line they are well equipped to introduce a performance incentive scheme. This is the next step in their performance tactical programme.

Create your own Personal Wealth

Do you agree that your business is a means to an end rather than an end in itself? If you agree then you have to have some idea where that end is. The logical commercial anticipation of what that end might be for you is creating wealth for yourself. You might also have some 'softer' reasons but I am focusing here on the cold, commercial reasons.

I often come across business people in their late fifties who have been in business for twenty plus years but who have created no wealth for themselves and in reality, having worked hard all their lives, have very little. It's quite sad and unnecessary in my view. If the majority of them had been exposed to some of the thinking and advice in this book, they could have been challenged and guided to understand that their business was a means to an end and not an end in itself. They could have moved substantially towards energising their vision and creating personal wealth.

The opportunity of a lifetime must be taken during the life of the opportunity.

Are you prepared to exploit this opportunity you are now being exposed to?
Yes_____ No_____

I would hate to think if I met you in ten years time that you would be in the above category. There is no need for you to be in that category provided you work a bit smarter. When I ask the question: 'Is your business a means to an end, or an end in itself?', too many people haven't thought out the essence of their answer. They become blinded by their business as they dig deeper holes for themselves and they lose perspective. They just dig faster and find it more difficult to climb out of the ever deepening hole. As I have said many times in this book, what gets measured tends to get done. It is very important for you to establish what you are worth, wealth wise. This is known as your Net Worth. It is calculated by recording the market value of all your assets and subtracting from this figure all your liabilities. The net figure is your current net worth or wealth. Don't be too worried about what your current net worth figure is. It is what it is. While you can't change that figure, you have some jurisdiction over what it is going to be as you move forward. The quality of your decisions and their successful implementation will be directly reflected in the growth of your wealth figure into the future. You should draw up a net worth statement and having reflected on it, decide on your action plan to achieve the SMART objective you will set about its growth. Monitor your progress against this SMART objective on a regular basis. You should repeat this net worth exercise at the same time every year and see your progress. The very act of measuring your wealth on a regular basis will focus your mind on the variables you need to manage, so that it grows at your planned rate.

It's an easy exercise to keep updated. The first time you do it, it will take more time and effort because you will have to gather together all your documentation about investments, insurance policies, securities, pension and bank accounts etc. You may find assets which you have forgotten about, such as dormant accounts, when you do this exercise. You should also write an instruction letter to your significant other with your wishes about how your personal and business affairs should be managed. You should put it in a sealed envelope and store it in this file. This is a very useful exercise and a good excuse to get your affairs in order. I would suggest that you send a copy of your Net Worth statement to your bank every year. It will help you to build up your brownie points, which will be useful in building your financial credibility profile with them.

I know a couple who own and run a business and are very successful at it. Like a lot of people, in the earlier years they were happy enough just to make a living. I sat with them about nine years ago and discussed their forward vision regarding their wealth. They decided at that stage that they needed to build wealth. They did this Net Worth exercise and set an objective for themselves to double their wealth every three years. They have done it. They are now into the third three year cycle. If they hadn't done this Net Worth exercise they wouldn't have created the personal wealth they have created because they would have been too busy running their business. The financial credibility that they built up in their business has afforded them the opportunity to build wealth outside the business.

Now, I know people who have set targets for themselves to double their wealth every four years and people who set a doubling target of eight years. That is what they want and I won't tell you how fast you should go, that's your own choice. What I will say is, if you don't have that down as a marker your chances of building the wealth that you need is unlikely. You are leaving it to chance rather than planning.

You don't have to do this net worth exercise if you don't want to but it will be a missed opportunity if you don't. Do it if you are looking to make an impact in both your personal and business life. I think five or ten years down the road you will remember this moment. I can remember the person who got me to do it some twenty five years ago for the first time. It was just one of those eureka moments; a life changing moment and I have consistently completed and managed the process every Christmas since.

I suggest that you should just pick a period, a particular time of the year that is appropriate for you and be disciplined enough to do it. It will work for you.

In relation to your business, you should have a shareholders' agreement if you have partners in your business. This agreement should reflect your wishes about how your equity is to be managed in the event of an exit, whether planned or spontaneous. One last piece of advice in relation to this wealth area is to ensure that you have key person insurance in the event that you hit an unexpected exit. If you have partners in the business, you should take out the key person insurance on each other and adjust your shareholders agreement to reflect this, so that in the event of an accident or death, the policy would be paid to the deceased's estate as compensation for their equity in the business. In such events, the existing shareholders generally don't want the deceased's estate representatives sticking their nose into the business, hence the above recommendation.

That finishes the financial section of this book. While it tends to be a boring subject, I have tried to make it as interesting as possible. Everything you do in your business turns up in finance. Keep the bits that are appropriate for you and use them.

I would encourage you to at least take and use the cash flow scheduling for your business and the net worth scheduling of your net worth (wealth) and consistently work them. If you do this on a regular basis you will gain a fantastic return on the time and effort you invested in this book. The following is a summary of the main learning points from this section.

Summary

- Cash can't be in two places at the one time.
- The faster you grow your business the more working capital you require because you are going to have more stock, more work in progress and more debtors.
- Manage as per your predicted cash-flow projections.
- The trend in the net current assets of your balance sheet is critical.

Section Three

Understanding The Dynamics Of This Business Model

Chapter **12**

Flaunt Your Propositions, don't hide them

The first line of your profit and loss account is your sales or revenue figure. This revenue figure is made up of two variables: the number of 'widgets' you sell multiplied by the average price of these 'widgets'. You won't have a business if you don't have sales. You certainly won't have a business if you don't have enough sales to justify your cost base. You must not only identify these variables, you must also understand how to influence them and manage them to your business's advantage. Your agreed marketing strategy will guide you on this journey.

Being a good marketer is about understanding the trends that are evolving, not the trends that are gone. Much of your business success depends on you deciding where you want to strategically position your business in relation to the evolving trends.

On a score of one to a hundred, with one being very weak and one hundred being excellent, how would you score yourself as a marketer?

I know that if I went out and surveyed one hundred business people and asked them where they felt they were weakest in relation to their input into their business up to eighty percent would say their weakness is in the area of marketing. In reality, I think that they are actually far better at marketing than they give themselves credit for.

I believe that the reason they feel they are poor at marketing is that they are comparing themselves with the wrong benchmark. Marketing, in all its manifestations, is in your face all the time. Every time you look at the television or open a magazine you are being bombarded with all kinds of messages and images, presented in a very innovative and professional manner. Then when you look at your own business and understand that you are not operating at this level, you conclude: I must be useless.

What is right for one business is not necessarily right for another. You have to market your business completely differently from your neighbour. Much of what you hear and see in relation to marketing is what the really big and renowned businesses are doing. These are the kind of case histories which are written about and drip fed to you at college and by the media. What they do is probably right for them with their large budgets but it is not necessarily right for you. The reason you feel so guilty or inferior is because you are judging yourself against an unrealistic benchmark. You have to look and decide what is right for your business. You are already marketing yourselves just by doing business with your existing customers, but you must step outside your comfort zone and expose your business offering to your larger targeted audience.

Unique Selling Proposition (USP)

Marketing is using many techniques and tactics to inform, educate and influence your target market about the advantage to them of purchasing your offering. If you and I don't know that the other exists and are unaware of the potential for trade between us then we will not do business. If we have more awareness of the possibilities then there is an enhanced chance that we will.

There is a concept in the general marketing/sales arena, know as demand pull versus demand push. Marketing is very much focused on the former, where, through your informing and influencing, your marketing is creating a pull for your offering. Sales on the other hand often focus in on pushing your offering on your targeted audience even if they don't have a real need for same. You have to decide which opportunity best suits your business.

The sequence to follow is:
1. **Ask**
2. **Listen**
3. **Produce**
4. **Sell**

Do you focus on marketing to create the demand pull or do you need to get out there and push, or which combination of both is right for your business?

What is your action plan to get from your present status to this visionary position?

191

From a time scale perspective, marketing is about informing and influencing, which has to be ongoing over the longer term. Sales can be very short term if you are into once off selling or longer term if you are into repeat sales.

How do you currently market your product/services?

_____

_____

_____

_____

_____

What percentage of your sales revenue do you spend on marketing?

In money terms, how much is this per year?

Do you have a plan on how to best spend this budget? If so what is it?

_____

_____

_____

_____

_____

I want you to keep the above profile as a reference point against which to judge your new marketing action plan, which you should consider putting together.

Marketing must be a fundamental business philosophy within your business. You have to have a company wide culture of putting the customer first. Larger, more professional businesses formulate and operate very effective promotional marketing campaigns. They put a lot of resources behind them in order to create this demand pull. The big question is, having spent all of those resources and attracting those customers into your business, can you deliver the promise? Many companies who are very good at step one are not very good at delivering their promise. Their professional marketing campaigns are creating an image and atmosphere that they are incapable, on a consistent basis, of actually delivering.

One of the banks run an advertisement every so often targeted at small businesses with the message: *'We are in business and we understand your business, so come in for a friendly chat.'* The message is, we will look after you. It is very subtle, and very professionally done. When you cross that threshold do they deliver that promise? If not then there is a gap between the image and perception that has been created and the reality on the ground. It is probably alright for them because they have the necessary resources and if they keep banging out the message they will condition a certain cohort of their targeted market to believe that they do deliver their promise in some form or other.

If your resources are limited you have to manage this gap very carefully. The image you are creating must be matched by your daily delivery of that promise. Every interaction between your business and your customers (and potential customers) is a *moment of truth*. These interactions can be personal direct contacts or less direct ones. Each of these *moments of truth* has the potential to be an image enhancing moment or the opposite. It is critical that you cause these hundreds of *moments of truth* to be handled in a professional and consistent way if you are to get the planned return on your investment from your marketing spend. This will enhance your possibility of developing the two **R's** of commerce: **repeat** business and **referred** business.

Strangely enough, as businesses grow, these moments of truth tend to get worse. It is one of the potential advantages smaller businesses have since they can have a lot more control over their consistency. This could be the foundation for establishing your competitive advantage over your larger rival. Instead of apologising because you are relatively small you should be making a virtue out of it.

Because you are relatively small you cannot afford to waste your resources on creating your desired image and then destroying it all at the same time.

It is often said that word of mouth is the best form of marketing. What I have found is that when you consistently deliver your promise the word spreads. This is like playing the two **R's**. However, it is also important to remember that the consequences of a bad moment of truth tend to travel nine times faster, so do be careful. We are very influenced by what other people say because it saves us the task of trying to find out for ourselves. There is the herd instinct in all of us. If you perceive a particular business is being supported, then you will likely do the same. Are you more likely to go into a restaurant with a lot of cars outside or one that appears to be rather slack?

Your moments of truth have to be perceived to be good so that you can influence the chatter that goes on behind your back.

I want you to identify a bad moment of truth experienced by your business in the last few months and what the consequences were for your business.

What have you learned from the incident?

What action plan have you put in place to avoid a repeat?

We are not good as a nation at either complaining or managing complaints. We tend to get very defensive if someone complains to us. How good are you at complaining or managing complaints?

If you went to a good restaurant at the weekend and it wasn't quite up to scratch, how would you handle it? Which strategy would you adopt?

It is important to remember that the chatter that goes on behind your back is critical in this influencing area. If you can influence it in your favour you will be very successful in business.

Business is always done between people; two companies do not do business. It is always done between people in one business interacting with people in the other business. The smaller your business the more people focused it is likely to be. This is why your marketing strategy needs to be quite different to that adopted by the bigger players. You cannot afford to go for the broad sweep and hope to pick up a percentage. You have to concentrate your scarce resources and focus on a strategy which satisfies your targeted niche. It is very expensive to get a new customer and when you do get one you need not only to deliver your promise but also to manage it. In business you must be able to manage expectations. If you create an expectation that you cannot deliver on, no matter what you do that moment of truth will be perceived as being bad.

People often use this as an excuse not to delegate to others. They want to remain in control so that they can ensure that the expectations are met. However I believe that this is short sighted. If you can't delegate effectively then your business cannot grow. You have to set the standard and then manage the variables including the team members, so that they understand this standard and that it becomes the culture of the business. It grows to become a deeply seated and shared principle. *Your role as a manager is to cause things to be done, as distinct from doing them.* If your business is too personal with your direct handprint on every delivery / moment of truth, then you cannot exploit leverage to grow your business. You have to deliver your offering standard via others. Your offering has to be more generic and less personal. Think in terms of the big Mac being served across thousand of counters across the world every minute. They have built their desired moments of truth into their delivery process. The same standard in the same way irrespective of language or culture. It is foolproof and quality assured. It is a live example of the concept of cause and effect discussed earlier in this book.

When I ask people what marketing is, up to seventy percent tend to say it is advertising. Marketing in my view is far more fundamental and pervasive than just advertising. Advertising is just one of the techniques or tactics that is used to get your message across.

Let me stress again that everything you do with your business washes out in your finances. You have to step over the line from being very passionate to being professional. If you want to grow your business you have to multiply and deliver that through other people. This is where good recruitment and training comes in.

Marketing embraces everything that is done prior to the actual sale: from product conception to manufacturing, packaging, advertising and promotion. It facilitates you in getting your offering into the 'last four foot space' of your potential customer. The last four foot space could involve being physically in front of your customer, being in phone contact or being in contact via other communication channels. Operating in this last four foot space is really your selling process, which is the next logical step of your commercial process.

As previously stated, you and I will never do business if we don't know each other exist. We still may not do business, but knowing of each other's existence means at least there is a chance that we will. The totality of what has happened prior to that point of contact, including all of the chatter, the recommendations and the promotional tactics are all part of your marketing. Advertising is just one step in your marketing process that gets you into that last four foot space in front of your targeted customer.

The core of your marketing is to understand who your target customers are and what their core needs are. The only reason a potential customer will give you a purchase order or write a cheque for you is if they perceive that they have a need for your offering and want it badly enough to justify the deal. The next dimension of your marketing is to understand your own competencies and see where they can be optimised. This is necessary so that you can deliver solutions to satisfy your targeted customers' needs more precisely and in a better way than your competitors. It is critical that your targeted customers perceive it thus. This is the anchor understanding you need to be crystal clear about before you develop expensive promotional interventions. You are trying to identify somebody with a need (pain) that will match the solution (tablet) you have available so that you can make a commercial deal to the satisfaction of both sides.

You need to really clarify your answers to the following three questions:

1. Who is your target customer? (I am not talking about names; I am talking about categories of customers.)

2. What needs/wants do they have that you are aiming to satisfy?

3. What competencies does your business have that facilitate you in satisfying those identified needs more precisely than your competitors (as perceived by your target customers, not as seen by you)?

When I talk about competencies I am referring to where you feel you have the edge over your competitors. Where do you think your customers feel you have the edge over your competitors?

One of the greatest motivators is clarity of purpose. The clearer you are about what you want out of your business and where you want your business positioned, the better the chances you have of being really successful. I don't think I have ever seen a business really successful that wasn't clear about what they were about. If you are not clear about what you want from your business, where your edge is or who your customers are, then what are you about?

There is a difference between needs and wants. Your targeted customer can have needs but from a commercial point of view, do they want a solution - or better still your solution - and are they prepared to write a cheque for it?

They may have a latent need which you must awaken to the point where it becomes a want; a want with such intensity that they are prepared to pay the price. Everything has a price. There is a price for doing and a price for not doing. The customer didn't know that they had a pain (want), but that old ditch was the pain. You had a particular solution which they went for. Somebody else may have had a different solution but yours was the one they perceived as best suited to their need.

Everybody has a different solution and this is where selling and influencing come in. When the customer perceives that your tablet is appropriate for their pain, that's when you have a commercial deal. The trick is transforming the identified need into a want. You need to know where your target market is positioned in relation to 'Maslow's Hierarchy of Needs' because you will have to play different games at each level. If you mismatch this you can waste your scarce marketing resources.

It is interesting to use this type of layered Maslow thinking to explain the development of the Irish market over the last thirty years. When I got involved in business in the early seventies, Ireland was quite a different country to what it is today. Most businesses were focused on the basic need. It was about survival and there was very little beyond that horizon. If you were in business then you had to play to this tune and focus on satisfying the basic needs of survival which was where your targeted customers were at. As Ireland moved on there were relatively good times in the eighties and the basic needs of companies and people were pretty well fixed. When those basic needs are satisfied it's the next level of need that is important. The area of people's social needs is introduced, where people want to be involved in clubs etc. Your marketing then has to reflect where your targeted customers are currently positioned in this hierarchy of needs.

Ireland has repositioned itself up through this hierarchy, especially during the last ten year Celtic Tiger era. The captains of industry and the people who have made it are now focused in on status. When you pick up any paper or magazine, who is looking out at you? For these people, and Ireland itself, status has become a critical need, and this in turn opens up opportunities for those of you who can satisfy this growing hunger.

If you view your targeted market and understand where these identified needs/wants are on the Maslow Hierarchy of Needs, it will facilitate you to fine-tune your business competencies so that you can deliver the required solution to your targeted market more precisely than your competitors. You can then build your business model from this very solid base line.

You may wonder if there is an issue when you have target customers on several levels of that pyramid. I don't think so. You could have your corporate customers at a particular level and your other customers at a different level. You need to know where you are going to anchor your 'offering' or otherwise you will stand for nothing. As a professional manager you need to understand that the dynamics of your targeted market keep changing, as it is being influenced from many angles. You need to be keenly aware of these movements and keep refining your anchored 'offering' in order to more precisely satisfy the emerging needs/demands variations. Your targeted market becomes more aware of their need variations and your solutions must reflect this. If you don't do it then your competitors will.

Clarity of Purpose

As you develop your business you are going to have to say no to a lot of options. This is the job of a manager. If you want to differentiate yourself or build an image or brand, you do have to say no. If you don't, there will be a lot of things your business will be associated with that will have a negative impact on your reputation or brand. This comes with stage two of your business.

Stage one of your business is very much about test marketing. You try a bit of this and a bit of that and to see where you can go with it. When you come into a stage two situation you really need to be a lot clearer about your business definition. Companies that put a lot of effort into trying to establish their brand name are very clear about avoiding anything that might have a negative impact or create any element of confusion. Branding is a critical statement about your defined positioning in your targeted market. As you build it, it becomes an intangible asset which may or may not be given a monitory value in your balance sheet. It has a value irrespective.

The real message for you is to start with the market. Do not create solutions for nonexistent 'pains'. Invention can be a means in itself, not a means to an end. This is one of the main reasons why a very high percent of patented products never successfully reach the market. Focus on a niche where you have, or can gain, competitive advantage. You need to establish an edge; an edge as perceived by your customer and not by you. This again is part of the problem with inventors.

They think they have created this wonderful invention and they cannot understand why the market cannot see it like they do.

You may have put in quite a number of years of effort to get your product or service to the market, but nobody can see it like you. Unfortunately, it doesn't matter a whit how you see it. The target customer is king. They decide whether or not you succeed. You can try to influence them by implementing your marketing plan but they have to want it badly enough to write a cheque for you.

Many businesses serve their clients beyond the call of duty. I don't agree with that but what I do agree with is delivering your promise on a consistent basis. You must strive to do what it says on the tin. You have to manage expectations. You have to be careful about delivering beyond expectation because it can cost you a lot of money. The trouble is, if you start to deliver beyond expectations then this standard becomes expected. This over-delivery will cost you. You have very scarce resources, whether it is time, money or effort. If you over-deliver in certain areas then by definition you are going to under-deliver somewhere else. So you really need to balance it out. If you have a successful marketing campaign and you create an expectation that you can deliver, then you have to do it. If you don't, then you are undermining your brand.

A number of years ago Perrier, the French water company pulled the product because of some scare. It probably cost them millions to pull the product but it was the best investment they ever made because of all the extra publicity that they got and the caring image they created.

Promotion

Your promotional activities should reflect the SMART marketing objectives you have set for your business. If you have ambitious sales targets in a particular market niche, or for a particular 'offering', then your promotional plan must support the achievement of same. The main promotional tools you can utilise are:

1. Advertising via the wide range of media options
2. E-marketing
3. Direct marketing
4. Public relations
5. Trade shows
6. Networking

For each of your SMART marketing objectives, decide what combination of promotional tactics will be the most effective for your particular set of circumstances. Allocate detailed budgets, responsibilities, targets and deadlines as appropriate. If any of your preferred promotional tactics are too expensive at this stage of your business cycle, look for more cost effective ways of reaching your targeted market, ensuring that your marketing activities work together to promote a consistent message to your targeted customers. This helps build awareness of your business brand so that it becomes almost automatic for your potential customers to decide to purchase from you. Your promotional activities will obviously need to change as your target market changes. Your marketing plan provides the launching pad to co-ordinate your total promotional package.

Summary

1. Understand that the role of marketing is to identify potential customers and influence them to consider doing business with you.
2. If you do this well, you will create a demand pull for your 'offering'.
3. You must clarify what your USP is.
4. You must develop a Marketing Plan and a budget that is right for your business. Don't try to mimic what the bigger boys are doing.
5. Don't be afraid to change your marketing interventions as necessary.

Chapter **13**

Being an Effective Salesperson

In the previous chapter I spoke about marketing and promotion. One of the points made was that both marketing and promotion represent the soft side of the exchange. What I want to talk about here is the hard side which is the actual selling and how you should operate in the last four foot space.

Selling is more important to you than marketing. Those of you who are not comfortable at selling probably spend more of your scarce funds on marketing and promotion in the hope that it will generate sales. But most likely it won't because you do not have enough marketing resources to make an impact. You have to depend more on actual selling than promotion and marketing. The core of marketing is: who is your customer, what are their needs/wants and where is your competitive advantage which allows you to gain the edge over your competitor, as perceived by your customer.

Our focus here is on how you are going to handle your targeted customers in that last four foot space. You only get one chance to make a first impression.

Are you a natural salesperson? Yes _____ No_____

How would you define a natural salesperson?

A pain in the neck?
A person who doesn't give a damn and is not afraid of being told where to go?
Someone who is prepared to get in front of potential customers in order to achieve their sale irrespective?
Someone who is resilient and not afraid to ask for the sale?

People often feel that they are not good at sales because they can't handle the rejection and being told 'No'. But the more often you are faced with a 'no' the nearer you are getting to a 'yes'. Even if you are not a natural salesperson you can still be a very effective salesperson. About two thousand companies have participated in our OMDP programme over the last twelve years. I would say that from these groups only about ten percent were natural salespeople. Natural salespeople generally make poor business people. To run a business successfully you have to have other skills in addition to the skill of selling. It is reassuring for you that while you may not be a natural salesperson, you can nevertheless be an effective salesperson and achieve your targeted level of sales growth.

The type of selling that I am going to outline can be learned and practised. The most likely reason you think you are not a good salesperson is because you are afraid of it. You are judging yourself against the wrong benchmark. If you change the word selling to negotiation, it will take a lot of the fear away from you. So forget that you are selling; you are actually a negotiator.

Again, if you look at your profit and loss account, the first line is your revenue and it is made up of two calculations. It represents the number of 'widgets' you sell multiplied by the average selling price per 'widget'. You don't have a business if you don't have an adequate sales margin to support your cost base.

Stage one of your business is probably the toughest section of the cycle. The wind is in your face as you push your way uphill. When you start the business you don't have any customers and you probably don't have a lot of experience. There are also a lot of other things that you don't have. There is a very steep learning curve with many slipping points which will test your resolve. How long stage one lasts depends on the business you are in. It could be six months or six years. The one thing that I can guarantee you is that if you can successfully come through stage one, stage two tends to be easier. At this stage you have built your reputation, you have a customer base, some good business and you have attained some mass. You may have a few specialists around you now who are undertaking some of the tasks you don't like, and who in any event are probably better at doing them. So you are starting to be a manager in stage two, as distinct from being an operator. It is lovely to see people who have participated in the OMDP programme over the years move on from being operators to actually becoming managers.

In order to achieve your revenue targets, how many customers do you need?

Is that a manageable number?

The extent of this number will determine the sales tactics you need to adopt. If you need fifty customers in order to achieve your revenue target and you are getting a ten to one conversion rate, that means you need to target about five hundred potential customers. Your conversion rate will depend on a number of variables such as your targeting accuracy, your selling techniques and your business and customer type.

The essence of business is: if you cannot sell a product don't make it. Even though it might be uncomfortable, you have to come through this phase and get out there in front of your targeted customers. You can research forever and come up with what appear to be rational excuses like 'we are not really ready yet'. Have a planned approach to decide how you are going to handle yourself in that last four foot space. If you practice often enough it becomes an everyday activity and the fear associated with it goes away.

If you believe in the integrity of your product it is very easy to sell it. If you think that what you have is shoddy, you have failed to sell it to yourself. If you believe that the product you are selling is the best product out there, then you will have absolutely no problems selling it. So, the first person you have to sell to is yourself. If you can't sell your own product to yourself mentally, you will never sell it to a customer. People can be good at selling for their employer but when they set up their own business they tend to lose confidence at selling their own products and services. There is something in the back of their mind that says: *I have created this, so it can't be that good.* They are apologising for whatever they have.

I want to hang the selling process on a couple of words. One of these is **matching**. Effective salespeople identify their targeted customers with more precision; they understand which customers are more likely to have the 'pain' for which they have the appropriate solution. If you can get a more precise matching between the customers' problem and your solution, then you have very little selling to do. You are facilitating them to buy from you. Success in selling is less about selling techniques than matching and negotiation. You must always be crystal clear about who your target market is; who has the problem that you have created the precise solution for. If you can do that more professionally then the situation is, rather than you selling they are purchasing.

There are three ways that you can grow your business. One is to increase the number of customers, the second is to increase the size of their individual purchases and the third is to increase the frequency that they deal with you.

As part of our consulting business I often sit in as an observer at sales meetings. The question that is generally asked is: *'How many new customers did we get last month?'*

Is this the right question? Yes_____ No_____

It is the wrong question. However, because it is the question that is frequently asked it becomes the area of focus. Remember my earlier advice *'what gets measured tends to get done'*.

Why do you think I am suggesting that it is the wrong question?

Primarily because it does not show adequate concern for their existing customers. You can get a lot more business out of your existing customers because you make more money out of repeat business. Setting up new customers is very costly: it is costly finding out where they are, speaking to them, building their confidence in you and getting them to say yes. When you look at the return on that investment it can be marginal for that initial transaction. If you can convert that costly initial event into a repetitive cycle you are establishing the potential to get a very attractive return on your investment in acquiring that first sale. I believe very strongly that most businesses don't look after their good customers well enough. I believe that they tend to take good customers for granted. Your good customers tend not to complain too much. They are the customers you make the most money from. If your competitor is any good, he should be targeting those customers as well.

The sales process comes back again to the concept of the 80/20 rule as the following case study illustrates:

The owner of a large supermarket chain was interviewed on a US chat show a number of years ago. The interviewer was having a tough time because the entrepreneur was being very defensive and replying with one syllable answers. I could observe the interviewer getting very frustrated because he was making little progress. However the tone of the interview changed when the interviewer asked the entrepreneur about the secret of his success. The entrepreneur suddenly became animated, saying, 'I often stand inside the door of some of my stores and observe the potential customers coming through. I visualise the figure $550 printed on their foreheads.' He then stopped talking again. The interviewer was somewhat puzzled but recovered and sought clarification on what he meant. The entrepreneur didn't answer immediately. Just as the interviewer was about to fill the silence, the entrepreneur began to explain as follows: 'We have worked out statistically that the *average customer coming through our doors spends $550 over their lifetime. If you had a customer coming into your business to spend $550, would you treat that customer differently to one that was spending $20?'*

It is a message with a great deal of depth to it. If you look at the lifetime business that your customers can give you, you would most certainly look at them differently. Many of your customers can give you a lot more business. You should be looking at them in terms of their lifetime business potential rather than just as a once-off.

What adjectives come to mind when people hear the word salesperson?

Sleazy? Pushy? Obnoxious? Loud? Fast talker? Professional? Slick? Expert? Over confident?

There are a lot of salespeople who are like that and they give the profession a bad name. If you are selling insurance from door to door you may need to have these traits. If you are selling your own business output you don't have to be like that. It is the wrong approach to take if you want to be an effective salesperson. Rather than apologise you should take pleasure in the fact rather that you are not like that. But you still must make the sales. You cannot go into the bank tomorrow morning and lodge promises.

Selling is about the ability to communicate. It is the ability to be persuasive but with a good attitude. Selling is a very personal game. It is a relationship building process, since your focus has to be on the life long business rather that the once - off battle victory. You need to be strategic and focus on winning the war, not just the immediate battle. The big secret in selling is how to play the two **R's (Repeat** business and **Referral** business) more effectively.

How much of your business is repeat business?
How do you know?
What targeted repeat figure are you setting for your business over the next five years?

In a mature business you will often find that a very high proportion of business tends to be repeat business. While this may reflect that they are doing a very good job it may also reflect that they are not pushing to get new business as well.

I know businesses that set SMART objectives requiring that fifteen percent of next year's sales must come from new customers. They may also set a SMART product objective, such as twelve percent of next year's sales must come from new products or services. In other words, they are trying to freshen up their business and keep it moving on, since all business has a finite life. If you want to maintain your business, you do need to extend it.

Young businesses have a very high proportion of their interaction coming from both new customers and new products/services. When they move into stage two of their business cycle that ratio tends to change. It is then that have to be very wary of the amber lights starting to flash which may be indicating the onset of staleness.

This often happens in second or third generation family businesses. Their traditional success formula can now become a liability because although the needs in their trading environment keep changing, they are often rooted in doing it the way it was always done: *'Sure my father always did it this way'*. Even if he has retired, his shadow is still around and is camouflaging the intensity of the dangerous red light coming down the track. Einstein says *'insanity is doing the same thing in the same way and expecting to get a different result'*. Business owners often live off of past glories and reserves. In other words they are living off the fat of their own business. There is a disease in cattle known as ketosis and it involves the animal living off her body fat rather than off fodder. As the fat of her body is burned off, she will obviously start to lose body condition and the clinical symptom is she gives out a sweet smell from her breath. If your business is starting to settle and everyone remains in their comfort zone and starts to exude sweet nothings, then it is time for you as manager to shake it up and face the reality of the emerging market place. Don't be afraid to throw a pebble into the still water and create a few ripples. This will help keep everyone on their toes.

We will come to the **how** techniques later. I am focusing here on **what** is involved in selling and its critical linkage to your business value chain. What one word best describes the business you are in?

If you are not in the solution business, you will not be in commercial business for long. What is your solution? What problem do you have a solution for?

If you are new to the business, you have to educate the market, which can be a slow and expensive process. Remember the saying, *'be not the first on who the new is tried, nor yet the last to lay the old aside'*. It's very difficult for the new boy on the block to get going. Statistically, it is often the second or third attempt that is the successful one. The first people into the market tend to run out of resources before they can successfully get their product to the market. You can be too far ahead of your market and this is what matching is about. It is all about timing. Can you live long enough to be commercially successful? I know of many businesses that died before their hour had come. One could ask whether they were poor business people. Many of them were pure entrepreneurs who saw all the advantages and opportunities but were naive about the reality of having the juice in the petrol tank to take them to their pre-determined staging post. In other words they just didn't have enough working capital to fuel the full length of stage one of their journey. You need a balanced, planned, integrated approach.

Some potential customers need to be hit with a crisis before they go looking for the solution. They are not sensitive to the amber lights flashing before the crisis point. Such a crisis would create an overnight demand **pull** for the solution and the selling status would change from demand push to demand pull. The market in this case would be looking for the product rather than the supplier trying to bang down doors. Someone in the security business once told me that a high profile robbery was great for business. Knowing this, they are always ready and able to fill the increased demand. I am not suggesting that you should create a crisis, but if one happens you then need to be in a position to exploit the opportunity. Remember my previous advice: the *opportunity of a lifetime must be taken during the lifetime of the opportunity*.

When a crisis happens in the public domain and you have a solution, you need to get on to the media straight away as the specialist offering expert opinions who by the way just happens to have the appropriate solution as well. You have to be innovative in how you optimise the opportunity for yourself.

There is a catalogue company that supplies a range of good equipment and they are very innovative in how they create their sales by optimising the matching principle. Any time there is a relevant national news item, they e-mail the appropriate product from their catalogue to everyone on their database. They are commercially exploiting this concept of matching their solution to the issue highlighted in the national media. This enhances their hit rate substantially.

I suggest that you should score yourself on a scale of one to ten, with one being poor and ten being very strong for each of the following profile parameters:

Profile of a Good Salesperson

	Your Score		
	1	5	10
Perseverance			
Empathy with potential customers			
Resilience			
Sincerity			
Open-mindedness			
Appropriate appearance			
Your Total Score			

When promoting yourself, how do you grab appropriate attention? How persistent are you? Are you good at building empathy? Are you resilient, open-minded, and properly presented? You need to measure yourself against all of these parameters. Is there something in there that you could be doing better? If I was to isolate out one, I would say it is perseverance. You really need perseverance, particularly when things are not going that well. You have to take a deep breath and keep going. When you work for yourself, self- discipline and working your SMART objectives are most difficult but they are also the crutch you need to use over this initial difficult ground.

It is important that you don't allow empathy to become sympathy. Remember, two companies never do business with each other; it's people in one company doing business with people in another. Resilience is closely related to perseverance. You must be resilient because there are a lot of knocks that may hit you.

I was with a company recently who are at stage two of their business cycle. Their business is supplying services to big outdoor events such as pop concerts. The company loses money delivering to many gigs but then makes a killing on a few, which balances the books. The owner notes: 'If you were not resilient you would be gone, because you may have two gigs with loads of money in it but then you can lose most of it in the other gigs.' He said if an accountant looked at this business he would have recommended closure long ago. But he has great resilience and he knows the next gig will make enough for the year. He has great confidence in selling himself and has the nerve to play the commercial game that is required

Appropriate appearance is very important in selling. If you are selling to somebody on a building site you wouldn't turn up in a smart pin stripe suit and nicely laundered coloured shirt. You need to dress in a manner appropriate to the environment you are trading to.

Ask yourself the following questions before you start selling:

1. Do you know enough about the product or service?
If you know too much about the technical aspects of your product it may be a bad thing. What is the core information relating to it? Know the information that this particular customer needs to know about the product and know it well.

2. Are you talking to the right people?
Who are the recommenders, the influencers, the supporters and deciders? This is important when you are bidding to institutions or organisations. The critical people are those who will influence the decision makers, so you have to know the politics of the organisation. Everyone has their own agenda and you have to be politically attuned enough to understand what the situation is. If you are dealing with a smaller organisation it is easier to see who the decision maker is.

3. Do you know what your target customer's wants and needs are?
This is critical. What is their pain? Why do they want your solution? Who are they currently buying from? How does your offering compare? It is important that you know the answers to these questions because it is going to be thrown back at you that Joe Soap down the road has a similar product. You need to know who Joe Soap down the road is and what you are being compared with. You have to differentiate yourself in some shape or form that is meaningful from your targeted customer's viewpoint. Why should somebody deal with your business rather than with Joe Soap? Even if you don't get asked that question you have to have the answer.

4. What is your unique selling proposition?
I'll ask the question slightly differently. Why would somebody write a cheque for you rather than a business offering a similar service or product? Why would somebody deal with you rather than with your competitor? Is it because your

solution is better? But what is that solution? It is not what you think that's important, it's how your targeted customer perceives your proposed solution versus your competitor's. You can influence that by the way you present your proposition to the market. Be careful about giving too many options; it causes confusion and leads to indecision. As a salesperson, you have to go from the general to the specific very quickly.

5. Appropriate language.

You are in an influencing game and therefore you must match the language of the people you are trying to influence. You are trying to get them to say yes, so match their language and appetite for detail. Just because you have created your solution doesn't mean that everyone else will see it in the same way as you do. That is often the problem with inventors. The inventor has this beautiful creation in his own mind and becomes very disappointed when everybody else doesn't see things like him. The customer doesn't really care, they have their own agenda. If you want to be commercially successful you must start to influence customers and play their game.

What does **WITFM** stand for in selling?

WHAT IS IN IT FOR ME?

The bell that is ringing in the customer's mind is asking what is in it for him. That is really the kernel of good matching or good selling. You have to help people to understand and buy from you, rather than you trying to sell to them. This process is known as **consultative selling.** Here you are consulting with your potential customer as to what their needs are and facilitating them to match your solution to address their needs and wants. Customers buy for their own reasons, not yours.

I remember when I started as a consultant some fifteen years ago. I had a hit list of eighty names which I had identified as potential customers. I knew all the businesses on that list and classed them as potential gilt-edged customers. I sought the advice of a well know businessman. His own company was on the list. He looked at the list and he told me that I would be very lucky if I did business with ten or eleven on that list. That was the last thing I wanted to hear. Regarding his own company he said that it would probably be a year or two before they would have a suitable project. He made the critical point that nobody is going to create a project for you. As I walked to the door quite deflated he called me back saying, 'I forgot to tell you something. There are eighty other companies that you are going to do business with that are not on that list'. He turned out to be very right.

He told me everything that I didn't want to hear but he was telling me the truth. We continued to create business with over eighty percent of companies who were not on that original list. There is an important message here. If we hadn't had that original list of eighty we would never have started our business. That is what gave us the initial comfort. We worked every one of those eighty over the following two or three years and learned (often at their expense) how to both position and present our proposition to the market. We did a review after ten years and found that we did business with just twenty out of that original list of eighty companies.

Think of the classic case of the mobile phone market. This product was initially pitched at people such as doctors and solicitors but very quickly it was Joe carpenter and Joe bricklayer that started to use them in the greatest numbers, people who were actually on the move in their daily work. They weren't on the original target list. Teenagers were not on that list and they became the biggest users of mobile phones.

People buy for two reasons. They buy for rational reasons and for emotional reasons. Businesses generally buy based on rational reasons. They are either trying to save money, make more money or save time and optimise their operation. You must reflect this in your selling technique. If you are focused in on the spontaneous emotional type purchase, then your selling technique must match this. You need to know the space that your targeted client is in and present your proposition accordingly. Present your proposition rationally to business type buyers. If you are in the fashion or flower business the customers often act impulsively and emotionally. For example the purchase of red roses on Valentine's Day is emotionally driven.

In selling it is very important to qualify the target

What does that mean?

You do not want to waste your time. Your resources are always scarce so you have to be careful that you don't waste them on the wrong target. You have to qualify the target. Do your targeted customers have the potential to give you the business you want? There is nothing more wasteful than being busy trying to service a poor customer. A poor customer in my view is someone who will not allow you to make any money out of your trade. They will shout loudest and most often and if you are not careful you will end up overreacting with the danger of over supplying.

You will have very little selling to do if you identify and understand who has the pain that your solution is best at sorting.

What is foremost in your mind if you have a toothache?

You want to get rid of the pain, don't you? You have an issue and you are looking for a solution to relieve it. If somebody comes along and presents a solution that is more appropriate than what is currently available then you will obviously purchase it. This is a win - win deal for both sides.

If your target channel to the end market is via the supermarket shelf you are faced with a difficult negotiation process because you are dealing with professional buyers. You must first get listed and then eventually get some shelf space. The entry barrier here is very high. A useful tactic adopted by smaller, new suppliers is to create an artificial demand for your particular product. This is done by arranging for a series of shoppers to keep asking their supermarket for your product. This bottom up pull will widen the hoops you are required to jump through. Having got onto the shelf, your product must then earn the required return from that shelf space. Every foot of shelf space in that supermarket is documented with a very SMART return objective set for it. What supermarkets are selling is shelf space, they are not selling products. They are basically landlords of your products. Financially they never own your product since they pay you after they have it sold. If your product doesn't successfully operate within their credit cycle then it looses its shelf space. Basically, they are leasing space to you.

Supermarkets create phoney price wars. If you take a reasonably large supermarket, they probably carry thirty thousand line items. They will create a false war over five or six items and make their budgeted overall margins from the rest of the line items which you will buy out of convenience while you are there. If you are a supplier, you will have to support their promotion once or twice a year, with you carrying the cost of the discounted prices while the supermarket maintains their margins. From the supermarket's perspective it is a great business model. Large international brands will not be exploited like this. They will be negotiating promotions from a more equal power perspective. No supermarket can afford not to have such brands as Kellogg's on its shelves. That is the value of branding. It is why supermarkets are pushing their own branding strategy, because it balances the power back in their favour. A small supplier in this equation can really get messed around.

I want you to reflect on these three real learning points about sales:

- Firstly I want you to realise that you can be quite an effective salesperson. You don't have to be a quick talking, sleazy kind of person. There should be a lot of comfort in this for you.
- Secondly I want you to understand the concept of matching and how you might exploit it more in your business.
- Thirdly I challenge you to optimise the two **R's.** What plan of action are you going to put in place to increase your repeat business and referred business?

To optimise your referred business you have to help your existing customers to generate more referrals for you. There is a format which works here. You should be asking your satisfied customer: *Who else around here should we be talking to?* The worst that can happen is they will say they don't know of anyone. They are far more likely to give you a few names and may volunteer to give you an introduction to them. This format actually works and the growth of your sales will reflect this. People often leave referrals too much to chance and in business you should never leave things to chance. Depending on the sensitivity of your business sector, it may not be appropriate to ask for referrals. You can gain advantage from a satisfied customer by listing other potential customers who match the profile of this satisfied customer. Then work this hit list.

One of the most important things about selling is knowing how to influence what people say behind your back. What other people say about your businesses out of earshot will be very influential in conditioning others to do more business with you. Satisfied customers are your advocates. You have to think through how you can influence this out of earshot chatter about your business. This manifests itself in scenarios such as: 'What are they like to do business with?' 'You should go into them, they are so helpful and they will look after you.' Advocates are your unpaid salespeople. They are spreading the good news about you behind your back.

When you empathise with a customer and develop a relationship it works both ways. When somebody perceives that you did something worthwhile for them, they want to reciprocate. By asking them *'who else around here should we be talking to?'* you are giving them the opportunity to do that. They are already open to the concept and you are actually giving them permission to do it for you.

It is important to identify your customers who are not referring your proposition. They may in fact be referring negatively. If you don't identify them you cannot remedy the potential damage they may be doing. Bad news travels faster than good news. You have to assist the good news to travel. The experts tell us that each dissatisfied customer will tell on average nine others. This is a lot of negative referrals. You need to identify it quickly and address it up front. The ostrich strategy is no good here, but unfortunately it is often adopted. For instance how do you handle customer complaints?

We often become defensive about customer complaints but remember, a customer who complains to you is giving you a chance to put it right. If you do it well you will have them forever more. Unfortunately, just as we are not good at complaining, we are not very efficient at handling complaints either. You can learn more from a customer that complains than from somebody who says you did a great job. Some of the complaints can open up all sorts of avenues, provided they are handled professionally.

What is the most awkward thing about selling for you? Write your answer below.

_____

_____

_____

Will you tackle that issue at least once this week?

Now I want to focus on the HOW to sell techniques. How should you manage yourself in that last four foot space, where you are in contact with your potential customer?
Follow this stepped process:

1. **Identify the target**
2. **Qualify the target**
3. **Make initial contact**
4. **Present your pitch**
5. **Empathise with the customer**
6. **Close the sale and thank the customer**
7. **Follow up**

I am assuming that you have made contact with your potential customer and you are now face to face with them. You have to look at how you manage this pitch and how to close this sale.

If you were to model your sales techniques on some profession out there, what would it be?

I think medicine is an area that you should look at for a role model to guide you in becoming a better salesperson. What is the difference between a good doctor and a bad doctor?

If I had a headache and went to a doctor how would he/she treat me?

_____

_____

My headache is only a symptom of something else that is out of sync in my body. It is my body's way of telling me that something is wrong. Now, if I go to a bad doctor he will give me a broad spectrum tablet to simply kill the pain. He is killing the symptom but failing to get down to the real issue. A good doctor will try to diagnose what the cause of the problem is. It is only after diagnosing that he will prescribe. This is the type of selling that you need to operate. We call it **consultative selling.**

It is a different form of selling to the fast talking type selling referred to earlier. Like a good doctor, a good salesperson will spend a lot of time diagnosing, trying to find out where the 'pain' is and what is causing it; they look for clues, they make a decision and then they treat. The bad doctor/salesperson just treats the symptom and doesn't spend time diagnosing. Adopt the consultative selling model if you want to optimise your sales.

You need to manage the customer contact timeframe using the following formula: (This formula works whether the contact timeframe is two minutes or two hours.) The first quarter of the timeframe should be given over to the small talk icebreaker. A generic non-controversial issue such as the weather is a useful topic for this stage. The next half of your contact timeframe involves what we call the consultative part of your selling. This is a critical step. The last quarter of the contact timeframe focuses in on closing the sale. You need to operate professionally in relation to these three aspects of selling.

In contrast, what does a poor salesperson do?

A poor salesperson spends three-quarters of the contact timeframe at small talk and then moves directly to the last quarter trying to force a sale. They fail to manage the middle fifty percent consultative phase. You have to manage this consultative section very well. This is important irrespective of the length of your customer contact timeframe. It costs you a lot to get in front of your customer and you have to manage the time you have well. During this fifty percent consultative section, I recommend that you use the **'Love with a Q'** technique to help you optimise your result.

Listen
Observe
Verify
Question
Empathise

What are you trying to do? What is your objective? You are trying to find out what are the needs or wants of the person you are dealing with. You are trying to help them to define the latent or acute pain they have. The more aware they are of their own pain the more open they will be to a cure.

What do you do when you ask a question?

Most of us, when we ask a question, tend to answer it as well.

Why do we do that?

Why bother asking the question if we are going to answer it ourselves?

The reason you answer your own question is because you are uncomfortable with the silence. Try it. Ask a question of somebody and then stop talking. See if you can do it. See if you can do it in a selling situation which is a slightly higher charged environment. It is very difficult but very effective if you can master it.

What message am I trying to get across with this face image?

Less is more in selling. There is something very obvious in the above picture. Nature gives you two ears and one mouth, and in selling you should use them in that proportion. The biggest problem with many salespeople is that they talk too much. The most effective seller gets the potential customer to talk. If you listen to them they will give you the hooks on which to hang your solution.

Going back to the **LOVQE** formula, when you ask a question or a series of questions what you are aiming to do is to find out what the needs or wants of the potential customer you are negotiating with are. You are trying to qualify that client in one sense or another. You are trying to find out where their pain is. You have to listen. If you listen you will be told. You also have to observe as the process is going on. Are you making progress or are you not? You will know very quickly if you have somebody's attention. Have you ever found yourself in a selling situation where your targeted customer is looking at their watch or fidgeting? They are basically waiting for you to go. You know it instinctively, don't you? What should you do in that situation? You need to be assertive and say to the person, 'I see that you are busy, how about if I give you a call later?' This indicates that you are confident and also respectful of their agenda. You have invested resources to get to this stage. You must get your return from this investment. If this negotiation has no potential, it is important for you to know so that you can focus on more fertile ground. So you have to observe what is going on around you. You also have to observe the environment that you are working in. If somebody has a very obvious plaque or medals up in his or her office, they are there for ego purposes. They are there because they want you to ask how they got those medals, so that they can play their ego script. This is part of the price you must pay with grace if you want to start developing the relationship. You do need to observe the immediate environment. There is always something that you can latch onto which will give you a cue for the first quarter ice-breaking phase of your sales cycle.

As the sales process continues, you need to verify what progress you have made.

What is verifying and why is it important in a selling process?

If you are listening, observing and asking questions, you will have quite a lot of information and you need to make sure that you are going down the right track. Verification is a process whereby you summarise in your own words where you understand the negotiation is at. The person who verifies takes control of the process. Verifying also gives you the opportunity to slightly warp what has been agreed to date in your favour. You are giving the potential customer the opportunity to agree or disagree with your analysis of the current state of play. Essentially, you are trying to get the potential customer to agree with your analysis. Even if they don't say yes, even if they say no, you have a chance to loop back and get it right. You have tried it and you are still pushing a small bit, not very obviously, but a small bit. The tactic you are using here is encouraging your potential customer to start getting used to saying 'yes'. It is very important to verify.

If you are involved with any organisation that you really want to influence, my advice is to become the recording secretary of that organisation. It is far more powerful than becoming the chairperson. The recording secretary can write the minutes with the desired 'slant' and once they are signed off then they represent the official line.

I recently coached a group of people in the art of negotiation. They were about to enter a very serious sales pitch and needed to achieve their objectives throughout the process. I got one of the team to volunteer to become the recording secretary. This became very valuable to them over the period of negotiations. An accumulation of slight variations can actually become something very serious down the road.

It is the same in a sales situation. If you are the person who takes control via the tactic of verification, you enhance your relative power. How often have you come away from a sales negotiation and wondered what was actually agreed? The other party may have quite a different interpretation of the outcome. This greyness may come back to haunt you later.

The last step of the **LOVQE** technique is to empathise. If you perform the other steps really well, you will start developing a chemistry between you.

By going through this consultative type process you are finding out from the potential customer what their real needs are. You are like the good doctor: diagnosing what the issues are before prescribing the appropriate solution.

While I have written these **LOVQE** parameters in a list for convenience sake, you don't always use them that way. You don't hold a list in your hand and mark the boxes. You have to develop a technique and use them as a guide in a very natural process. Managing silence is what you will find most difficult. Until such time as you develop the habit, you will have to use some prop to remind you to stay silent after asking a question. The prop I used in the early days was to pinch my forefinger with my thumb as I asked a question. The pain of the pinch reminded me to manage the silence. I don't have to use it anymore as I have naturally developed the habit.

Silence is also uncomfortable for the person on the other side so they will respond in order to relieve this pressure. As they respond they will provide the 'hooks' upon which to hang your proposition.

Most people love to talk about themselves and their business. As you go from the general type of questions to the more specific, listen and observe. Good doctors use the questioning technique. They go from the general to the specific as they strive to diagnose your real problem. They talk about your family history, any previous health issues and so forth. As they move from the general to the specific, they are focusing in on a more accurate diagnosis and are thus better equipped to match it with the most appropriate medication. They only prescribe after diagnosis. As an effective salesperson you too need to adopt this stepped process. You are trying to create business for life if at all possible. You are looking for repeat business and you are looking for referred business. The only way you can get those two **R's** working for you is to perfect your technique based on personalising this **LOVQE** technique.

During the first quarter of the sales contact timeframe, after the initial chit chat, you are asking what are called open-ended questions such as: *tell me more about the business*. You follow a trail going from the general to the more specific type questions as your potential customer throw out 'hooks' to you. Eventually you get down near enough to 'yes and no' types of questions or at least more quantifiable questions. You have to try to take control of that process as the other side may be playing games with you as well.

The person that asks the questions and verifies the progress to date tends to control both the pace and the content of the negotiation. The better prepared you are for this type of game the more successful you will be at selling. You need to practice these skills. Debrief yourself after each encounter and challenge yourself to list what you would do differently if you had the opportunity of replaying that last sales negotiation.

There is nothing in this sales process that you can't do. Even if you are not a natural, you can still be a very effective salesperson. If you adopt my suggested techniques you should be able to squeeze at least a further five percent success out of your sales negotiation. That is all that you need. The difference between a highly successful and a less successful sales negotiation is generally down to something relatively small. You need to identify this critical **Trim-Tab** issue (a trim-tab is a mini rudder which has a multiplier enabling impact on the main rudder in guiding the ship in a planned direction, irrespective of the prevailing navigational circumstances) and develop an action plan to address it to the professional satisfaction of your potential customer. How your customer perceives your ability to manage these issues will be the clincher for you. You need to conduct yourself professionally. Your end purpose is to close the sale.

Be interested rather than interesting

What does that mean to you within the context of your sales role?

A lot of salespeople think they are magicians or actors. They think they are great fun. You are there not to be interesting but to be interested in your client's issues so that you can prescribe a solution. If you can help your client to achieve his objectives, you in turn will achieve your objective, which is to secure the sale. You have to be genuinely interested in trying to understand and bring to the surface your client's real needs. If you are not it will show in your body language and other signals.

Your potential customer's cry is: To you who call on me, resolve to get to know me and my pain by listening to me. Don't take me for granted. I want to buy, not to be sold to and I want your promises matched by follow-on delivery.

1. Don't take your potential customer for granted
Your potential customer is king. He can decide whether to support you or not. His decision often turns on something fairly simple. Generally he will not do business with you if he doesn't like you, except if you have a monopoly position.

2. Boost their morale

What is the best way to get someone to really appreciate you and have a good opinion of you?

The best way is to ask them their opinions.
And when you ask somebody their opinion on something, what should you do?

Listen.

Stop talking. Listen for the answer because when you ask somebody their opinion on something, what you are doing is *acknowledging that they are an expert in this area and you value their opinion*. If you are trying to influence your potential customers to do business with you, you have to get them to try and feel good about you. That is why you are asking their opinion on something and listening to them. People love to give their opinion on things. Try this with your significant other and see if it works.

How can you build a working relationship with a potential customer that you don't like and feel threatened by?

I was taught how to deal with people that I feared or disliked in business in the following crude way. Understand that they too have to use the toilet. In other words they are just the same as you. When you go face to face with them, visualise this toilet scenario. Another possible solution is to visualise the person you have a problem with sitting there in his/her 'birthday suit'.

Are you prepared to pay the price, so that you can get the order?

Mirroring

In sales you also have to work the law of reflection to your advantage. If the potential customer is more left brained then you need to communicate your proposition in a factual way as this is what he will appreciate. If your potential customer is more right brained then they are more into images, colour etc. and therefore you need to present your proposition in this mode. By matching the styles you are enhancing your possibilities of developing a working relationship and follow-on business. So you have to come into both the physical and the personality space of the individual in order to do business. You have to play the game differently at different stages. Have you had any experience acting on stage? Let's say a show is running for three or four weeks. It is the same show, the same script, the same actors and setting but with different audiences every night. Good actors try to gauge their audience in the first ten minutes. Based on their instinctive analysis, they will act slightly differently in order to reflect the mood of the particular audience. In selling you have to be just as sensitive.

Suppose you have gone through the sales process in a professional way but have not achieved a positive outcome. Just as you are at the door, you come back for one last bite since you have nothing to loose at this stage. You say to your now fading potential customer: *'What do we have to do for you so that we can do business?'* and then stop talking and wait for his response. The worse thing he can say to you is 'nothing'. There is more than a possibility that he will list out his real needs. You then have to make a judgement call as to whether you can commercially meet these or not. At least now it's your choice. If you decide that you can meet this purchase criterion, you don't just say so. You must be smart here. What you do is you say to him, *'If we will operate as per this list, will you give us the business?"* and again stop talking. Now the balance of power has come to your side, as you have challenged him to commit to the business or not, before you commit yourself. This is a very powerful and smart way to play this 'relative power' game.

Your observation and understanding of the signals being given through body language is also very important. Is what he is saying supported by his body language? Verbal communication at best only represents about fifteen percent of the communication process. We communicate through our body's five senses and the observation of these in selling situations is very important. Good salespeople are very sensitive to understanding these subtle messages. Even if you are not a natural, you can still acquire the necessary skills. Studying the area of body language will help you to be more observant. You have to observe if, for example, your potential customer is adopting a defensive stance. If that is the case you have to break this barrier before you can achieve the sale. The trick is to adopt the body mirroring technique, whereby you adopt the same stance and gradually and naturally open up your stance. Subconsciously, he will follow you into a more receptive stance. When you have got him to that point you have significantly increased your chances of making the sale. Having got to this more receptive mode, the next tactic is to try and get him to engage. You can do this by asking him questions and managing your silences. If you can get to the point where you are using the word 'we' and bending in and working on the same document or drawing, then you are both developing a mutual solution to address the identified issue.

With body language, observe the eyes in particular. People can make a reasonable effort at controlling their body movements as they lie, but they cannot control their eyes. I'm sure you've heard the saying that someone is 'lying through their teeth'. If they try it through their eyes it will be transparent. That is the reason why you should never negotiate with someone wearing dark glasses. You need to see their eyes as the deal gets to crunch time.

The second **R** of selling which you need to optimise is referral. Your potential customer will place more credibility on what an existing customer will say about your offering than what you will say. You should be confident enough in your own product or service to encourage them to check you out. You shouldn't be trying to hide from that. If you are new in your business and don't have reference sites this can become a major mental block for you. The following SMART tactic will take you over this block. If you are fairly new in the game and somebody needs references and you don't have any, tell the person that you work on a confidential basis with your clients; that you don't talk about who you are dealing with and neither will you talk about his business to anyone else. That will get you over that initial barrier. Later, when you have a list of good customers you may change your tactics to using reference sites, but first your business must live long enough to be successful. You must be SMART at adopting the appropriate tactics for the particular stage of the business cycle you are at.

Listen to potential customers' unstated objections. Some potential customers are just afraid of change. They may also be lazy. Once you have established them as a customer you have to do something really negative to them before they move on. This is both good and bad in business. It is bad if you are new in business and you are trying to wrench your targeted customers away from their existing suppliers. It is good when you have those customers because eighty percent of them will stay with you pretty well irrespective of how you treat them.

You must also establish as early as possible if the person you are negotiating with has the authority to make the deal. If you deal with bigger organisations, the young professional buyers will present themselves as having a lot of authority and will put you through hoops as they climb up their corporate ladder. The vision I carry around in my head about these young people is that they are full of their own importance and operate in suits and shoes which are too big for them. You must do whatever is necessary for you to get that sale.

Observe how the professionals do it. From a male perspective, I find the real professionals we encounter are the old boys selling you a new suit of clothes. I am sure the same applies in ladies boutiques. They observe you as you approach. They have you already profiled by the time they talk to you. They go from the general to the specific very quickly as they show you the whole range. They are playing a numbers game, and they finish up with two suits and say, '...*which one of these will I put in the bag for you?*' They assume you are buying. They have very quickly gone from a general look at what is available down to just two. They have simplified the decision process by reducing the options to two. If they left four options they would be less likely to sell to you. When selling you too need to bring your options down to two as quickly as possible. There has to be a contrast between the two options so that there is an automatic decision to purchase forthcoming as soon as possible. You are really only using the other option to provide a contrast to show up the targeted option in a better and more attractive light.

When they have the suit in the bag then they sell the shirt and all of the other bits and pieces (which they tend to make most margin on). What are the selling messages for you here?

Never come away from a sales negotiation without agreeing the next step. If you have agreed to do something, make sure you do it within the agreed timeframe. Keep control of the pace of the process by agreeing to come back to them rather than letting them have the initiative of coming back to you, which may never happen.

Operating on a face-to-face basis is to your advantage. It is more difficult for the other side to say 'no' to your face. Younger people are losing this critical skill because they have got into the habit of addressing awkward issues via texting or e-mail. There will be a price to pay for this supposed convenience further down the road.

Payment and payment terms are critical and you should establish them before you give the price.

I recently dealt with someone who was under a bit of cash pressure in their business. His client's quantity surveyors were using all sorts of excuses so that they could delay final payment on the contract for as long as possible. My client was so desperate to get the money, his negotiating resolve was weak. Ultimately he accepted a considerably discounted amount. The discount washed out all of his budgeted margins.

Remember, in selling you are always trying to get your potential customer used to saying yes as you move to the point of asking for the business. Once you have asked for the business, stop talking and play the silence tactic. When the sale is completed get out of there. If you stay around and chit-chat it will cost you; if your now confirmed customer is any use, he will leverage something else out of you. This then will come straight out of your planned net margin and it is the accumulation of these bits of extras which become very costly over the longer term. Good buyers agree the sale and then they open negotiation again and they get you. Many a good deal has gone astray by delay.

The first exercise you need to do is create a hit list of your targeted customers. Then you need to qualify them. By this I mean that everybody on that list should fit the profile of what you are targeting. If you are in a one-to-one selling situation you should work the quarter, half and final quarter timeframe tactic suggested earlier. The most important part of that timeframe is the consultative part, where you are trying to get the potential customer to talk about their wants and needs. It is only when you fully understand these that you can prescribe the most appropriate solution. You need to be very good at questioning and listening. You need to observe what is going on around you. You need to verify the progress made at critical points of the process, whilst all the time building empathy. As you condition your potential customer you will start to test the closing of the sale: *Which colour do you want? Which of these will I wrap for you?* Depending on the reaction, you may have to loop back through the above stepped sales journey to continue the conditioning process, until your targeted customer is primed for the deal. If the sale is not to be completed that day, agree how you are going to keep control of the next phase.

You do need to continue sowing seeds, which is spreading the word out there that you are in business. They will tend to germinate at different time lags. A potential customer you speak to tomorrow may not be in a position to purchase until later but you will never do business if you don't know of each other's existence. It is a great discipline to continue to sow seeds even when you don't want extra business. Your pipeline of potential sales may not always be as healthy. You can get lazy about it and get out of the habit of prospecting. I would advise you to allocate some time to prospecting. It allows you both to sow seeds and to gather useful data from the ever changing market place.

Remember the 4 by 4 sales tactic from an earlier chapter? Make four cold calls plus four follow-up calls a day. Send out four pieces of literature and follow up on four quotations. If you calculate that cycle out over a year you will have made contact with over one thousand potential clients.

This chapter will have shown you that even though you may not be a natural salesperson you can still become a very effective salesperson. If you model your sales techniques around the guidance given here you will increase your hit rate by at least five percent. This improvement could make all the difference to your sales performance because you are probably already doing it reasonably well through your own technique. Modelling yourself as suggested will push you over the line more often. This is where the rainbow touches the ground. It is the last twist of the nut that really secures the beam.

Have your hit list of potential customers and work through it at an appropriate pace. As your business grows, your business model must be built around the two **R's:** repeat and referred business. In relation to repeat business, you are negotiating so as to reduce slippage because you make the most money from your existing customers. You cannot leave the tactic of referred business to chance either. As mentioned previously you should be asking your satisfied customers: *'Who else should we be talking to about this product / service?'* And then listen. Eighty percent of the time they will give you at least one warm lead.

Operating these two **R's** partly opens new doors which allow you to leverage your initial investment over the follow-on sales. This facilitates the reduction of unit costs and thus helps both your margins and your competitiveness. Facilitating your satisfied customers to become your advocates (unpaid salespeople) is the real trick.

Summary

1. You can become an effective salesperson, even if you are not a natural.
2. For many of you, selling is more important than marketing. Because of your relatively scarce resources your marketing possibilities are restricted so you need to get out there through the more direct route of selling.
3. By internalising and practicing the LOVQE technique you can develop your own effective selling skills.
4. Model your technique on the stepped process performed by good doctors.
5. Understand the importance of matching; it is fundamental to the development of selling effectiveness.
6. Customers buy for their own reasons. Get to know these reasons and respond accordingly.
7. Be resilient and disciplined.
8. You can do it.

Chapter **14**

The Art of Negotiation

There are a number of tactics you can use in order to get your own way. You can achieve it through negotiation, political action or manipulation. Through negotiation you can use one or other of the following sub-tactics: bluff, threat or promise. Your usage of these will depend on how skilful a negotiator you are.

Selling is just another form of negotiation. Where do you think your natural style of negotiation is on this matrix?

There are different ways of resolving conflicting issues.

You can resolve it my way, your way or our way. It depends on what strength you have in the market. If you have a monopoly on something which your target market demands then you can solve it your way, at least in the short term.

Management Resource Institute

Negotiation is about getting people to agree. Successful negotiators aim to win an agreement, not the argument. It generally involves a series of offers and counter offers. You know when you enter negotiations that the other person will give a bit and you will give a bit. The whole process depends on how much give is on both sides and where both sides stand. You state your position, they state theirs and there is always a gap in between. You use your negotiation tactics to close this gap in your favour. The more modern form is to negotiate about both side's interests rather than their positions.

Firm offers must be clearly distinguished from teasers. Good salespeople often throw out some proposition just to get a reaction. Studying the body language of the other party to your 'way-out' proposition will give you some signal of the outer limits of a possible deal.

Strong words, attack or apparent loss of temper are accepted as legitimate bargaining tools, provided you know how to manage them. There is quite a difference between an emotional outburst of aggression and a calculated usage of aggression. Emotionally aggressive people make poor negotiators because they lose their shape and sense too easily. In the process they let themselves become very exposed to the calculated tactics of the other party. Calculated aggression can often be used to 'soften up' the other side; it is done very coldly and in a calculated manner. You have to decide whether the person is having a go at you emotionally or adopting a calculated aggressive tactic to soften you up. The final agreement needs to be crystal clear regarding all the relevant parameters.

Different people have different styles of negotiation. Some will throw out a completely unrealistic starting position and then pull back. Others will open very close to where they want to be and just anchor themselves at that point.

One of the first and real tactics of negotiation is never to give away anything for nothing.

Secondly, always put in a couple of things that you have no interest in so you can allow yourself to have them negotiated away from you. At worst you will pick up a few brownie points.

Negotiation is a most important function in business because if you get it wrong at the beginning you can spend the rest of the year or more trying to get it right.

You should never go into negotiation without having made the two following decisions. Firstly, what is your ideal outcome and secondly, what is your walk away position or bottom line. Don't try to decide your bottom line when you are in negotiation because at that stage you are in an emotional state and you are not in a position to make rational decisions. If you have decided your walk away position beforehand you will be a far stronger negotiator because the worst thing that can happen to you is that you get the deal at that point or no deal. This gives you psychological strength.

Again, before you enter into negotiations, decide what concessions you can use as bargaining chips. What is your opening offer? What arguments are you going to use to support your case? Understanding what the real needs of your client are helps here. Time is a big issue in negotiation. If you can sense that somebody has a very tight timescale, their power is very low at that stage.

Know what the other side's weakest point is. If there are two or more people on your negotiation team it is very important that only one speaks and the other/s observe and interpret the real messages and signals being given out by the other side. We have often seen cases where, in the heat of the process, two or three people on the same negotiation team end up arguing amongst themselves or making conflicting points. Have good eye contact. And remember silence is a great way of pulling somebody into the conversation.

If the other side have a negotiation team you should try and scatter them by sitting amongst them. Positioning is very important. More often than not, you will have the opportunity in any room to manoeuvre yourself into the right position. I know the Chief Executive of a Plc who refuses to go to a negotiation meeting if he hasn't some rights over where to position people. He considers it very important. But there is a potential weakness in that as well because if he can't get his way it puts him in a weaker psychological position. If the opposition know his style then they should be smart enough to out-manoeuvre him by taking up their own preferred positions first or make some excuse to scatter his preferred positioning.

Try and sit your enemy or strong opponent to your left. This psychological positioning originates from the Roman times, where it was always advisable to keep your enemy on your left so that you could draw your sword with your right hand and kill them in one sweeping movement. Even if this proposition is not factually correct, if you believe it is, then it will work for you. Back to Henry Ford again:
'If you believe it can, or you believe it can't, you are right.'

Just look at the seating arrangements in the various chat shows. Is there a correlation between this and the quality of the programme?

It is all about timing and positioning.

In any negotiation you can adopt either a soft approach or a hard approach. A soft approach is where everybody is very friendly. A hard approach is where you state your position and you anchor yourself at that position. You will have power at some point along the way and if you don't optimise it, it will cost you in the long run. You have to be prepared to stand behind it.

In the modern type contract of design and build, you need to be professional enough at the outset to include all the necessary variables since the option for extras are seriously reduced. In the traditional type contract, you could be a poorer initial negotiator because you knew that you could patch up the gaps with extras. Even in the design and build model, the client often has requirements that were not included in the original drawings. This presents you with the opportunity of negotiating extras. You need to be professional enough to hold your ground until you get a PO for these extras / variations. If you don't have the paper trail correct, some quantity surveyor will work you over some months later when you are trying to get paid. Their motto is: *Show me the paper.* The primary job of the quantity surveyor at this point is to try and ensure that the client pays the least amount possible at the latest date possible. What often happens is that without a PO you can end up arguing and while that battle is going on, your money is still in your client's bank account rather than in yours. This is a particular type of negotiation, where you have allowed yourself to slip into a very poor bargaining position because of your lack of paperwork. You were probably too generous or foolish in agreeing to do the extras at your client's panic point. Some months later in the cold light of day, your generosity / stupidity will be trampled on by the quantity surveyor who incidentally wasn't there at the critical moment you decided to rescue your client.

I know of one situation that is going on for the last eighteen months. The quantity surveyor on the other side is coming up with all sorts of issues in an effort to delay agreeing a final account. In the meantime this subcontractor's money is in the bank account of the developer, resulting in a serious working capital deficit in his account. Eventually this type of negotiation often drifts towards getting a payment at a seriously discounted rate, rather than optimising your bottom line. The focus then becomes minimising losses rather than optimising surpluses - which is what you all should be in business for.

You will not achieve what you want to achieve if you can't move yourself into a more powerful position. There are two ways of manoeuvring yourself into a more powerful position. Firstly, if somebody becomes more dependent on you, you have more power over them.

Isn't that right? Yes _____ No_____

You have to look at your business proposition and work out how you can manoeuvre your clients so that they become more dependent on you.

The second option is to work out how you can become less dependent on your client.

If you want to become more successful in business you have to learn how to play this power game. You must devise strategies and tactics to play both sides of this power equation to your advantage. What can you do in your particular situation?

_____

_____

_____

_____

_____

Devise a strategy where your targeted customers become five percent more dependent on you and a strategy where you can become five percent less dependent on whoever has you in a squeeze at the moment. If you can get both of these strategies going in opposite directions, you will achieve a multiplier effect on your relative power position. With this enhanced power position you are equipping yourself to optimise your bottom line.

This is the most fundamental business lesson I can expose you to. If you can really internalise this concept and determine the angles that are relevant to you, you will have gained a fundamental 'tool' that will be as important to you in twenty years as it will be in twenty days. Like all business people, you need to keep challenging yourself about what return on your investment (ROI) you are going to get from reading and reflecting on the learning points in this book. If you have decided that you only want to take away one learning point then might I suggest that this be a serious contender. Knowing the point is just theory; applying the principle to your business is where its real value comes in.

I recently came across an example of where the power game was very evident. The company had a staff member who has accumulated a lot of relevant information and data but was unwilling to share it with the rest of the team. Because he held that knowledge he could do what he liked in the company and the company allowed him to manoeuvre his way into that position. Now the only strategy that can be adopted in that kind of a situation is that the system within the company has to be changed. This guy is running on the parallel server to the main server if you know I mean.

Negotiation is about repositioning yourself into a more powerful position. With this enhanced relative power base you have options to optimise your bottom line.

DERRY: I have worked with a lot of project engineers. Generally they operate under severe pressure deadlines, trying to manage all the variables in an organised way so that the project can be delivered on time and within budget. If you can build a trusting professional relationship with them so that they are confident that you can deliver your contract every time, then this is another variable they don't have to micro-manage. This makes them more dependent on you and thus enhances your power position. With power all things are possible.

BLAISE: Yes, if somebody trusts you they don't question you anymore. You get what is called 'referent power': they refer to you.

There are a number of behavioural strategies you can use during your range of negotiations. Don't respond to the opposition's proposal with your own counter proposal. Instead dissect theirs, find its 'soft underbelly', expose it and then pull it apart. By implication you are undermining their total proposition. Don't get into an attack / defend cycle. Just ignore their attack. Let it go over your right shoulder but not through your head. Don't give too many reasons. If you do, you are diluting your argument. You are also giving the other side too much ammunition to attack you. If they are any use they will focus in on your weakest argument, pull that apart and thus undermine your total argument. Play for time by seeking further information. It will at least keep the other side busy. You can control both the pace and the content of the negotiation by asking questions and waiting for answers.

Reflect on what you can do in your business to enhance your power position.

What is your action plan?

_____

_____

_____

_____

The power can sometimes just be in your own head but that is very often all you need as that is frequently where the first barrier is. I can't ever convince you of something unless I am first convinced of it myself. You just won't believe me. I might even get the script right but you won't believe me because you will somehow pick up that I am not really genuine about it. If you are targeting somebody on the phone and that person has never met you, you might get away with it. But even over the phone it can come across that you are not convinced. Most serious negotiations get to a face to face scenario at some stage.

When somebody is going for a job their CV is only equivalent to a brochure. Its only purpose is to get you to interview stage. After that you are into a selling situation; a negotiating situation. Then it is all down to relatively small things. It could be your response to some scenario put to you that will be the clincher. A useful tactic to use if you haven't got the nod is to have a meeting with your targeted customer and ask them what you should have done in order to get the contract. By really listening you will equip yourself to be smarter the next time.

Summary

1. We are always negotiating, even though we tend to think of negotiation as being those once-off big events.
2. To be more successful you need to fine tune your negotiating skills.
3. Personalise the negotiation tactics addressed in this chapter so that you too can appear to be a natural.
4. Enjoy the enhanced results.

Chapter **15**

Pricing for Profit

In this chapter I will address how to price your product or service so as to optimise your profits.

My experience is that pricing, particularly in SMEs, is very poor. I certainly can't remember any case in my time as a consultant where I visited a company and observed over-pricing as a problem. I have however come across the opposite where under-pricing is a serious difficulty. Of all the things that are going to have an impact on your bottom line, pricing is the most critical.

There are many market structures in the market, ranging from the fragmented through oligopoly to monopoly structures. In fragmented markets there are many players some of whom are involved in all sorts of sharp practices, which in turn tend to seriously affect your pricing structure. Thus the approach to pricing tends to be fragmented and difficult to pin down.

This happens particularly where barriers to entry are low. As your niche gets over populated all kinds of sharp practices tend to creep in. You need to try and differentiate your product in a meaningful way so that you can carve out a tightly defined market niche where you can become a bigger fish in a smaller pool. As well as giving you an enhanced position this will also establish the opportunity for stronger pricing. You need to get away from being part of the mass; otherwise you are going to be in a fragmented market where it is very difficult to get consistent margins.

The other extreme market structures represent a very concentrated market where one or two players are in control and thus it is easier to support strong pricing.

Pricing is more of an art than a science and you need to be creative in this critical process. There are all sorts of scientific accounting formulae that you can use as a guide to establishing the price you should charge. But these accounting formulae are just an aid towards pricing. As a businessperson you need to understand the dynamics that are going on in your targeted market and use these formulae as an aid rather than a foolproof mechanism.

Pricing is a most transparent management tool. What does this mean to you?

If I want to go in and compete with you in your business, the easiest thing in the world for me to do is to compete on price and gain market share. Now if your 'edge' was based on something other than price, then it would be more difficult for me to compete with you, in the short term at least. Your 'edge' is now based on some less transparent angles thus making it more difficult to copy or compete with.

This is where many SME type businesses are weak. They think that the only advantage they have in the market is price, which is often a false premise. I have stated that pricing is an art. It is based on guesswork, judgement, experience, costings and where the market will take you. It is based on all those parameters, not just on an accounting formula.

As your 'offering' matures the price gets more elastic. What does that mean?

Did you study economics in school?

If you did, then you were exposed to the concept of elasticity of demand. This means that some products and services are more price sensitive than others. If the demand for your product changes substantially as you make small price changes, then your 'offering' is price sensitive or very elastic. If something is price sensitive and you change the price by a small amount it has a disproportionate impact on the volume demanded. If on the other hand, the demand for your product doesn't change much as you juggle around with your prices, then your 'offering' is less sensitive or inelastic. This affords you real opportunity to be creative with your prices as you optimise your bottom line.

The price of a pint of Guinness went up by five cents recently. It will be price sensitive for about a week as people complain about it. After that it will become price inelastic once again as they settle into their pints of the black stuff.

From our experience of operating with a large range of businesses, nothing is as price sensitive as you think it is. Because you are a small operator, don't assume that if you increase your prices your customers will walk away. More often than not it is your psychological weakness rather than the market reality which is preventing you from charging the optimum price. You have to win this debate in your own head before you can win it with your customers. You can do your own figures to calculate the impact on your own bottom line of making slight adjustments upwards on your prices.

Price is determined by the intersection of the demand and supply curves. As demand increases it takes time for supply to catch up, hence the initial rise in prices. As the supply levels catch up with and eventually exceed demand then prices weaken. This is an ever dynamic repositioning. You can never know for sure where this relative dynamic between demand and supply is, hence my contention that pricing is more of an art than a science.

As your 'offering' matures it tends to get more price sensitive because at that stage there are likely to be many more operators in the market and many more 'me too' substitute products. As this happens your 'offering' is likely to be slipping towards the commodity end of the market, where margins get very thin and your competitive advantage has to be built on efficiencies of operation, so that you have some advantage in unit cost.

Nothing is as price sensitive as you think. I want you to write down the current price of the following:

1. Pint of Guinness: ------------------
2. 500g tub of butter: ------------------
3. Litre of milk: ------------------
4   Standard sliced loaf of bread: --------
5. A litre of petrol: ------------------
6. A thousand litres of heating oil: ------------------
7. The daily newspaper: ------------------
8. A bottle of water: ------------------
9. A coffee: ------------------
10. A scone: ------------------

I suspect that you knew the exact price of very few of the above. What is that telling you? These are basic commodities that you are buying almost every day. They are items that one would expect to be very price sensitive and thus you should know the price of each.

What is the message for you here?

If you don't really know the price of these everyday items then why are you assuming that your customers are any more informed about the pricing of your product? It is very likely that their purchasing decisions are based on other criteria such as convenience, attraction of the packaging, brand image etc. This is a fundamental decision point for you.

I'll give you an example of something I came across just a couple of months ago.

I was in a particular business waiting at the trade counter for the MD. While I was waiting there was an argument going on between the salesperson and a customer. When the MD arrived I asked him to stand back and observe the sales process going on at the counter. The potential customer went off after about twenty minutes without buying the machine they were negotiating over. When we talked to the salesman to tease out the issues involved, it transpired that the price on the machine was wrong. It was priced at twenty percent too low. Neither the salesperson nor the potential customer knew that the machine had been marked under price and yet they had the same arguments over the price.

I believe that this happens several times every day in the business world. When people say to me that customer X will spot the price and will argue, I say of course they will. It is like a bad playing record. If you are not careful you will be too influenced by a few awkward customers who tend to know the price of everything but the value of nothing. If you adjust your prices to strive to satisfy these people then you are missing an opportunity of doing good business with the majority and optimising your bottom line. Don't adjust your prices down to try and satisfy the vocal minority. Focus on the silent majority and win.

The real tactic for you is to sell the 'difference' your product offers. If you do this the focus for your customer is on value as distinct from just price. As you become more expert at selling your 'difference' you are positioning your 'offering' on to the less price sensitive plane. This is when you really start to optimise your bottom line which after all, should be your main reason for being in business.

If you are a weak seller, you will have a tendency to drop prices in the mistaken expectation that this will solve your problem. It is usually the wrong solution. Remember the guy arguing about the price of the machine which was priced incorrectly? There is always going to be a certain proportion of the buying public who will make these arguments and if you are too sensitive to them you are going to drop your price.

I have witnessed that scene played out so many times over the last fifteen years.

I was sitting in a client's office some time ago and the salesperson came in and said to the boss, 'what can we do with that?' meaning how much could she reduce the list price by. I had started to discuss issues around margins with her boss but obviously he hadn't internalised my point because without thinking, he said to the saleswoman that she could drop the price to around €900. 'Hold on a minute, you're not listening to what we've been talking about' I said. 'Why don't you try €1,050 and see how she gets on?' He said okay and the woman went out and finalised the sale. The message here is that if you are not careful, your salespeople will tend to sell at the bottom of their price range rather than at the top. They may think it is easier, but it is your margin they are playing with.

Discounting and cutting prices destroy your margins. Some people just don't understand the maths. They believe that if they drop their prices by say twenty percent, they are cutting their margins by the same amount. This is not correct. They may in fact be eliminating all or most of their net margin. Always remember that your margin is calculated as a percentage of your sales price. Mark up is calculated as a percentage of your purchase price and is thus a much lower figure. If you want to optimise your bottom line, then do the maths for your particular business for both the mark up and your budgeted margin and compare both. When you understand it, adopt the appropriate pricing tactics. If you drop your price by say ten percent, you need to calculate how much extra sales you need to generate in order to give you the same gross income. Depending on the margin possibilities in your business, I think many of you will be quite frightened by the extra volume of sales you will need to cover for this price drop.

Some people say to me, 'Why aren't we making money?' They are not making money because their net margin is too low.

Which pairs of the following words go together do you think?

Cheap, Select, Nasty, Expensive

All the research indicates that there is a strong correlation between what you charge for something and what the perceived value of that something is.

Price is an indication of Quality

The worst thing that you can do for your business (in my view) is to charge the wrong price. If you are promoting yourself as being the best in your niche and then charge a less than average price, you are in fact confusing the market because you are giving out two different messages. For credibility, you have to back up your premium image with strong pricing. If you don't, you will lose.

Many people judge the product by the price they pay. This proposition is frequently proven in 'blind-tests' carried out by market research companies. Here the tasters mentally use the falsely published price as one of the main deciding factors as they line up the samples in priority order.

If you go into a store tomorrow morning and you see something on the shelf and the price hits you as being cheap, what is the first that goes through your mind? I believe you will wonder what is wrong with that product.

If everyone is as price conscious as we think then why are there such variations in prices for the same product?

It is because of all the other factors that come into the purchase decision process. Take the example of any petrol convenience store. They don't make money on fuel sales because margins have dropped to two or three percent. They make something between fifteen and twenty two percent in the shop. What you are paying for is the convenience and most people are prepared to do so. If everything was as price sensitive as we think it is, wouldn't everybody be buying at discount stores?

I know of a landscape designer who was pitching for a large job. She had put a big effort into the design and was very anxious to get this contract, but she was frightened of the client's reputation. He had indicated that if she got the contract he would accept no messing. She showed me the quotation and had a range of prices worked out. As a result of her fear, she was starting to lose her nerve and was losing the debate in her head. After discussing the issues with her and giving her some guidance on negotiating tactics, I convinced her to go in at her top price and to be prepared to walk way from the contract if she couldn't get it at this price. I prepared her for the fact that part of the price she had to pay in order to get the contract was to listen to his ranting. He frightened her the first day as he told her he would sue her if she didn't perform. She was completely frightened of him and that's what these guys do.

That guy wouldn't have a clue about the proper price, as it was a once off, but that wouldn't stop him abusing and using whatever arguments he could. I guess that's natural. That's the bad playing record that I was talking about earlier and we are too influenced by it.

What she did was to suck him into her unique design. Once she had achieved that the price wasn't really the issue, but that didn't stop him moaning and groaning. He set her up the first day and nearly got away with it. Believe me it's happening out there all the time and you are giving away your margin. It is only a tactic used by your potential customer and you need to understand this and work around it.

Many people in business give their margins away too easily. They are too sensitive to the tactics being used. Understand that it is a game and like all games you need to prepare yourself to win. If you are not prepared to defend your line by being prepared to walk away, then you will continue to be a weak seller and thus continue to earn poor margins.

In a situation where you are not just selling time but you are selling expertise, you must charge accordingly. Take the scenario of a car break-down service: the installation of a new bolt may have only take thirty minutes, but the mechanic knows both the problem and the solution. Therefore they are selling expertise and they must charge well for it, otherwise it will not be appreciated. What you give for free will not be appreciated. How often have you heard, 'we couldn't charge that amount'? You must get over this barrier and start to value yourself. If you don't value yourself then how do you expect the market to value you?

Many retailers are using the same old pricing formula for years. They are marking up their product by 2.4 times to cover both their vat and margin. What is so magical about the factor 2.4? Why not 2.5 or some other figure. Often it has nothing to do with what the market is willing to pay. Remember, I spoke at the head of this chapter about pricing being an art.

It is important to realise that everyone sees the world quite differently. Just because you are a small business there is a perception out there that you need to sell cheaper and that you can do so because your cost base is small. This is a wrong assumption. While your cost base may be low, so too are the number of 'widgets' going through your system. Because of this lack of scale, it's very likely that your unit costs are higher than the big operation down the road which has a far larger absolute cost base but in turn is pumping out 'widgets' at a rate which reduces their unit costs below your more modest volume.

If you have to sell at various price points, then you must adjust your production costs so that your net margin is maintained. Neither should you over-deliver on portion size or quality. If you do you are eating into your margin. Your motto has to be to deliver your promise in a professional consistent manner, no more or no less. *The consistent drip on the rock wears the rock.* Your rock here is your chosen market niche which you must wear into the shape you want.

Remember, there is no such thing as perfect competition or perfect pricing. The market is very segmented. People buy for all sorts of reasons and price is only one of those. As sellers of your own 'offering' you are sometimes too shy about appropriate stiff pricing. As indicated earlier, your pricing is a real statement about your standing in your market niche.

The two critical pricing messages here are:

- Your natural instinct is to try to come up with logical arguments in your own head in order to try and reduce your prices.
- Every time you discount think of how much your margin is being reduced. If you don't have a margin then you don't have a business long term, full stop.

The one certainty about business is that every day that you open your business it is costing you money. You only start to make money when you have all your costs covered. If you can't cover your costs you won't stay in business too long.

Never apologise for being commercial. Be proud of your 'offering' and act accordingly. Keep selling the difference and not the price, unless you are positioned at the commodity end of the market and your competitive advantage is built on very competitive pricing.

$$P_x V - C = \text{your business future.}$$

Do you understand what this formula is saying?

Your average price multiplied by your number of widgets sold less the total cost of producing them equals the surplus you generate for your business. You can then continue to build your business off this surplus base. I have represented the price using a capital P because of the impact that pricing has on the output of this formula.

What is the widget equivalent in your business?

How many of these units do you sell each year?

This is a very important exercise for you to do. If you sell a large number of units then start juggling around with small price variations and see what the positive impact on your gross income will be. For instance, if you produce 500,000 units, then every one cent increase in price will wash out as €5,000 extra income per year. A €1 adjustment would increase your gross income by €500,000 per year. The resultant extra income goes straight to your bottom line because you have already covered all your costs with your current pricing policy. Therefore the extra income generated increases your net profit on a one to one basis, provided you were already creating some surplus. Do your own sums, see the impact and decide your own pricing action plan. The real money is always made by the last twist of the nut.

What Action Plan are you going to put in place to exploit this concept?

What positive impact will it have on your net profit for the coming year?

Is this worth the effort of you getting out there and selling the difference?

Are you committing yourself to doing it?

Remember, commitment means *doing the things you said you were going to do, long after the mood in which you said it has left you.*

If you are limited, capacity wise, to a given number of units which you can either produce or sell, then your net return per unit becomes even more critical. I am saying that your pricing strategy has an inordinate impact on this unit wash out.

To be continuously successful you must obviously continue to operate the business professionally and really sell the difference.

I'll give you an example of a previous programme participant who owned a corner shop, which in her view was trading poorly. She told me one day 'I am a going to give up this game because there's nothing in it.' During a site visit to her business I quickly observed that there was a real looseness in the management of the business and all the family seemed to be going to the cash till and taking money for various living needs without any records being kept. When questioned she admitted: 'Oh yes, we all live out of the till but we don't make any money.' I got her to keep an exact record of what was being taken out of the till for a month by the various family members. She came back to me the following month with her schedule and was shocked. After the analysis, she agreed that she would need a job paying €1,200 per week to be equivalent to her current business. Having got over this shock, she kept saying 'but we are still making no money.' Next I got her to work out the number of units (widget equivalents) they sell yearly. After a lot of analysis she came back with the figure of 600,000 units. I then got her to start calculating the impact on her bottom line from small price adjustments. In her case each cent adjustment on average was adding €6,000 to her bottom line.

She is much smarter today and far more confident as a businessperson. Small successes build on themselves and result in real improvement in both your own self worth and your balance sheet.

The challenge for you now is, are you going to apply this principle to your business or will you just salute this concept in passing?

Accountants tend to use the 'cost plus' method of pricing. This involves working out the cost of producing the unit and adding a mark-up to give you the recommended selling price. But how do you know with certainty how many of those units you are going to produce? Are you going to produce two thousand units, two and a half thousand units or three thousand units and which figure are you going to base your calculation on?

From our experience many people assume the highest figure. They will decide their price based on the highest figure because the resultant cost plus formula then throws out a lower recommended price. You all know what the word 'assume' means when you break it up into its three component parts. It tends to make an **ass** of **u** and **me**. Be careful in calculating your cost plus formula in assuming that you will achieve your optimum number of units. At worst you need to build buffers in there. Do you have the necessary number of units to drive your unit costs lower relative to your competitors? If you do, then you have the option of following a low price high volume strategy. If you don't, then you need to follow a lower volume higher price strategy. In either case you have to be crystal clear about where your relevant competitive advantage is and really sell this difference to your targeted market niche. Your potential customer will be your final adjudicator and they will either vote with their business or with their feet.

Ryanair operate their low price strategy which is built on them having the lowest unit costs. This is based on handling a much larger number of passengers per head of staff or per physical seat numbers than their competitors.

You have to try and differentiate yourself in some meaningful way as perceived by your targeted customer and then sell that difference at a premium price. You don't have enough units going through your system to follow the low cost low price strategy.

I remember visiting a client who had an old established business which was in financial trouble. As the crisis meeting progressed, the business owner wasn't accepting reality and wanted to continue to live off the reserves built up over the years. The bank's representative was getting frustrated and he eventually said 'What sign is on your front door?' The owner (Pat) was taken by surprise and had to think about it. The bank rep then answered his own question: 'When I was coming in here this morning I didn't see "Charitable Organisation" written up on your door. But you are running this business as a charitable organisation.' It was a telling comment and created in Pat a 'felt need' to face reality.

I believe many owners run their businesses as charitable organisations to some extent. They are not commercial enough. Believe me the market is never as sensitive as you think it is. It is sensitive because you are not selling the difference. When I addressed the issue of selling earlier in the book, I challenged you to go away with two learning points. One was the tactic of **matching** and the second one was how to use **silence**. I'm still saying that these are the core skills you need to perfect in this crucial area of pricing for profit. If you have a problem with pricing at the moment you are probably matching incorrectly. You are not targeting the right customer category. Neither are you using silence very well in your negotiation with yourself in the first instance and with your targeted customers.

Don't believe all market rumours and customers who say your prices are too high. Don't assume that when your sales drop it is because of your price. There are many other variables in this purchasing mix. Value and price are two very different things but people tend to confuse them. You should be focusing on value, not price. If you are serious about your business then this is one of the variables you'll have to start managing.

The whole strategy around sales is to find out what the parameters are that are costing your customers money and to be able to demonstrate where you are going to save them money. You are in the solution business. In essence, it has nothing to do with cost, but it has everything to do with the value you are bringing to your particular client. They need to optimise their own ROI so this is the card you must play.

Finally, to repeat the message which I have been trying to challenge you with: Nothing is as price sensitive as you think it is. You are the barrier to stiffer pricing, not the market. You should look at your business and reduce it to the lowest common denominator. Work out how many units you actually sell in the year, then challenge yourself to make small price adjustments and calculate the yearly impact on your bottom line. You will be surprised with this impact. It will be more impressive if you are already operating at greater than break-even point as any extra then goes straight to your bottom line. And that is why you are in business; to optimise your bottom line and create wealth. Remember, pricing is an art more than a science. You have to be smart in order to optimise your margins and price is a critical variable in the mix.

If you take the lessons from this chapter on board, redefine them in a way that is meaningful for your business and draw up and implement an appropriate action plan, then reading this chapter represents a watershed business moment for you.

Summary

1. Pricing is more of an art than a science.
2. You must understand the impact that pricing levels and discounting have on your bottom line.
3. There is a very strong correlation between price levels and one's perceived value of the 'offering'.
4. Nothing is as price sensitive as you think.
5. You are the limiting factor in your pricing, not the market.
6. Build your confidence to price strongly and manage your targeted customers' expectations.
7. Enjoy the enhanced returns.

Chapter **16**

Building and Managing Your Team

In order to achieve your business objectives you will need to gather together the necessary resources and manage them in the optimum way. One of your major resources is the team you build around you, whether they are directly employed by you or you are operating another model such as franchising or subcontracting in.

I want to focus in on the issues involved in building and managing your own team. If you don't have any employees at the moment, these issues are still relevant to you based on the expectation that you will grow your own business into the future. Having employees can lead to a lot of problems if these issues are not given professional focus.

Currently there are in excess of twenty different pieces of legislation governing the hiring, managing and firing of staff. While it may be impossible for you to be up to speed on every angle of this range of legislation, you must nevertheless be professional in this area and use your common sense. You often hear managers say at business events that their staff are the real assets of their business. Do they really mean it?

What do you believe?

Jack doesn't want to know anything about this range of legislation and its implications for his business. His decision is to manage his team by instinct and if he gets caught on technical breaches of the legislation he is prepared to suffer the consequences. While he has got caught a few times he reckons that on average it works out better for him this way. This is a rational strategy as he sees it for his business.

Are you like Jack, or do you think he is playing with fire?

Jack's is one approach but I think it is very dangerous. I believe that you should be more professional about this most important area and proactively manage it so that your business objectives can be achieved. To keep this engine running smoothly and productively you need to have proper procedures in place so that there is consistency for both parties. In order to do this you need to understand the implications of the relevant basic legislation.

The process starts with good recruitment. Before you hire anybody, decide if you actually need that person. Just because somebody has left your team doesn't mean that you should automatically replace him. Have a look at other options such as subcontracting in. Can you upgrade your technology to do the required job rather than hiring a replacement? As businesses grow at speed it is very tempting to just keep adding people rather than re-engineering the systems and structures. Adding people is a quick fix but it is not necessarily the best tactic in all cases. If you keep adding people to a system that is not working it can lead to disaster and the quicker that business is growing the more likely it is to get into that disaster area. The one certainty of hiring a staff member is that they are costing you from day one. There is no certainty that you will get an adequate ROI from that person.

I was with a company some time ago which had just taken on two travelling salespeople. Based on their cost and the gross margin percentage earned by this business, each salesperson would need to generate extra sales of €200,000 just to pay for themselves. So the first €400,000 of sales is of little advantage to the company. Only after each of them had sales of €200,000 were they in a position to make a real contribution to the company.

The individual yearly sales targets they are setting is €500,000. Whether they will achieve or exceed these targeted sales or not, only time will tell. The one certainty is that their cost clock starts to tick the morning they start their new job. This business will need to be able to finance them for at least the first three months before the fruits of their input start to generate funds for the business.

Assuming you have worked out that you do need to hire someone, the first thing you need to do is prepare a job specification, with particular attention to its planned outputs. You must also be specific about the type of person that you need to fill this vacancy. People prepare very well for interviews; it is possible to groom somebody to get a job. They may be useless later but they can sell themselves very well at interview. If they are better prepared for the interview than you are there is every likelihood that they will sell their version of the job to you, rather than you promoting the version that is right for your business.

The second reason for writing a specification for both the job and the ideal candidate is that you need it to put together a score sheet so that you can score one candidate against another under each designated heading. Under the Freedom of Information Act candidates can request the reasons as to why they were not interviewed or why they were not offered the position. Having the scorecards facilitates you to be transparent in this process.

It is advisable not to hire a candidate based on one interview. It is best to invite those on the short list back for a second discussion and have someone else interview them on this occasion. Your interview team should be gender balanced as women are so much more perceptive than men and perception and intuition are critical in the recruitment process.

Having gone through the recruitment process and made your decision after due reflection, you must then record your job offer in writing. In many cases your prospective employee will require a copy of his employment contract at this stage. In other situations, your new employee may have started to work for you before they get a copy of their employment contract. You are legally required as an employer to give a written employment contract to your new employee within the first month of their employment. Your employee has a contract even if they do not have the piece of paper. It is obviously more difficult to prove a verbal contract. The circumstantial evidence will be more important in this scenario.

The contract of employment basically sets out the job description, what the expectations are; the conditions of employment, grievance procedures and so forth. Larger companies have a company handbook detailing their rules and regulations. Their letter of offer would reference the company's rule book for the generic conditions and just flesh out the specific details pertinent to this candidate.

You might say that you have somebody working with you for the last ten years, he has no contract of employment and he is no problem, so what should you do? My advice to you is to be sensible about it. Don't disturb your relationship by trying to force an employment contract on him. Inform him of the legal obligation on you to have such a contract in place before giving him a written contract and then keep proof of same. Thereafter, ensure that you follow the correct procedures with all new employees.

If you are using advertising to attract applicants, then you should follow the basic **AIDA** Formula. This will help you to grab **A**ttention and generate some initial **I**nterest and **D**esire to take **A**ction by applying for the position. Be truthful in relation to both your business and the job. It is professional to do so and you could expose yourself to being accused of misrepresentation if you are not. If you are using an application form as part of your recruitment procedure, be careful that you don't ask any personal questions. This is to prevent potential employers discriminating against candidates under any of the nine discrimination headings. Insist that all candidates submit a CV as all of that personal information is generally volunteered within a CV. If there are noticeable gaps in the CV they are generally left out rather than forgotten. These are potential amber flashing lights which you should focus in on.

Interviewing is not an exact science by any means. I am sure you have been on both sides of the table at different times. It is a reasonable process provided you are well prepared beforehand. You should have both the job and the person specifications and what you are doing is trying to match the applicants against these profiles. It is a matching process: what is the culture of your business and will this person enhance it or not.

It is important to note that the same laws apply whether you have just one employee or a hundred. The reason we have laws in the country is to control the minority. Most people are law abiding and it is the same principle in relation to employment law. The majority of employers will never need any of these procedures. The rules and regulations are there in order to regulate the minority of bad employers and employees.

I would suggest that you open a personal file for each employee. The file itself is not a legal requirement but you are legally bound to keep what is in the file. It makes good housekeeping sense to do so. The records in this file should include the person's CV, job and person profile, letter of offer, signed employment contract, training received; details of attendance, time keeping, holiday records, disciplinary record, copies of any correspondence referring to previous disciplinary procedures and notes on the exit interview. If you have the misfortune to be called in front of an employment tribunal or other such body, you may be required to present all these documents and without an organised filing process they may be difficult and time consuming to amass.

Exit interviews are useful in distilling the real reason for leaving and maybe also show signals of issues simmering within your team. It also helps in that the person leaving is less likely to have unresolved issues and no place to discuss same.

If you look at your team you have about 20% stars, 70% good soldiers 10% idlers.

You should not have the 10% idlers. If that 10% were a machine you would replace it. A lot of employers are so afraid of the legislation in this whole area that they don't manage this resource properly and instead complain and put up with things. They have heard all the horror stories about unfair dismissals cases. Unfortunately they often only receive very scant and biased reports on these cases, which usually come from parties only interested in the one side. As a result of this, they frequently avoid taking the necessary decisions and follow-on actions and this in turn has a very negative impact on their businesses. If you approach this real management issue in a commonsense way, there is no need to get to this point. The only way to start curing your fear is to address it upfront.

Induction is carried out very poorly in some small companies. The typical induction is 'go down there to Mary and she will show you what to do' and that's about it. The one certainty is that once you hire somebody they are costing you money from that morning on. The sooner people are inducted properly, the quicker you are going to get a return on that investment. For those of you who are operating in a dangerous type of environment, your safety statement will dictate that you cannot let somebody onto your factory floor before they have read and understood the safety statement and have signed off to that effect. It is equally important to get your new employee up to speed as quickly as possible. You should spend a bit of time welcoming the person to the business. First impressions are very important. Also, you have gone to the time, trouble and cost of taking on this person and you and your business need this relationship to work. You should have a procedure for inducting new employees so that the person understands where they are and what is expected of them from day one. It is not unknown for a new person who has either been miss-sold the job or who is not properly inducted to quickly decide this business is not for them and to exit as quickly as they entered. Allowing this to happen is bad management as it will have cost you considerably.

The process of appraisals is another area which tends to be badly managed in many smaller businesses. In some cases it is simply not done at all. Appraisals are an excellent opportunity for two-way communication between your employee and yourself in a more formal, professional setting. They can be done once per year or more often as decided. In management speak we tend to talk about the **Key Performance Indicators (KPIs).** The first step of this agenda is to review the employee's performance against these KPIs over the previous timeframe and to distil the relevant issues which are supporting and blocking this planned performance. If their performance is good, it's a good opportunity for you to acknowledge that. If their performance is lagging then this is the opportunity to address the issue in a rational and professional way.

The next step of the agenda is to agree the KPIs for the following period and agree the action plan to energise them. This is also the employee's opportunity to articulate any issues bothering them and to seek both guidance and help on same. It is best that the employee has a few days notice of these meetings so that they can prepare for them. Don't ambush them. It is useful to have a template score card so that both the employer and employee can separately score the employee under the various performance headings. Both sides can then bring their respective score cards to the appraisal meeting. You can then focus on the gaps between the individual scores and get answers and follow-on commitment.

There is a very important date that you need to keep in your head and that's **a year and a day.** Within the law at the moment, if somebody is with you less than a year the law is reasonably on your side. After the expiration of one year's employment it is very much against you. If someone is on their third back-to-back term contract, they are entitled to be offered a permanent position.

I know a company with an employee whom they decided they weren't going to hold on to. They operated a seven to eleven type business. They didn't pay overtime but people could build up time credits. By the time they decided to give this employee her notice she had enough time credits plus outstanding holidays to bring her total served time to the equivalent of over a year plus a day. Because of this they had to pull back and work through each step of the grievance procedure.

If it takes you a year to find out whether the person is suitable for the job or not then you are not very observant or professional in this area. With proper evaluation of the person's performance you should be able to pick up these symptoms earlier. If you feel uncomfortable facing these personal issues up front you will busy yourself doing something else. You are trying to fool yourself but deep down you know you are avoiding the real issue.

What people issues are you currently avoiding?

Are you now embarrassed enough to do something about it?

If your answer is yes, what is your proposed Action Plan?

Within that initial twelve month period you have reasonable flexibility. You can't ambush somebody in the tenth month and say 'you are no good', because there is such a thing as natural justice and it will be on their side. If an employee is not performing to your required standard then you must inform the employee and give them both the opportunity and the resources to operate to your standards. If they cannot consistently do so, or if they are in breach of some other company procedure, then you must operate as per the steps of your grievance procedure. This process should be detailed in their contract of employment or referred to in the employee handbook, if one exists. The normal steps are as follows:

- Verbal warning
- Formal verbal warning
- Written final warning
- Dismissal

Never reprimand employees in public. If you have the opportunity to praise them, try and do this in public. As an employer be strong, consistent and fair. This professional approach will give you a better return on your people investment.

There may be situations which are serious and justify immediate dismissal or suspension, such as striking another employee, theft, working while under the influence of alcohol or drugs etc. These serious grievances and the consequences of same should be clearly listed in your contract of employment. The importance of having these serious offences documented in the contract is that the offending person cannot say that they weren't made aware of them. The evidence is there to show that they have signed the contract and accept its conditions. In relation to theft, make sure that you have proof of same before accusing someone. If you suspect someone, you can lay a trap and wait. If you can't wait to gather all the evidence, you could call the person in and insinuate that you have gathered more evidence than you actually have. You can ask for a full disclosure and indicate that if it is not forthcoming you will pass all the evidence to the police. When faced with this scenario nine out of ten guilty parties will break. You can then decide how you want to proceed with the matter.

Constructive Dismissal refers to a situation where somebody gets to the point of saying: 'You have made it impossible for me to work here'. You haven't sacked them but in their view you have created an environment that they can no longer continue to work in. It is the only situation in this whole HR legal quagmire where the employee has to prove their case. In all other situations, the employee has only to claim that they were unfairly dismissed and as their employer you are obliged to prove that you were correct and lawful in taking that action. However, in the case of Constructive Dismissal the opposite applies. Natural justice helps the employer here. An employee can't just walk out of work some day and just win the case. They must give the employer the opportunity of rectifying the identified issue. There are more and more of these constructive dismissal cases coming through as the stress levels in the workplace grow more intense. These cases generally end up being adjudicated on technicalities, so having a paper trail in the form of good records in the personal files as suggested above is crucial.

If you are using the redundancy mechanism to downsize your business remember that you are making the position redundant rather than the person. In other words you cannot replace the redundant person with a colleague or a new employee the following day. By giving proper notice, you can claim back up to 60% of the statutory redundancy paid to the exiting employee, using Form RP50. It is calculated on the basis of two weeks pay per year of employment plus one extra week's pay. It is calculated on a weekly pay ceiling of €600 at the time of writing this book. If you want to pay severance pay over and above the basic redundancy payment then you cannot claim any percentage of this back from the state. I am just giving you the basics here. Negotiation is what happens after that. The outcome of this process will indicate how good your negotiating tactics are and your relative strengths versus those of whomever you are negotiating with. But remember, there is no state subsidy available for the sum negotiated beyond the statutory sum. Big companies such as Aer Lingus and Irish Ferries paid severance pay to their departing employees in the region of five to seven weeks per year of employment. They were striving to restructure their historical layered businesses into slimmer, flatter and more flexible businesses in order to make them more attractive to the market. In such cases this once off payment probably represented a good investment.

Would you be able to pay any level of severance pay?

There is no legal obligation on you to do so. Be careful of 'pub knowledge' about these issues. It is not always accurate. If in doubt source accurate, relevant information for your particular set of circumstances.

The majority of employees and employers are decent and professional in their respective dealings. As stated earlier, the only reason you need to have rules and regulations is to try and control the difficult minority. The grievance procedures documented above are there to give clarity to all sides about the stepped journey to be travelled if there is a problem. Troublemakers tend to know the law and their rights better than their employer. Be careful at the recruitment stage that you don't buy in potential trouble. Many employers are afraid of holding their ground. While they may be right about the fundamentals of the case, they may not be up to speed on the technicalities. Many of these cases tend to fall during the process due to technicalities and the lack of paper trails, rather than on the rights and wrongs of the case itself. The possibility of bad press often weakens the resolve of employers to face down the real issues.

The Employment Equality Act lists nine criteria under which you cannot discriminate. They are as follows: 1) Gender, 2) Marital Status, 3) Family Status, 4) Sexuality, 5) Name, 6) Age, 7) Mental or Physical Disability, 8) Member of the Travelling Community/Race/Culture/Nationality, 9) Religion. Do not use any of these criteria in employee disputes. Be careful also that you are not being set up for a potential later claim. There are a minority of people who operate all different types of schemes in order to get easy, unearned income. They are using their knowledge of the law to exploit hard-pressed employers who are just trying to keep their businesses going. This area is tightly marshalled and the adjudicated cases tend to be well publicised.

One of the issues mentioned above is age. If you get a CV and the person's date of birth is not included on it, it was either left out by accident or by design. You have to suspect it was left out by design. If somebody is over fifty they tend to omit their age from the CV because age is often used as a screening process. Be aware that you cannot screen somebody out of a job just because of their age.

Again this demonstrates why it is so important that you have the job and the desired type person profiled out prior to starting the recruitment process. You are then judging the applicants against these profiles. Being a business person you will obviously only recruit the right person to fill your vacant position.

If an applicant had a physical disability that prevents him from being able to do the particular job, would it be appropriate not to offer him the job?

Yes, provided it was a genuine barrier. If the applicant's particular disability didn't prevent them from doing the particular job then you couldn't use it as criteria for rejecting the applicant. If you are looking for a jockey and the applicant just wasn't physically able to ride a horse, obviously then they are not suitable for that job. While on the subject of disability, you should also remember that when interviewing for a job, the interview venue should be wheelchair accessible, otherwise you could be seen to be discriminating against wheelchair bound applicants.

In relation to maternity leave, understand that the person on leave holds all their rights and are entitled to return to their old job or its equivalent. They are entitled to their holidays and public holidays while on leave. As an employer you are not legally obliged to pay the person on leave. They can claim via their social insurance, which at the point of writing ranged from € 207 to € 280 per week. Some larger companies continue to pay the difference between this insurance rate and the person's normal pay so that the person on leave will continue to get their gross normal income between both sources.

All of these matters and others need to be spelled out in detail in your contract of employment. This prevents any later dispute regarding interpretation.

In addition to the employer/employee contract, there are two others of interest to you. They are known as a fixed term contract and a fixed purpose contract.

The **fixed term contract** is where you take on somebody for a specific period of time, which is documented in their contract. The downside is that you are obliged to continue to honour this contract even if the work dries up before the end of the contracted period.

The **fixed purpose contract** tends to be used where you take on somebody to do a specific job but you are not too sure how long that job will take. The contract lasts as long as the job is there.

If you are working as a subcontractor, be careful to maintain your status as a subcontractor as per the revenue guidelines. If you don't have a C2 card then your main contractor employer is obliged to deduct 35% of the face value off your invoices and return same to the revenue. It is up to you then to sort your tax affairs with the revenue. For others delivering services to public bodies, you will need to have a current tax clearance certificate, otherwise the public body cannot issue you with either a purchase order number or a payment.

Harassment is defined by the person who feels they are being harassed. As an employer it is your responsibility to provide a safe environment for your employees. You should have an harassment policy in place and a procedure for handling incidents. It is always best if these incidents can be sorted informally between the concerned parties. If this is not possible, then your documented formal stepped procedure must be put into action. My main message here is don't ignore any complaint made to you.

Every company should also have a policy and a supporting procedure to regulate the use of the Internet. The downloading and distribution of offending material can be considered as harassment, which may or may not be sexual harassment. Different people will have different tolerance levels for this kind of offending material. What might be very acceptable in a building site hut wouldn't necessarily be acceptable in an office situation. You as employer must respect these degrees of sensitivity. The downloading of child pornography material is illegal and must be reported to the Gardaí.

Cain runs a small computer servicing business. Recently one of his engineers was called out to fix a computer problem in their best customer's offices. After due analysis, he found the offending virus and sorted it. During the course of his investigation he found that the boss had downloaded child pornographic images and imported the offending virus in the process. He was very worried and he called Cain and asked him for guidance. The law says that he should report this to the Gardaí, while the commercial implications of doing same were very transparent to him. Cain decided that they had to obey the law and thus risk losing his best customer and possibly others within Cain's network.

What would you do if faced with this type of scenario?

Conclusions

The future success of your business depends on your ability to manage.

You are the most important person, but also the limiting factor in your career or business. This is a positive statement because you have more opportunity of improving your own capacity than you have of changing the other variables which you have little influence over.

If your dream is to be more successful in building your career or business, this book is a must for you. It offers you a unique opportunity to gain valuable practical exposure to a range of ideas, methods and techniques which will both challenge and guide you. By reading and internalising the issues addressed in this book you will uncap your latent potential and maximise your management skills. This enhanced capacity will better equip you to successfully tackle the opportunities and threats that may arise as you move your business forward.

Clarity of purpose is the first critical link in your future success chain. The challenges and guidance in this book will facilitate you to clarify your purpose. They will help you to focus the lens on your life. You will then attract the resources and circumstances necessary to make it happen. This is accomplished via the law of attraction.

Some of the key learning points addressed in the book are:

1. You are the master of your own destiny – be open to change.
2. No one has a monopoly on good ideas.
3. Clarity of purpose is the bed-rock for your future journey.
4. Only you can define what success means for you.
5. Don't sweat, get smart – successful people are smart not sweaty.
6. The market pays you based on your output (not input).
7. What gets measured gets done.
8. Are you prepared to pay the price?
9. Eating the elephant – remember, one bite at a time.

Extract your own learning points from this book. Your return on investment will come from your successful implementation of these learning points.

The focus of this book is on facilitating and challenging you to reach your enhanced output targets. My aim has been to provide you with the knowledge and skills to enable you to reposition yourself from where you are now to where you need to be. I have successfully come through the hard knocks of business life, from which I have learned very valuable, practical lessons. It has been my privilege to share these with you and to facilitate you in energising your dream.

You can't change yesterday, but you can choose to make today a better day and tomorrow even better.

Bibliography

Peters, Thomas J. and (Sr.), Waterman, Robert H.
In Search of Excellence: Lessons from America's best-run Companies
New York: Harper and Row, 1982.

Porter, Michael E.
Competitive Advantage: Creating and Sustaining Superior Performance
New York: The Free Press, 1985.

Acknowledgements

Aer Lingus is a Registered Trademark of Aer Lingus, Aer Lingus Corporate Head Office, Dublin Airport, County Dublin, Ireland.

Coca Cola is a Registered Trademark of the Coca Cola Company, 121 Baker Street, Atlanta, GA 303131807, U.S.A.

Cuisine de France is a Registered Trademark of Cuisine de France, Belgard Square North, Tallaght, Dublin 24, Ireland.

Dunnes Stores is a Registered Trademark of Dunnes Stores, 46/50 South Great George's Street, Dublin 2, Ireland.

Guinness is a Registered Trademark of Guinness & Co., St James's Gate, Dublin 8.

Kellog's is a Registered Trademark of The Kellogs Company of Great Britain, The Kellogs Building, Talbot Road, Manchester, M16 OPU, Great Britain.

Kerry Foods is a Registered Trademark of The Kerry Foods Group, Charleville, County Cork, Ireland.

Perrier is a Registered Trademark of Nestlé Waters France, 4 avenue du Maréchal Juin, 92364 Meudon-La-Foret, France and the Nestlé Waters Group, Nestlé Waters M.T., 12 Boulevard Garibaldi, TSA 40001, 92793 Issy Les Moulineaux Cedex 9, France.

Ryanair is a Registered Trademark of Ryanair Ltd. and Ryanair Holdings Plc., Ryanair Corporate Head Office, Dublin Airport, County Dublin, Ireland.

Superquinn is a Registered Trademark of Superquinn, Superquinn Support Centre, Newcastle Road, Lucan, County Dublin, Ireland.

As one of Ireland's top practical business advisors, Blaise Brosnan has successfully conducted consulting and training assignments for over two thousand businesses both here in Ireland and internationally.

In *'You are the Limiting Factor'*, Blaise presents a proven, powerful and practical guide to rapidly improve your management capacity. Using a unique approach which will create within you a real desire to change, he explores the issues facing you and your business and presents practical guidance to facilitate you on your journey forward. Each successful step of this journey is a small victory. The accumulation of these personal victories will build your confidence and your future success.

Blaise uses a number of exercises, business models and case histories to help you to better understand both yourself and your business. He demonstrates how very ordinary people can be, and are, very successful and instructs you in developing action plans to close the identified gaps between those people and you.

If your dream is to build your business more successfully, this book is a must for you. It offers a unique opportunity to gain valuable practical exposure to a range of ideas, methods and techniques which will both challenge and guide you to substantially increase your self-management and uncap your latent potential.

You are the **limiting** factor

You are the **limiting** factor